Henry Fanshawe Tozer

The Church and the Eastern Empire

Henry Fanshawe Tozer

The Church and the Eastern Empire

ISBN/EAN: 9783337274474

Printed in Europe, USA, Canada, Australia, Japan

Cover: Foto ©ninafisch / pixelio.de

More available books at **www.hansebooks.com**

THE CHURCH

AND

THE EASTERN EMPIRE

BY THE

REV. HENRY FANSHAWE TOZER, M.A.

FELLOW AND TUTOR OF EXETER COLLEGE, OXFORD
AUTHOR OF 'THE HIGHLANDS OF TURKEY'
'TURKISH ARMENIA' ETC.

SECOND EDITION

LONDON
LONGMANS, GREEN, AND CO.
AND NEW YORK: 15 EAST 16th STREET
1893

All rights reserved

Epochs of Church History

EDITED BY THE

REV. MANDELL CREIGHTON, M.A.

THE CHURCH AND THE EASTERN EMPIRE

PREFACE.

IT has often been said that the Eastern Church has no history independently of the State; and this is so far true, that during long periods the annals of that Communion have little else to show than lists of patriarchs. At the same time, at certain intervals episodes of great interest and importance occur, and from first to last the influence of the Church on the social and religious life of the Eastern Empire is a subject well worthy of study. To relate, however briefly, those episodes, and to trace the working of that influence, is the object of the present volume. The early period, that of the first four General Councils, belongs to the history of the Church at large, and therefore is only touched upon here as far as subsequent events depended upon it; it is the later, or Byzantine, age of the Eastern Church which we have especially to consider.

The works which I have used in compiling this volume, and to which I desire here to express my obligation, are the following: Gibbon's 'Decline and Fall of the Roman Empire;' Finlay's 'History of

Greece;' Neander's 'Church History;' Milman's 'History of Christianity to the Extinction of Paganism,' and 'History of Latin Christianity;' Stanley's 'Lectures on the Eastern Church;' Neale's 'History of the Holy Eastern Church;' Krause, 'Die Byzantiner des Mittelalters;' Rambaud, 'L'Empire Grec au Dixième Siècle;' Léger, 'Cyrille et Méthode;' Jireçek, 'Geschichte der Bulgaren;' Mouravieff, 'History of the Church of Russia;' 'Edinburgh Review,' vol. 107, art. 'The Eastern Church;' 'Christian Remembrancer,' vol. 10, art. 'History of the Church in Russia,' and vol. 42, art. 'More Studies of the Eastern Church;' and the Dictionaries of Christian Biography and Christian Antiquities. I have also availed myself of some of my own writings.

The subject is a large one, and can only be treated superficially in a work of this size. It presents us also from time to time with problems of some difficulty and intricacy; but these are worthy of attention even from the point of view of general history and modern politics, for they are more closely connected with the 'Eastern Question' than is generally supposed. In speaking of the Eastern Church I have endeavoured to represent it truthfully, neither exaggerating its faults, nor painting an ideal picture. My hope is that even this slight contribution may be of service, if it enables the reader to understand more clearly the position and antecedents of an important section of Christendom.

H. F. T.

CONTENTS.

CHAPTER I.

THE EASTERN EMPIRE.

Foundation of the Eastern Empire—Constantine's administrative system—Taxation and disarmament—Its injuriousness—Its advantages—Constantinople—Its political importance—Its Greek inhabitants 1

CHAPTER II.

OUTLINE OF THE HISTORY OF THE EMPIRE.

Greatness of the Byzantine Empire—Constantine to Justinian—Reign of Justinian—Justinian to Leo III.—The Byzantine Empire—Saracen and Bulgarian wars—Iconoclastic period—Macedonian dynasty—The Comneni—The Crusades—Latin Empire of the East—The Palæologi—Retrospect 11

CHAPTER III.

THE ORTHODOX CHURCH.

Dignity of the Eastern Church—It was the parent of theology—Influence of the Greek language—Contrast of East and West—The Arian controversy—Title of the 'Orthodox' Church—

Its stationary character—Causes of this—Its austerity—Its love of mystery—Position of the laity—Fondness for learning—Types of character which it produced—Its organisation—Description of an Eastern Church—Liturgies and vestments 29

CHAPTER IV.

THE CHURCH, THE STATE, AND THE PEOPLE.

Union of Church and State in the Eastern Empire—Questions of doctrine—Reasons for the Union—Influence of the Union upon the State—Effect upon the Church—Judicial power of the bishops—Comparison with the Western Church—Popular character of the Greek Church—Origin of this—Influence of orthodoxy—Formation of Modern Greek nationality—The clergy and the people—Charitable institutions—Attitude towards slavery 52

CHAPTER V.

THE ORTHODOX CHURCH AND THE HERETICAL CHURCHES.

Causes of separation—Churches of Syria and Egypt national—Suspicion and persecution—The Nestorians—Their missions—Their present state—The Jacobites—Their later history—The Egyptian or Coptic Church—Its decline—The Abyssinian Church—The Armenians—Their history—Their influence—The Monothelite controversy—Martin I. and Maximus—Sixth General Council—The Maronites—The Paulicians—Their leaders—Their persecutions—The Bogomilians—Their treatment by Alexius Comnenus 71

CHAPTER VI.

THE ICONOCLASTIC CONTROVERSY.

PAGE

The principles at stake in it—Growth of image-worship—The Emperor Leo III.—His decree against images—Pope Gregory II.—St. John Damascene—Constantine Copronymus—Treatment of the monks—The Empress Irene—Tarasius patriarch—Second Council of Nicæa—Fate of Constantine VI.—Leo the Armenian—Theodore Studita—Death of Leo—Michael the Stammerer—Theophilus—Restoration of images—Effects of the controversy on society—Attitude of the West—Statues and pictures—Hymnology of the period—Rules of composition—The leading hymn-writers—Specimen and translation 100

CHAPTER VII.

THE MISSIONARY EFFORTS OF THE EASTERN CHURCH.

Conversion of the Slavs—Cyril and Methodius—Mission to the Khazars—St. Clement's remains—The Moravians—Visit to Rome—Methodius archbishop—The Bulgarians—Conversion of Bogoris—He hesitates between Rome and Constantinople—Clement of Ochrida and his work—Subsequent fortunes of the Bulgarian Church—The Russians—Early conversions—Vladimir—Embassy to Constantinople—Baptism of Vladimir—Peaceful conversion of the people 132

CHAPTER VIII.

THE MONASTIC SYSTEM OF THE EASTERN CHURCH.

Permanence of the system—Mount Athos—Eastern monastic life—Contrast with the West—Phases of monastic life—Hermits and Stylites—System of St. Basil—Love of tranquillity—The Hesychasts—Incidental uses of the monasteries—Their unfavourable side—Strange monastic abodes . 155

CHAPTER IX.

THE SEPARATION OF THE GREEK AND LATIN CHURCHES.

Early tendency to divergence—Political differences between the Greek emperors and the popes—Ecclesiastical differences between the two patriarchates—Papal claims of supremacy—Ignatius and Photius—Counter-excommunications of the two churches—Doctrinal differences—The *Filioque* clause—The question of *azyma*—Renewal of the strife by Michael Cerularius—The final schism—Effect of the Crusades—Attempts at reunion—Council of Lyons—Council of Ferrara—Removed to Florence—Repudiated by the Greeks 171

CHRONOLOGICAL TABLE OF PRINCIPAL EVENTS REFERRED TO 191

INDEX 193

THE CHURCH AND THE EASTERN EMPIRE.

CHAPTER I.

THE EASTERN EMPIRE.

Foundation of the Eastern Empire—Constantine's administration system—Taxation and disarmament—Its injuriousness—Its advantages—Constantinople—Its political importance—Its Greek inhabitants.

THE circumstances under which the Eastern Roman Empire was founded permanently affected both that empire itself and the Church which was associated with it. Before the time of Constantine the Great the impossibility of satisfactorily administering the affairs of the civilised world from a single centre of government had been sufficiently proved; and the establishment of a New Rome, as the head of the eastern portion of the empire, though it was anyhow a stroke of genius, was an arrangement towards which previous events, such as the residence of Diocletian at Nicomedia, seemed to be pointing. But the immediate and determining cause of this change was the conversion of Constantine to Christianity. What-

Foundation of the Eastern Empire

ever may have been his reason for adopting that creed —whether it was genuine conviction, or policy, or, as is most likely, a combination of those two motives— there can be no doubt that in doing so he was conforming to the faith of a large part of his Eastern subjects. No stronger proof is needed of the power that Christianity exercised over them than the subsequent failure of the Emperor Julian to revive paganism. But at the same time Rome was still the headquarters of the old religion, with which Constantine by this step was brought into antagonism, and it became a political necessity that he should free himself from the entanglements which such a state of things involved. Thus it came to pass that the new capital was from the first a Christian city, and that the empire of which it was the head was closely allied with the Christian Church.

But, at the same time that he adopted a new religion and established a new centre of government, Constantine introduced into the imperial administration reforms of such magnitude as to amount to a revolution. He rendered the military power, which had hitherto been the terror and bane of the state, subservient to the civil power; and the emperor, who up to this time had held office as commander-in-chief of the army, henceforward became primarily the political head of the government. He reorganised and consolidated the administration of justice throughout his dominions; and the boon which he thus conferred on his subjects reconciled them to many severe grievances, because they felt that, whatever temptations there might be to rebellion or to joining the barbarians, this advantage could not be obtained

Constantine's administrative system

elsewhere. So conscious were succeeding emperors of this, that strictness in maintaining impartiality in the law-courts was observed until quite a late age of the Byzantine empire. He also centralised the executive power in the emperor; and that the chief of the state might be regarded as being of a different order from the people, he was surrounded by that lavish Oriental splendour and ceremonial for which the Byzantine court was afterwards noted. Further, with the view of counteracting the danger arising from pretenders to the throne, the offices of state were made magnificent prizes, and thus opened out to ambitious persons a road to advancement, which was safer both for themselves and for the empire than civil war. Henceforth the world was ruled by the emperor and his household, forming a narrow bureaucracy, whose administration was wholly irresponsible; but this portion of the system also was most skilfully designed, for these officers were no chance adventurers, but a body of highly trained officials, thoroughly organised in their various services, so that each department of the state formed a profession of itself. In this way a large amount of ability and experience was secured for the public service, and the fruits were seen in the long succession of able administrators who were thus produced, and who came to an end when this system began to be disused, at the commencement of the eleventh century.

The two remaining features of Constantine's scheme were of necessity highly unpopular. In order to meet *Taxation and disarmament* the expenses of the court and government, and at the same time to maintain a powerful army, an elaborate system of taxation was required, and the inhabitants of the empire were impoverished for objects in which they had no direct concern. With a view to this the Roman municipal system was introduced into Greece, notwithstanding the existence of a national and traditional organisation in the ancient city communities of that country. According to this each town, with the agricultural district in its neighbourhood, was administered by an oligarchical senate called the *curia*, elected from among the landed proprietors; by them the municipal officers were appointed, and the land-tax collected, for the amount of which they were made responsible; while those who did not possess land, such as merchants and artisans, paid the capitation tax, and formed an inferior class. The oppressiveness of this arrangement was more and more felt as wealth declined, for the private property of members of the *curia* was confiscated when the required amount was not forthcoming; and at last, in order to prevent a further diminution of the revenue, an elaborate caste-system was introduced, which fixed the condition of every class, and required a son to follow the calling of his father, lest the number of persons liable to a certain kind of taxation should decrease. With the same view the free rural population came to be tied to the soil, to prevent the ground from falling out of cultivation. The other harsh measure which Constantine introduced was the general disarmament of the population, which was intended to render unavailing the discontent which the system just described was certain to produce. The possession of arms was now made a thing apart, the military class being separated from all others; and, for the same reason, barbarians were much used as troops, because they could have no sympathy with the citizens.

Our judgment of this system will differ according as we regard it from the point of view of those who were immediately affected by it, or from that of the world at large. If statecraft consists in conducting government without reference to the wishes of the governed, no arrangement ever more thoroughly deserved the name than this. Its relentlessness caused general poverty and deep-seated hatred of the central government; while its suspicion of the people was the origin of the weakness of the empire, because the provincials, who were really stronger than their invaders, were never allowed to defend themselves. By it the life-blood of the people was drained by slow degrees. It is important to remark this, in order to understand the influences by which the character of the inhabitants of the countries included in the eastern empire was formed; because it is unjust to attribute to degeneration in the people themselves changes which were the inevitable result of the circumstances that surrounded them. The prohibition to carry arms necessarily renders a people unwarlike; and the loss of the resources which would be expended on maintaining roads and other means of communication isolates them from others, and prevents the interchange of ideas and other movements by which the intellect is quickened. It was this narrowing and depressing influence by which the Greeks were gradually lowered, and thus a barren soil was left in which religion might germinate—a condition of things which has gone far towards determining the leading features of Eastern Christianity amongst the people at large.

Its injuriousness

Constantine no doubt foresaw that this system would involve a continual struggle between the rulers and those whom they governed, because the interests of the government were unconnected with those of any nationality or any class among its subjects. But long before his time the emperors, absorbed as they were in the constant labour of administering and defending the empire, had ceased to regard themselves as belonging to any particular country, even to Rome, and had learned to consider that to be provincial which to the people themselves was national. Still, whatever we may think of the immediate effects of such a mode of administration, we cannot but admire the foresight that devised a system which proved itself to be endued with such extraordinary vitality. As we look down the long vista of centuries during which the Byzantine empire lasted, we feel that nothing else than this high-handed centralisation could have prevented dissolution. Had it been in the power of the provincials to bear arms, the centrifugal tendency which existed among so many heterogeneous elements and conflicting interests must have made itself felt, and would have caused them either to overthrow or to break away from the body politic; and if sufficient resources had not been forthcoming by means of taxation, the successive attacks of powerful enemies could not have been repelled. If we can persuade ourselves that the Eastern empire conferred an inestimable blessing on the world —and this is the lesson of history, for without it the face of Europe would probably have been changed by the overwhelming power of Mahometan conquerors, whom it kept at bay—then the system which main-

Its advantages

tained it must be considered in the long run to have been a beneficent one.

The name of the founder of the Eastern Empire is for ever associated with the city which he established is its capital—Constantinople. This place, which was destined to outlive the empire itself, occupies perhaps the finest position in the world. The response of the Delphic oracle, which stigmatised the people of Chalcedon, on the opposite coast of Asia, as 'the blind men,' because they overlooked a site of such excellence in their immediate neighbourhood, was amply justified by the sequel. It occupies a triangular peninsula which lies between the Sea of Marmora and the long and deep inlet of the Golden Horn; and when the triple line of walls was built, which stretches from sea to sea, and defends its western side, it was almost impregnable to resist any force that could be brought against it in ancient times. And as long as it was safe, the empire remained intact. The Persians, the Saracens, and the Seljouks overran the Asiatic provinces, and on the side of Europe the Bulgarians advanced up to the walls of Constantinople; but the city itself was not taken, and in due course of time the lost territories were regained to the state. In the concluding period of this history, it is hardly too much to say that the capital survived the Byzantine empire by a century. From a commercial point of view also its position was unrivalled, because all the trade between the Black Sea and the Mediterranean must needs pass by it, and it was the natural *entrepôt* for the goods which were transmitted from the continent of Asia into Europe, or in the opposite direction; while at the same time the

Golden Horn formed a harbour in which innumerable vessels could find safe anchorage. And though it could not then have presented the superb appearance which it now wears, with its mosques and minarets crowning the central ridge, yet it must always have been imposing, from the nature of the seven hills which intervene between the two seas. Nor must we forget the beauty of its surroundings—the picturesque windings of the famous 'ocean-stream,' the Bosphorus, which joins the Propontis in front of the city, the verdant slopes both of the European and the Asiatic shore, the smiling group of the Princes' Islands close at hand, and in the distance the heights of the Bithynian Olympus, which during a great part of the year are covered with snow.

But it was the political influence of Constantinople which was of especial importance to the state, as the name 'Byzantine,' which came to be applied to it, sufficiently testifies. A glance at the composition of that empire will show that it consisted of two distinct parts, the European and the Asiatic provinces, which were alien to one another in their interests, their feelings, and their associations; nothing could have held them together and neutralised the forces that drew them asunder, except the attraction exercised by this central point, which was neither European nor Asiatic, neither Western nor Eastern, but stood on the confines of both continents, yet remained distinct from both. By the assimilating influence of its administration, its language, and its civilisation, the various races that inhabited both these areas were combined into one state. Greeks, Illyrians, Thracians, and Slavonians on the one hand, and Phrygians, Cappado-

Its political importance

cians, and Armenians on the other, became merged in a common Byzantine nationality. Adventurers of ability from all those peoples found their way to the seat of government; and, while they made their own fortunes, contributed to the administrative talent of the empire. The titles of Leo the Isaurian, Leo the Armenian, and Basil the Macedonian—the last-named a Slavonian of humble origin—show that even the dignity of emperor was within their reach. Thus the blood was continually flowing from the extremities to the heart of this vast body, and returned thence with quickening power to organise, to refine, and to stimulate those semi-barbarous elements which, from age to age, were incorporated with it.

The New Rome at the time of its foundation was Roman. Its senators were transplanted thither from Old Rome; the language of the court was Latin; and the condition of the lower classes was assimilated to that of the old capital by their being exempted from taxation and supported by distributions of grain. But from the first it was destined to become Greek; for the Greeks, who now began to call themselves Romans—an appellation which they have ever since retained—held fast to their language, manners, and prejudices, while they availed themselves to the full of their rights as Roman citizens. The turning-point in this respect was the separation of the empires of the East and the West in the time of Arcadius and Honorius; and in Justinian's time we find all the highest offices in the hands of the Greeks, and Greek was the prevailing language. But the people whom we call by this name were not the Hellenes of Greece

Its Greek inhabitants

proper, but the Macedonian Greeks. This distinction arose with the establishment of Greek colonies with municipal government throughout Asia by Alexander the Great and his successors. The type of character which was developed in them and among those who were Hellenised by their influence, differed in many respects from that of the old Greeks. The resemblance between them was indeed maintained by similarity of education and social feelings, by the possession of a common language and literature, and by their exclusiveness, which caused them to look down on less favoured races; but while the inhabitants of Greece retained more of the independent spirit and of the moral character and patriotism of their forefathers, the Macedonian Greeks were more cosmopolitan, more subservient, and more ready to take the impress of those among whom they were thrown: and the astuteness and versatility which at all times had formed one element in the Hellenic character, in them became the leading characteristic. The influence of this type is traceable in the policy of the Eastern Empire, varying in intensity in different ages in proportion to the power exercised by the Greeks: until, during the later period of the history—in the time of the Comneni, and still more in that of the Palæologi—it is the predominant feature.

CHAPTER II.

OUTLINE OF THE HISTORY OF THE EMPIRE.

Greatness of the Byzantine Empire—Constantine to Justinian—Reign of Justinian—Justinian to Leo III.—The Byzantine Empire—Saracen and Bulgarian wars—Iconoclastic period—Macedonian dynasty—The Comneni—The Crusades—Latin Empire of the East—The Palæologi—Retrospect.

IN writing the history of the Church in other parts of Christendom it would be natural to presuppose in the reader a knowledge of the secular history with which that Church was associated; but, owing to the general neglect of Byzantine history, this is not the case in treating of the Church in Eastern Europe. It will therefore be necessary, before proceeding farther, to give a brief sketch of the course of events in the Eastern Empire, though the first four hundred years which elapsed from its foundation to the commencement of the Byzantine period, properly so called, early in the eighth century, may be passed rapidly over. The neglect of this important field of history arises from the prevalent error—which is mainly due (strange to say) to a writer gifted with the remarkable insight of Gibbon—that this state, during the greater part of its course, was weak and effete. How far this is from being true is proved by the great things which it accomplished, and the services which it ren-

<small>Greatness of the Byzantine Empire</small>

dered to the world. It was this empire which beat back for centuries, and ultimately survived, first the Saracens and afterwards the Seljouks, both of which peoples would otherwise have overrun Europe; and, even in its decline, it kept at bay, for more than a hundred years, the Ottomans when at the height of their power, thereby providing the western nations with a breathing space, without which the career of Turkish conquest would certainly not have been arrested at Vienna. From the eighth to the tenth century, its military power was the strongest in Europe, and its long succession of able emperors and administrators is such as no other monarchical government can show. Its commerce was widely extended both by land and sea. The Byzantine art of painting, however cramped and rigid it may now seem, was the parent of the schools of Italy. Its architecture has exercised a greater influence than any other style, an influence which is traceable from Spain to India, and from Egypt to the north of Russia. Finally, in that which is the best evidence of a highly developed system, in the excellence of its social and political organisation, its superiority to other mediæval states is shown by the attention paid to education, by the regularity of its administration, and by the steady maintenance of the legal standard of the coinage.

The period that intervened between Constantine and Justinian (330–527) was marked by three events of primary importance in their subsequent effects —the establishment of Christianity as the religion of the state by Theodosius the Great (380), the partition of the empire between his sons and successors,

<small>Constantine to Justinian</small>

Arcadius and Honorius (395), and the extinction of the empire of the West (476). By the first of these events paganism, though it continued to number many adherents, and was not altogether extirpated for several centuries, was forced into a secondary and insignificant position. The second consummated the tendency to divergence between the older and the newer state, which had existed ever since the foundation of the latter, and caused them to pursue their respective fortunes independently of one another. The third, the end of the Western Empire, was the most important of all, because it rendered the eastern branch the sole representative of the Roman Empire, so that for the time it became the depository of the traditions, and the inheritor of what were supposed to be the inalienable rights of that state. So fully was this recognised in succeeding centuries, that when Charles the Great established himself as emperor (800), he asserted his position as head of the Roman Empire, not by professing to revive the Empire of the West, but by getting himself recognised as, in some sense, the representative of the Eastern emperors; and in order to effect this with a semblance of legality, he professed that he was the legitimate successor of the Eastern emperor, Constantine VI., who had been deposed. Thus Charles is spoken of, in the annals of the time, as the sixty-eighth in order from Augustus, Constantine VI. being the sixty-seventh. As regards the external history of the state, the period of which we are speaking was the time of the barbarian inroads, which fell with even greater severity on Italy. The Goths, at the great battle of Adrianople (378), defeated and slew the emperor Valens, and afterwards, under Alaric, became the terror of the Greek provinces through their plundering expeditions. The Huns also penetrated through Armenia into Cappodocia, and overran Syria, Cilicia, and Mesopotamia (395); and, under their king Attila, in the reign of Theodosius II., they ravaged the country between the Euxine and the Adriatic, and penetrated as far as Thermopylæ (441-447).

The long reign of Justinian (527-565) has naturally attracted the attention of historians, on account of the important events which it comprised. By the brilliant campaigns of his generals, Belisarius and Narses, the kingdom of the Vandals in Africa was overthrown, and Sicily and Italy were recovered to the Roman empire, after which time the Greek possessions in Italy were governed by an exarch, who resided at Ravenna. A more enduring monument was raised by the compilation of the *Pandects*, the *Code*, and the *Institutes*, a work which has left indelible traces on the legal systems of Europe. Art also enjoyed its triumph in the erection of the church of St. Sophia, a building which has never been surpassed in the unity and completeness of its design, and which served as a model for subsequent buildings in the Byzantine style. Justinian himself was a man of moderate ability, but was gifted with a remarkable power of making use of the talents of others, and his inordinate ambition impelled him to give encouragement to every project which would add lustre to his reign. But the effects of his administration were disastrous on his dominions. In order to meet the demands of his lavish expenditure on foreign conquests, splendid public buildings, and an

Reign of Justinian

extravagant court, he impoverished the people by taxation, and seized the revenues of the free cities of Greece, until at last the fortifications fell into disrepair, and a great part of the army was disbanded. Thus the empire was left almost undefended, and in the year 559 the Kutigur Huns advanced within seventeen miles of Constantinople. His suspicious policy also caused him to disband the provincial militia, which to some extent still existed in Greece. The state of the empire under his immediate successors proves how demoralising his reign had been.

The century and a half which followed witnessed the overthrow of the Persian power of the Sassanidæ.

Justinian to Leo III. This great dynasty, which arose in A.D. 226, during the reign of Alexander Severus, on the ruins of the old Parthian kingdom, had maintained a long and successful struggle with the Roman empire. The emperor Valerian was taken prisoner by the second of its princes, Sapor I. (257), and a century later Julian lost his life in fighting against the same power. In Justinian's time, owing to the ability of his great opponent, Chosroes Nushirvan, a struggle of twenty years' duration ended to the advantage of the Persians. Subsequently the greater part of the Asiatic provinces was laid waste, and a Persian army was for a time encamped on the shores of the Bosphorus; so that for the moment it appeared as if the Roman empire was about to be conquered by Persia. From this fate it was saved by Heraclius, who was at once an able administrator and a great military commander. In seven brilliant campaigns, which carried the war into the heart of the enemy's country, he dealt a deathblow to the Persian power (622–628). The conflict was unavoidable, and Heraclius was not, like Justinian, a prince who sought renown by unnecessary contests; but the result proved almost as ruinous to the Romans as to their adversaries. The year 571 had witnessed the birth of Mahomet, and the Saracen power, which was destined to propagate the religion which he founded, was now rising into prominence; so that the exhaustion of the two great combatants who had previously contested the supremacy of western Asia left the field almost open for the Saracens. Within half a century, in the reign of Constantine Pogonatus, Constantinople was besieged by land and sea for seven years by the forces of the caliph Moawyah (672–679), and it was mainly due to the recent invention of the Greek fire that he was forced to desist from his enterprise. Meanwhile a large portion of the European provinces had been incorporated in the kingdom of the Avars. When they disappeared, their place was taken, at the end of the seventh century, by the Bulgarian monarchy, which lasted for nearly 350 years, and had already begun to menace the capital. At home rebellion prevailed at this time in the army, and anarchy in the government, six emperors having been dethroned within the space of twenty-one years. Thus the same causes which had overthrown the Western empire seemed to be threatening that of the East with destruction.

The evil day, however, did not arrive, in consequence of a number of vigorous reforms, which were The Byzantine Empire introduced into almost every branch of the administration, and caused the Eastern State to enter on its period of greatest prosperity. Though some of these changes were commenced somewhat earlier, yet the person who systematised them, and in whose time their effects became apparent, was Leo III. (the Isaurian); and, therefore, the Byzantine empire— as the Eastern Roman empire thus modified was thenceforth called—is most rightly to be regarded as having commenced with his reign (716). The division of the country into *themes* for purposes of defence was introduced by Heraclius, but was reorganised by Leo, and bore somewhat the same relation to the previous arrangement in provinces that the departments in France bear to the earlier distribution of that country. In these themes the various bodies of soldiers were stationed, each with a general of its own. By this means local defence was provided for, and the danger of rendering the military commanders too influential was avoided. In respect of finance, while he succeeded in raising more money than his predecessors, he caused the burden to fall less heavily on the people. This arose from the taxation being brought directly under the emperor's own cognisance; for all local agencies for collecting the taxes were abolished, and their functions were transferred to the imperial officers. He also codified the military, agricultural, and maritime laws; and in order to obviate the difficulties which had arisen in the administration of Justinian's elaborate enactments, he published in Greek an abridged manual called the *Ecloga*. This system, with some modifications, lasted until the overthrow of the state.

During the three succeeding centuries (716–1025), the Byzantine empire was both the strongest and the wealthiest state in Europe, and far surpassed all others.

in civilisation and the arts of life. At this time it was constantly at war with the Saracens in Asia, and the Bulgarians in Europe, and after having long kept them in check, ultimately witnessed their destruction. Within a year after Leo III.'s accession, the attempt to capture Constantinople which had been made in the time of Constantine Pogonatus was renewed by Moslemah, brother of the Caliph Suleiman. Notwithstanding the enormous host which he brought against it, his attacks were baffled owing to the skill of the besieged in military defence, which was equal to that of the Romans in their best days; and a winter of extraordinary severity ensuing ruined his army. The victory of Charles Martel at Tours has often been regarded as one of the turning-points of the world's history; but it was insignificant in its results as compared with this siege. The Saracen empire was now at its height; and it was the brunt of this power, in full tide of conquest, that was resisted at Constantinople. But it was not merely in defensive operations that the forces of the empire were skilled. The troops of which its armies were composed were so powerful and well-disciplined, that during the long ages in which Asia Minor was the battle-ground of these opponents, the Saracens would never meet them in the field except with far superior numbers; and the Byzantine nobles were distinguished for their military spirit and personal prowess. The hostile power on the other side of the Bosphorus—the Bulgarians—was closer at hand, and hardly less formidable. In the time of Constantine Copronymus, the successor of Leo III., it required all the military talents of that

<small>Saracen and Bulgarian wars</small>

strong emperor to repulse their attacks. And in the beginning of the ninth century, their king, Crumn, defeated and slew Nicephorus I., and converted his skull into a drinking-cup. After an interval of peace, when war broke out afresh, owing to the heavy customs which were imposed on the Bulgarian traders, the treaty between their king Simeon and Romanus I. was made under the very walls of Constantinople (923). At last, in the reign of Samuel, a man of great vigour and ability, the Bulgarians extended their conquests over Macedonia and Thessaly, and, finding that the plains of Bulgaria were unfavourable to them, owing to the superiority of the Imperial cavalry, they transferred their seat of government to Achrida, on the confines of Macedonia and Albania, until the territory they occupied was as extensive as the European portion of the Byzantine empire. But Basil II., who was Samuel's contemporary, was one of the greatest of the emperors, and the period was the culminating point of Byzantine prosperity. By his victories over this people, Basil obtained for himself the title of 'Slayer of the Bulgarians' (Βουλγαροκτόνος); and in his time the whole nation submitted to the dominion of the Greeks (1018).

The period of which we are now speaking naturally divides into two almost equal parts, the first century and a half (716–867) being mainly occupied by the iconoclastic controversy, while the remainder (867–1025) contains the reigns of the great emperors of the Macedonian dynasty. The history of iconoclasm belongs to the annals of the Church, and will be treated of separately in a subsequent chapter; and the civil history of the time is so closely bound up with

Iconoclastic period

it, that it can hardly be spoken of independently. One or two events, however, should here be noticed, which affected the general course of the history. In the year 747, during the reign of Constantine Copronymus, the empire was attacked by a fearful pestilence, which, both in the mortality and the demoralisation of society that it produced, must have rivalled the most terrible plagues that history has recorded. The ultimate effect of this on the population of Greece proper was very great. In consequence of the destruction of life in the capital, the Emperor induced many families from that province to emigrate thither, with the prospect of an advantageous position; and while the middle classes from the Hellenic cities thus flocked to Constantinople, the inhabitants of the villages made their way into the towns to supply their place. By this means, and at the same time by the depopulation caused by the pestilence, the rural districts were left almost unoccupied; and it is from this period that we must date the extensive immigration of Slavonic settlers, who spread themselves over the face of the country. The old Greek names of places began to disappear, and that process of mixture of races commenced, which has resulted in introducing a large ingredient of Slavonic blood into the veins of the modern Greeks. Another event of some importance, which occurred about the same time as this visitation, was the loss of the exarchate of Ravenna to the Eastern empire. Before this, though Byzantine influence in Central Italy had waned, and the popes had become more important personages than the exarchs, yet justice was administered in Rome by Byzantine judges, and the officers of the empire were allowed to reside there. As the power of the emperors was too remote to be a source of dread, while the Lombard king was a formidable enemy in their immediate neighbourhood, the popes threw their weight into the Byzantine scale, and for a while enabled the exarch to maintain his position at Ravenna. This, however, was but a temporary respite, for in 751 that city was captured by Astolph, king of the Lombards, and the Byzantine rule in Central Italy ended. A century later, Sicily was conquered by the Saracens. But the loss of these outlying provinces can scarcely be said to have weakened the empire, for the revenue derived from them hardly covered the expense of the force required for their defence, and it was of the first importance to concentrate the resources of the state.

The Macedonian dynasty witnessed the introduction of considerable constitutional changes into the empire. Its founder, Basil I., converted the government into a pure despotism by abolishing the senate, which, though now a shadow of its former self, continued to exercise a certain influence in controlling the absolute power of the emperor. He also tacitly inaugurated the principle of legitimacy in succession, which had never up to that time been recognised. With a view to this he established the custom that his descendants should be born in the 'porphyry chamber,' so that the name 'Porphyrogenitus' might become a title of legitimacy. The result was that his dynasty was of far longer duration than any that had preceded it. Among his successors may be mentioned Constantine VII. (Porphyrogenitus), the imperial author of the *De Thematibus*, the *De Administrando Imperio*, and the *De Cæremoniis Aulæ Byzantinæ*; Nicephorus Phocas,

<small>Macedonian dynasty</small>

who was so successful in his wars with the Saracens, that he recovered the city of Antioch, which had been in their power for 328 years (968); John Zimisces, who triumphed over both that people and the Russians, who under their leader Swatoslav had invaded the empire from the North (971); and finally the ruthless but ascetic monarch Basil II. His death was followed by a period of feeble administration, during which two fatal errors were committed, which contributed greatly to the subsequent decay of the state. One of these was the abolition of the system of training officials to conduct the various departments of the government—a system which had secured efficiency in the public service ever since the foundation of the empire. The posts which they had held were now entrusted to eunuchs of the imperial household, and the conduct of the administration was consequently impaired. The other mistake was the destruction of the Armenian kingdom of the Bagratidæ. The safety of the eastern frontier of the empire had long been guaranteed by Armenia, a country admirably adapted for defence, whose population were a hardy race of Christian mountaineers. To encourage them was the reasonable policy of the Byzantine government, especially at that period, since the Seljouk Turks had begun to appear in that quarter. But Constantine IX. thought otherwise. By him the Armenian kingdom was overthrown (1045), and thereby his dominions were laid open to these invaders, who before long had overrun all the inland part of Asia Minor, and had established their capital at Nicæa, in the immediate neighbourhood of Constantinople (1080).

We have now arrived at the time of the Comneni, which was a period of decline, though the outward signs of this can hardly be said to have appeared. The three great emperors of that dynasty, Alexius, John, and Manuel Comnenus, whose long reigns extend over an entire century (1081–1180), were men who would be distinguished in any age, on account of their literary culture, their political sagacity, and their personal courage. The first and last of these were hardly characters whom we can admire; for Alexius was vainglorious, unprincipled, and fond of artifice, and Manuel, whose fine gifts were spoiled by the early possession of absolute power, was passionate in temper and ill-regulated in mind. But the second, John Comnenus, was a hero of the finest type—a man irreproachable in morals, open-hearted, prudent in council, and pious without superstition. As long as men like these were at the head of affairs, the government was efficient; but the neglect of the proper education of the officers of state, which has just been mentioned, had the effect of rendering the emperors almost the only capable men, and when the supreme power passed into the hands of a thoroughly profligate sovereign like Andronicus Comnenus (1183–1185), the empire was ruined. The commerce of the Greeks, also, was seriously injured by the trading privileges which were conceded by Alexius to the Venetians, and by Manuel to the Genoese and Pisans. Piracy became prevalent, in consequence of the money that had been contributed by the commercial communities for the maintenance of local squadrons of galleys, being ordered to be remitted to Constantinople. The army, too, declined in efficiency, partly from the growth of luxury among the nobles, which rendered them indisposed towards military pursuits, and partly from the habit of disbanding troops at the end of a campaign, in order to save money to defray the expenses of the court.

The principal enemies whom the Byzantines had to encounter at this time were the Seljouks in Asia Minor, and in Europe the Wallachians, who established a kingdom in Thrace and Macedonia, and the Normans of Southern Italy, who on several occasions made inroads into the empire. The most famous of these attacks was in 1185, when Thessalonica was besieged and taken by the forces of that people, and the population were treated with great indignity and cruelty. But the events of this period which produced the most permanent effects were the Crusades. If we regard those great movements from the point of view of the Western nations, we may find much to admire in them, from the element of heroism and religious enthusiasm which they contained, and the enlarged ideas which they introduced into men's minds; but to the Easterns they seemed hardly better than marauding expeditions. The First Crusade, indeed (1095), was partly undertaken in consequence of the solicitations of Alexius Comnenus for aid against the Seljouks, and by means of it that people were forced back into the interior of Asia Minor. But the undisciplined bands of which the crusading force was in part composed pillaged the population; and in the Second and Third Crusades the natives took every opportunity of showing their ill-will to the soldiers of the West. The mutual animosity that was thus generated at last came to a head in the disgraceful buccaneering expedition, which is dignified with the name of the Fourth Crusade, when a force, which was assembled for the purpose of fighting the infidels, turned its arms against the most important Christian city of that time, and, after having stormed and captured it, partitioned its dominions between the nations who took part in the attack (1204). From this blow Constantinople never recovered.

A Latin empire of the East was now established, which continued to exist, though with gradually decreasing vitality, for nearly sixty years. Meanwhile the Greeks, though driven from their ancient capital, did not resign their claim to be the rightful rulers of the country. Theodore Lascaris, who had been acknowledged as Byzantine emperor before the capture of the city, took up his abode at Nicæa, and succeeded in maintaining himself there in opposition both to the crusaders and to the Seljouks of Iconium. From that post his successors jealously watched their former heritage, lest, when the weakness of its Latin occupants had reached a critical stage, it should fall into the hands of other competitors. At last, in 1261, Constantinople became the prize of Michael Palæologus, who founded the last dynasty that ruled the Greek empire. But that empire was for the future only a shadow of its former self. The northern coasts of Asia Minor were formed into a separate dominion by the Comneni of Trebizond; and other Greek states for a time existed in Epirus and at Thessalonica. The islands of the Ægean were held by Venice and other Italian states; the greater part of

Latin Empire of the East

the Peloponnese was a Frank principality; and Athens, with the neighbouring provinces of northern Greece, was in the hands of the family of De la Roche. Subsequently other powers came to prey on the weakness of the enfeebled state—the Catalans, who arrived in the character of auxiliaries, and then plundered those whom they had undertaken to serve; the Knights of St. John, who occupied the island of Rhodes; and the Servians, who, under Stephen Dushan, established an important kingdom, which lasted until it was destroyed by Sultan Amurath at the great battle of Cossova (1389). Still, the restored Byzantine empire continued to survive for nearly two hundred years; at first, in consequence of the weakness of the neighbouring states, and afterwards through the strength of the capital, until, after a a long death-agony, it was captured by Mahomet II. (1453).

The Palæologi, who occupied the throne of Constantinople during the whole of this period, were the most ignoble sovereigns whom its annals have to show. As a rule they resembled Michael, the founder of their line, who was intriguing, selfish, and unscrupulous. Their chief object was to maintain their despotism, and they cared little for the welfare of their subjects, as was shown by their debasing the coinage. It was through the jealous policy of Michael, who denuded the passes of Mount Olympus of the protection of the warlike mountaineers who occupied them, that the Ottoman Turks, when still an unimportant tribe, were allowed to pass through from Phrygia into the lowlands of Bithynia, where they made the city of Broussa their capital, and in course of time passed over

The Palæologi

into Europe (1354). The conquest of the empire by the Ottomans, when it appeared almost unavoidable, was unexpectedly delayed by the appearance of the Tartars under Timour, who defeated and captured Bajazet, the most powerful of all the Ottoman rulers, at the battle of Angora (1402), and thereby gave the Christian state a new lease of existence. When they were once more hard pressed, the Greeks applied for succour to the Western states of Europe; and, as a preliminary condition, negotiations were carried on at the councils of Ferrara and Florence (1438) for the reunion of the Eastern and Western Churches, the separation of which had taken place nearly 400 years before (1054). This measure amounted to the submission of the Greek Church to the Pope; but though it was ratified, it was productive of no benefit to those who made the sacrifice, and only aroused indignant opposition at home. The closing years of the empire were overshadowed by gloom, arising from dissensions within the city, and the advance of an irresistible foe; but in the midst of this one bright ray appeared in the heroism of Constantine XI., the last emperor. With a spirit worthy of the representative of a long line of distinguished sovereigns, after receiving the Eucharist in St. Sophia's, he went to meet a certain death in the breach made by the Turkish artillery, and there fell fighting amidst a heap of slain.

In the course of this rapid review we have seen how the empire founded by Constantine the Great continued to exist for eleven centuries, and even to the last was an important factor in the history of the world, as being the outpost which defended Europe against Asiatic invasion. We have followed the

Retrospect

history of its contests, first with the Persian monarchy and the Goths, afterwards with the Saracens and the Bulgarian kingdom, and finally with the Seljouk and Ottoman Turks. We have watched it diffusing civilisation, arts, and learning among peoples of inferior cultivation; amalgamating nationalities of various origin and affinities; and thus impressing a stamp of character peculiar to itself on a considerable section of the human race. We must now proceed to examine the leading features which characterise the Church, which was associated with it and shared its good and evil fortune.

CHAPTER III.

THE ORTHODOX CHURCH.

Dignity of the Eastern Church—It was the parent of theology—Influence of the Greek language—Contrast of East and West—The Arian controversy—Title of the 'Orthodox' Church—Its stationary character—Causes of this—Its austerity—Its love of mystery—Position of the laity—Fondness for learning—Types of character which it produced—Its organisation—Description of an Eastern Church—Liturgies and vestments.

THE Eastern Church, though at the present time it has retired into insignificance in comparison with more active and more aggressive communions—though the sixty-six millions of souls which it includes, notwithstanding their imposing number, are on the whole an unprogressive element in the world—is, nevertheless, the most lineal representative of the primitive Church. As the starting-point of Christianity was Judæa, it was to be expected that the lands which lie about the eastern basin of the Mediterranean would first be converted to that faith; and, as a matter of fact, it was in those countries that it spread most widely during the first three centuries. The Jews of the Dispersion, who were settled in those regions for purposes of trade, contributed not a little to this result; because they had propagated the doctrine of the unity of the Godhead, and had diffused a knowledge of the contents

Dignity of the Eastern Church

of the Old Testament scriptures, among the Gentiles in the midst of whom they lived; so that by their means many were prepared to understand and accept the truths of the new religion. Even the Church at Rome was itself at first Eastern in its character, being mainly composed of Greeks, or Greek-speaking Jews, as is shown by all the extant literature of that Church up to the middle of the third century being written in Greek.

But, however much the importance of the Eastern Church may have been due to its geographical position, it is as the parent of theology that it may claim a pre-eminent place. The doctrines of the Gospel, as they were originally communicated, were unsystematic in their character; and the documents in which they were set forth, consisting as they did of narratives and letters, by their nature precluded a methodical form of statement. So, too, the earliest summaries of Christian belief, of which the Apostles' Creed is the most familiar example, confined themselves to a simple statement of the facts and doctrines, the knowledge of which was considered to be necessary to salvation. But it was impossible that the study of the subject should rest here. The questions with which Christianity occupies itself are among those that exercise the greatest attraction on the awakened human mind. Besides this, the theosophies and other forms of speculative or mystical religion, which were rife throughout the East at this time, were certain before long to come into collision with it and to force it to determine the position which it occupied towards them. The relations of the Persons in the Godhead to one another, the union of the Divine and human natures in our

Blessed Lord, and similar points of doctrine which belong to theology, properly so called—that is, the science of things divine—were canvassed; and from the erroneous views which were conceived concerning them arose various forms of Gnosticism, Sabellianism, and other modes of heretical teaching. It became the duty of the leading Christian divines to confute these, and to set forth the true doctrine in contradistinction to them. But it was mainly in the Eastern Church that the learning and the subtlety of intellect necessary for this purpose was to be found. There the widespread study of Greek philosophy had accustomed men's minds to deal with such questions. There it was that the science of Christian theology arose, and the doctrines of the Gospel were stated in a more precise and definite form.

The agency which more than anything else conduced to this result was the Greek language. That wonderful tongue, by its flexibility and the richness of its vocabulary, was an admirable instrument for conveying religious truth; and the varied movements of Greek thought had provided it with expressions which were serviceable for explaining the mysteries of the Christian faith. The continuous possession of that language by the Eastern Church throughout the whole of its history gives to that communion a claim of direct affinity to primitive Christendom such as no other Church can show. In Greek the Scriptures of the New Testament were written. In the hands of a profound thinker, like St. Paul, it served for the purposes of subtle argument; while, at the same time, the etymology and associations of the words thus employed could not fail to affect in some degree the form in which the

Influence of the Greek language

writer's ideas were expressed. The works of the great majority of the early fathers of the Church were composed in it. If we would estimate aright the service which it has rendered to Christianity, we may compare it with the other great language of antiquity, and reflect what would have been the result if Latin had taken the place of Greek as the vehicle for transmitting Christian doctrine. The rigidity of Latin, and its unfitness for the treatment of philosophical subjects, are fully admitted by Roman authors. Lucretius, whose skill we admire in reproducing the tenets of Epicurus in Latin verse, more than once in his great poem complains of the poverty of his native tongue for such a purpose. Seneca speaks with equal candour of the impossibility of finding Latin words to express ideas suggested by Plato's speculations. Even in Cicero's philosophical treatises, notwithstanding that orator's unrivalled skill in the use of language and in distinguishing the meanings of the terms which he employs, we feel that he is engaged in a constant struggle with an intractable material. The same difficulty became still more apparent when the formulas, drawn up by Christian councils held in the East, had to be translated for the use of the Churches of the West. Had Latin been the original language of Christianity, the result might have been an ambiguity in doctrinal statement which would have caused endless confusion.

The contrast which has thus been drawn out between the Greek and Latin languages leads us to consider *Contrast of East and West* the corresponding difference between Eastern and Western Christendom in respect of the point of view from which they regarded theological questions. This was determined to a great extent by the character of the dominant races, the theology of the East being, like the Greek mind, speculative, while that of the West was, like the Roman intellect, practical. It is in the subjects of discussion on which they were respectively engaged that this difference makes itself especially apparent. The Eastern Church, as we have seen, occupied itself chiefly with transcendental questions, by which the West was but slightly affected, though it afterwards approved the conclusions which its sister had arrived at, and accepted the definitions proposed. But the controversies in which the Western Church became involved turned almost entirely on questions relating to man and his destiny. This was the case with all the subjects which were discussed in connection with Pelagianism—original sin, predestination and freewill, and the influence of divine grace on the human soul. These were at the time, and for ages afterwards, the absorbing questions of the divines of the West, while in the East they were regarded almost with indifference. The writings of the great opponent of Pelagius, St. Augustine, if they were known were not understood by the Easterns; and the controversy in which he was so prominent is not named by the Greek ecclesiastical historians of the period. The same contrast, arising from inherited diversity of character, may be traced, without fancifulness, in numerous points of detail. It is not without significance that the Beloved Disciple is known in the West as St. John the Evangelist, in the East as St. John the Divine (ὁ θεόλογος).

The occasion on which the power which the Eastern Church possessed of dealing with abstruse theological questions became most conspicuous, and on which it rendered the most signal service to the Christian faith, was the Arian controversy. The struggle which that contest involved was one for life and death; because on its result depended the maintenance of the most cardinal of all Christian tenets, the true doctrine of the Incarnation. How great the danger was, may be seen both from the power exercised by Arianism at the time, and by its subsequent influence. Constantine himself in his later years inclined towards it, and two of his successors, Constantius and Valens, openly declared in its favour. It seemed at one period to have so pervaded the Church, that its great opponent, St. Athanasius, stood alone as the champion of the true faith. Afterwards, through the preaching of an Arian missionary, Ulfilas, the vast Gothic nation accepted that form of Christianity, and the important kingdoms which they established in Italy, in Gaul, and in Spain, professed that belief. The same was the case with the Vandals, when they founded the great monarchy in Africa which it was reserved for Belisarius to destroy. Had it not been for the intelligence of the Eastern theologians when the controversy arose, and their power of distinguishing exactly the points at issue, aided by the learning, the acuteness, and the indomitable courage of Athanasius, the world, humanly speaking, must have become Arian. The Nicene Council, by which the primitive doctrine was set forth in such a way as to exclude an Arian interpretation, though it was a General Council of the Church, and its decrees were accepted as universally binding, had unmistakably an Eastern character. Though over three hundred bishops took part in it, not more than eight of these came from the West. The place where it was held was in the neighbourhood of Constantinople. The language in which the discussions were carried on, and in which the Creed which it ratified was written, was Greek. The triumph in which it ended was a triumph of the Eastern Church, as the question which it debated was an Eastern question.

In the same manner as 'The Catholic Church' is the name appropriated by the Church of Rome; the appellation which the Eastern Church applies to itself is that of 'The Orthodox Communion,' ('Η 'Ορθόδοξος 'Εκκλησία). It was during the period of the General Councils that that Church assumed the characteristic on the strength of which it claims that title. More and more the office of asserting the true faith, and maintaining it unimpaired against the assaults of error, fell into its hands. If the Nicene Council was Eastern in its character, much more were those that succeeded it. At the second of these assemblies, that of Constantinople, by which Macedonius was condemned, and the Nicene Creed was reduced to the form which, except for the addition of the *Filioque* clause by the Latin Church, it has since retained, not a single Western bishop was present. The views of Nestorius and Eutyches, which were debated and disallowed at Ephesus and Chalcedon, were connected with Oriental modes of thought, and affected in the first instance the Eastern Church; though at Chalcedon, undoubtedly, the influence of Leo the Great, after he had been appealed to on the subject in dispute, was the predominant feature. The fifth and sixth councils have been hesitatingly acknowledged as œcumenical by the Western Church, the seventh not at all; but all three are ranked in the East along with the preceding ones as establishing the foundations of the faith. It was the absorbing and widespread interest which these controversies for centuries excited, and the peculiar mode of thought which the discussion of them created, that caused the desire of doctrinal orthodoxy to become almost a passion in the minds of Eastern Christians. But to this feeling, as time went on, a political influence was superadded. The question of heterodoxy, as determined by certain of the Councils, especially that of Chalcedon, became in some of the provinces—*e.g.* in Syria and Egypt, as we shall hereafter see—a national question; and when these countries were either loosened in their allegiance, or from external causes were severed from the main body, the empire thus restricted in its area clung to its orthodox belief as a badge of patriotism. Later still, when barbarian settlements had introduced heterogeneous elements of race, and the emperors themselves and other leading men were frequently of Slavonian or Armenian origin, the bond which had been previously formed by Greek nationality was replaced by that of orthodoxy. In proportion as learning declined, the traditional tenets were adhered to with increasing intensity. In consequence of this, the General Councils have been, and are, regarded in the East with a reverence which finds no parallel in the West. One who discusses points of theology or of religious observance with a member of the Greek Church at the present day, finds that his ultimate appeal is, not to argument, nor to Scripture, but to the Councils. Frescoes representing those assemblies, painted in accordance with traditional types, may be seen on the walls of some of the more important Byzantine churches. In the vestibule of the great church of the monastery of the Iberians, on Mount Athos, there is a series of these. In that which depicts the Council of Nicæa, St. Athanasius is introduced as a young man stooping down to write the Creed, while Arius is in the act of disputing between his two great adversaries, Spiridion and Nicholas. On the right hand of this group is a band of Arians, dressed as philosophers, some of whom are coming into the council-chamber to recant their errors, while the rest are being driven into a prison, by a man armed with a club. The leading facts, it must be allowed, are here set forth with much truth, even to the civil penalties.

Another feature, besides that of orthodoxy, which is strongly marked in the Eastern Church, is its stationary character. In this respect it stands in striking contrast to its more flexible Western sister. The watchfulness of the Roman communion for new fields of activity, on which to exercise her energy; her adaptation of her machinery and her public worship to the needs of the time; the development within her pale of extraordinary agencies, like the Mendicant Orders; her eager outlook over the political world, in order to discover opportunities for advancing the interests of Christianity—all these are singularly absent from the Church in the East. Such as she was in the eighth century—we might almost say, in the time of Justinian—such she has continued to be, with but slight modifications, ever since. Her services not only retain, like those in use in the West, an impressive element of antiquity, but are wholly cast in an antique mould.

Its stationary character

No attempt has been made to adapt them to the needs of any age or any people, and their immense prolixity and wearisome repetitions render them unedifying to an ordinary congregation. Her patriarchates and other territorial divisions remain unchanged. Her monastic system has hardly altered since the time of St. Basil. The ordinance of preaching, that most powerful instrument for maintaining religious vitality, has been almost wholly neglected. With this immutable character is closely connected the formalism which, 'heavy as frost,' has overspread the spiritual life of the Eastern Communion; and though depressing causes have latterly deepened its influence, there is every reason to believe that this plague-spot dates back for many centuries.

For all this the Eastern Church itself, no doubt, must to some extent be held responsible; but yet much is attributable to external causes. The first of these is its connection with the State. Owing to this it was deprived of that education in independent effort which is experienced by a self-acting body; from leaning on the support of another it lost that spontaneity which is required in order to set on foot any important movement, or to organise any great reform. To this it should be added, that the State with which it was associated was intensely despotic, and regarded with extreme jealousy any attempt to claim freedom of action, from whatever side it might come. Secondly, progress was hindered by the depression of the people at large, which was caused by the suspicious nature of Constantine's centralising policy, and was aggravated, from Justinian's time onward, by the disregard which the government showed for the

<small>Causes of this</small>

interests of the provincials, and by the devastations caused by barbarian inroads. The vigour of the plant must depend in no slight degree on the nature of the soil in which it grows; and when the discouragement offered to municipal institutions, and the neglect of the means of communication which arose from want of funds to maintain them, caused thought to stagnate beyond the limits of the chief cities, it was natural that religion also should be affected with lethargy. That only a stimulus was needed is shown by the renewed spiritual life which accompanied the enthusiasm evoked on both sides by the iconoclastic movement. Thirdly, this stationary character was further promoted by the isolation of the Eastern Church, and the defensive attitude which it was forced constantly to maintain. On the one hand, during a great part of its existence, it was engaged in a struggle with Mahometanism; on the other, it became alienated from, and at last hostile to, the Western Church. Its religious point of view thus became one of antagonism; and by this means it was thrown in upon itself, the healthy influence of criticism and comparison was excluded, and it was forced stiffly to maintain its own traditional position.

Austerity is another distinguishing characteristic of this communion. Nowhere else is so little attempt made to recommend religion by putting forward its more attractive side. This has often been noticed in respect of its religious paintings, which from first to last present the same severe types as those from which Cimabue copied. Whereas in the ecclesiastical buildings of the West the mind of the beholder is often elevated or subdued by representations of

Its austerity

divine tenderness or unearthly holiness, the walls of the Eastern churches are covered with frescoes of gaunt saints and naked hermits, which seem to communicate an ascetic character to the buildings themselves. In the icons of the Russian Church, a softer mode of treatment has been introduced, but such pictures seem to be out of place in the midst of the surroundings of a Byzantine place of worship. The same thing is still more marked in the performance of the services, and especially in the music that is employed. The nasal, drawling intonation, with which litanies, psalms, and anthems alike are chanted, possesses no quality that can gratify the love of pleasing sound, or, as far as one for whom it has no habitual associations can judge, can inspire a higher feeling of devotion. Here, again, the Russian Church represents the more progressive element in the Eastern Communion, for the music which it uses is singularly harmonious. But in Russia, as in Greece, instrumental music is rigidly excluded, on the ground that the employment of an instrument in the place of directly human and personal agency, is derogatory to divine worship. Again, in respect of fasting, no other Church has imposed such severe rules. 'Long as Lent' (μακρὸ σὰν μία σαρακοστή) is a modern Greek proverbial expression; but in the Greek Church there are four great periods of fasting during the year. In addition to the usual Lent, there is the Fast of the Apostles, which commences on Whit Monday, and, though latterly it has been shortened, originally lasted for seven weeks; the fast of fourteen days in August, which precedes the festival of the Repose of the Virgin (κοίμησις τῆς Παναγίας); and the Fast of the Nativity, which corresponds to our Advent. In the whole year, 226 days are observed as fasts, and the rigour of these is extremely severe. Not only is meat forbidden, but fish also, except the bloodless kinds, such as limpets, mussels, and other shell-fish, and the octopus, which is largely eaten in the Greek islands; and eggs, cheese, and milk. So far is the abstinence carried, that in the monasteries, during the first three days of Lent, those whose constitutions can stand it, eat nothing. But the whole population, and especially the lower classes, are very strict in their observance of these rules.

One other feature remains to be mentioned, the love of mystery. This is nowhere more strikingly seen than in the manner of celebrating the Eucharist. In the Roman Church it is desired that this service should be performed in the sight of the congregation; so that it is a merit in the construction of a church that it should admit of the altar being in view of as many as possible. But in a Greek church the whole of the sanctuary is concealed by a lofty screen or *iconostasis*; and behind this, the Liturgy (ἡ λειτουργία), as the Communion service is called, is celebrated, so that it is almost entirely out of sight of the people. This was a Byzantine, and not a primitive custom; for the *iconostasis* took the place of a light and open screen, and in its present arrangement certainly does not date further back than the eighth century. The sacred buildings themselves produce something of the same feeling. Unlike the spacious churches of the West, they are almost always small and dark, St. Sophia at Constantinople being a remarkable exception. Many domes, covered with paintings in sombre colours,

<small>Love of mystery</small>

the gilt and inlaid woodwork, and the numerous chandeliers and pendants crowded into so narrow a space, inspire the mind by the multiplicity and gorgeousness of their details, not so much with awe, as with a sense of mystery. In like manner the elaborate ceremonial of the services, though impressive, is hardly intelligible, having lost its meaning in the course of ages; and at any time it must have been difficult for the ordinary worshipper to understand. In seeking an explanation of this peculiar characteristic, it is hard to avoid tracing it, at least in part, to the associations of the court ceremonial, the object of which was to invest the person of the emperor with a halo of almost superhuman majesty. The intimate affinity which existed between this and some of the ecclesiastical observances, is clearly seen in the *De Cœremoniis Aulæ Byzantinæ* of the Emperor Constantine Porphyrogenitus, in which work elaborate instructions are given as to the procedure of the court in the matter of divine worship on the occasion of the high festivals. The two went hand in hand, and the character of the one would easily affect the other.

Yet, notwithstanding these traits of austerity and mysteriousness, the Eastern communion has shown far more regard for the position of the laity, and consideration for their independence, than the Church of Rome has done. She has assumed no such power to dominate men's consciences in respect of belief as is involved in the doctrine of Papal infallibility. Her claim to rest her authority on the earlier utterances of the Church is sufficient to prevent her from adding anything to the deposit of the faith. Though the worship of the Virgin and the invocation of saints, as

Position of the laity

practices, exist hardly less in the East than in the West, yet the doctrines connected with these have never been formulated there, and no attempt has been made to impose on believers such a dogma as that of the Immaculate Conception. In the administration of the Holy Communion, the laity as well as the clergy communicate in both kinds. No impediment has been placed in the way of reading the Bible in the vulgar tongue. Though the ancient Greek, which is in use in public worship wherever Greek is spoken, is only partially intelligible to an ordinary congregation, yet they understand it sufficiently to follow the prayers; and the Slavonic and other branches of the Orthodox Church are at liberty to translate all the services into their own tongues. The existence of a married clergy also is advantageous to the laity, because it places the priest and his flock in the same domestic position. This it was which the venerable Egyptian bishop, Paphnutius, contended for at the Nicene Council. Socrates the historian (i. 11) describes how, when a proposal was made on that occasion to require that all who were in holy orders should separate from their wives, whom they had married prior to their ordination, this confessor, who himself lived in strict celibacy, protested against any such rule, on the ground that rigid continence is not suited to all men. He advocated the maintenance of the custom already existing in the Church, that none should marry after they were ordained, but objected to making the rule more stringent. Thus the practice was sanctioned, which still continues in the Eastern Church, that the parochial clergy should be married, but that they should enter on the estate of matrimony before becoming priests. By this means not only were the hardships and the scandals averted which are apt to result from enforced celibacy, but a link was maintained by which the clergy and the laity were bound together.

Fondness for learning was always an attribute of the Byzantine Church, as it was of the Byzantine Empire. The style employed by the authors which it produced may seem to us stilted and pedantic, and their ideas conventional; but it was their taste for literary subjects, however faulty, which maintained the high level of cultivation that distinguished this state from all other contemporary states during the middle ages, and caused the ancient literature to be preserved. The Byzantines have been aptly called 'the librarians of the human race.' They added little to the stock, it is true; but they preserved and handed down what they had received, after guarding the precious deposit against innumerable attacks of barbarians and the ravages of time. If we would estimate aright the service they have rendered to civilisation, we should reflect that without them our knowledge of ancient literature would be confined to what existed in Western Europe in the fourteenth century. In keeping up the interest which was thus felt for learning, the ecclesiastics took a prominent part, and this process reacted on themselves and maintained the standard of intelligence of their order. This state of things continued until a late period of their history; and some of the prelates of that time, who were known for their learning, were of service also to their contemporaries in other ways. Such a character was Eustathius, bishop of Thessalonica, the famous commentator on Homer, in the latter half of the twelfth century. Before he was made bishop he filled the office of professor of rhetoric at Constantinople, and his extant works prove that he possessed a most extensive knowledge of Greek literature. It was during his episcopate that Thessalonica was captured by the Normans in 1185; and when the hostile soldiery brutally ill-treated and insulted the population, it was through his prudent conduct in conciliating the generals that their licence was restrained. Another such, a generation later, was Michael Acominatus, brother of the historian Nicetas, who was archbishop of Athens at the time of the fourth crusade. When the central government at Constantinople was paralysed by that attack, Leon Sguros, the governor of Nauplia, took advantage of the general disorder, and endeavoured to make himself master of Athens. But the archbishop animated his flock to maintain their independence, and organised the defence of the Acropolis, so that the usurper was forced to raise the siege.

The types of character that were developed in the Eastern Church, as might be expected, were not of the very highest. There was among them no St. Francis, no St. Louis. The uniformity which pervades everything Byzantine prevented the development of such salient characters as are found in the West. It is difficult, no doubt, to form a true estimate of the influence of religion on men's lives in Eastern countries, just as it is of their domestic relations, and even of the condition of the lower classes, because such matters are steadily ignored by the contemporary historians. But all the evidence tends to show that individual rather than heroic piety was fostered by the system which prevailed there. That at certain periods a high tone of spirituality prevailed among

Types of character

certain classes is sufficiently proved by the beautiful hymns of the Eastern Church, many of which, thanks to Dr. Neale's singular felicity in translation, are in use among ourselves. But the loftier development of their spirit took the form of asceticism, and the scene of this was rather the secluded monastery, or the pillar of the Stylite, than human society at large. But if the Eastern Church did not rise as high as her sister of the West, she never sank as low. No Alexander VI., no St. Bartholomew's Day, disgrace her annals. And in respect of constancy when exposed to persecution, her members have held, and still hold, a high position. This has been especially conspicuous in the latest and lowest phase of her existence, that which succeeded to the Ottoman conquest. To mention but one of their trials; no more grinding instrument of persecution was ever invented than that of the tribute of Christian children, who, from the time of Sultan Orchan, the founder of the system, in 1329, until it was legally abolished in 1685, were taken from their parents and educated in an alien creed, in order to form the force of the Janissaries, which was the most powerful engine for the enthralment of their race. Speaking of the religious sentiment of the Eastern Church, Dean Stanley says: 'If it has produced few whom we should call saints or philosophers, it has produced, through centuries of oppression, whole armies of confessors and martyrs.' 'The eighteenth century,' says Dr. Neale, 'which added few, here and there, to the glorious catalogue of Western martyrs, was full in Greece and Anatolia of such triumphs for the East.' The resistance to the temptation to apostasy, when a change of creed involved an immediate change of political status and innumerable social advantages, is in itself a proof of the strong influence which their religion exercised on the Greek people.

<small>Organisation</small> At an early period the Eastern communion comprised the four great patriarchates of Constantinople, Antioch, Jerusalem, and Alexandria. As time went on, however, partly owing to the schisms that followed the condemnation of Nestorius and Eutyches by the Councils of Ephesus and Chalcedon, and partly in consequence of the conquests of the Saracens, the three last-named divisions of the Orthodox Church became more and more restricted in their area. At the present day the office of patriarch in them is hardly more than titular, and the holders of it do not reside in their famous ancient sees. Thus the patriarch of Constantinople came to be the head of the whole Eastern Church, and in that character he bears the title of Œcumenical Patriarch. The area which owed allegiance to him was divided into four dioceses, which were administered by exarchs—viz., Pontus, Asia, Thrace, and Eastern Illyricum; and each of these was subdivided into numerous metropolitan and other sees. The patriarch was originally elected by a local synod, and confirmed by the emperor; but at a later period the synod selected three persons, one of whom the emperor appointed. Though the head of the state possessed no legal power by which he could compel a patriarch to resign, yet it was generally easy to bring such pressure to bear as would render it unavoidable. Since the fall of Constantinople, the sultan has claimed the right of investiture, and from this have arisen simoniacal

practices, a sum of money being more or less habitually paid for the office. Though, as we have seen, it became a universal custom for the parish priests to be married, such marriage having taken place while they were still laymen or deacons, yet celibacy is required of the bishops, and consequently, unless they happen to be widowers, they must be taken from the monasteries. The evils of this system are self-evident. The persons who are thus set in authority are men who have had no experience of ministerial work, who have nothing in common with the parochial clergy; and their ignorance of practical life renders them especially liable to be led into intrigues.

A few words may be added respecting the places of worship and the liturgies in use in the Eastern Church.

Description of a church As the best-preserved specimens of Byzantine churches are to be found on Mount Athos (the Christian edifices in the cities having been converted into Mahometan mosques), the central church in the monastery of the Iberians on that Holy Mountain, of which the following is a description, may serve as a typical instance:—

'Entering at the west end, we find ourselves in the *proaulion*, or porch, a corridor supported on the outside by light pillars, running the whole width of the building: in this part are represented scenes from the Apocalypse, especially the punishment of the wicked. Passing inwards from this, we enter the first *narthex*, or antechapel, which contains pictures of various forms of martyrdom: on either side of the central door, which leads into the second *narthex*, are figures of SS. Peter and Paul. These narthexes, which are divided from one another and from the body of the church by walls rising the whole height of the building, were originally intended for catechumens and penitents; as it is, they are employed for the celebration of the more ordinary services, and when the body of the church is too small for the number of worshippers, they serve to provide additional room. In the second narthex are frescoes of saints and hermits, who look down in grim solemnity from the walls: the hermits especially are most striking objects, being almost human skeletons, and stark naked except for their long grey beards, which reach to the ground. From this we pass into the main body of the church, which is in the form of a Greek cross, with a central cupola supported on four pillars, which symbolise the Four Evangelists. At the east end and in the transepts are semi-cupolas, but the whole of the sanctuary is concealed by the *iconostasis*, a wooden screen reaching nearly to the roof, and elaborately carved and gilt, in which are set pictures of Our Lord and saints. The sanctuary is divided into three parts, with three apses at the eastern end corresponding to them. The northernmost of these is the chapel of the *prothesis*, where the sacred elements are prepared; that towards the south is the sacristy; while the central compartment contains the holy table ($\dot{\eta}$ $\dot{\alpha}\gamma\iota\alpha$ $\tau\rho\dot{\alpha}\pi\epsilon\zeta\alpha$). The position of two of the frescoes in the body of the church is always the same: in the cupola is a colossal figure of the Saviour, and over the western door of entrance a representation of the Repose ($\kappa o \iota \mu \eta \sigma \iota s$) of the Virgin. Other parts of the walls are covered with Scripture subjects, and in one of the transepts is a group of young warrior saints, among whom St. George is conspicuous. From the drum of the cupola hangs an elegant brass coronal, and from this are suspended silver lamps, small Byzantine pictures, and ostrich eggs, which are said to symbolise Faith, according to a strange but beautiful fable that the ostrich hatches its eggs by gazing steadfastly at them: within this coronal again is a large chandelier. The floor is ornamented in parts with *opus Alexandrinum*, a kind of inlaid work in white marble, porphyry and *verd antique*; and here and there are placed lecterns, elaborately decorated with mother-of-pearl and tortoise-shell. The stalls are ranged all round the sides, and are provided with *misereres*, which, however, are seldom used, as the monks generally stand during the whole service.' We may further notice that in churches which were not monastic, a women's gallery was sometimes provided, to which the female sex were confined, in accordance with the traditional ideas respecting the seclusion of women in the East. An instance of this, on a large scale, is found in St. Sophia at Constantinople: others (to come down to a much later period) may be seen in the churches of St. Demetrius and Pantanassa at Mistra, near the site of ancient Sparta, both of about the fourteenth century. Where such galleries do not exist, the women stand at the back of the church, apart from the men.

The Liturgies, or Communion Offices, in use in the Church of Constantinople are those of St. Basil and <small>Liturgies and vestments</small> St. Chrysostom. The beauty and spirituality of the prayers which they contain are familiar to many English churchmen through the medium of Bishop Andrewes's 'Devotions,' which work is to a great extent compiled from them. That of St. Chrysostom is by far the most commonly used, but it is an abbreviation and new edition of that of St. Basil. In addition to these there is a third liturgy, that of 'the Presanctified,' which is said from Monday till Friday of every week in Lent. This is so called because it is a communion with no consecration; the five holy loaves necessary for the purpose (one for each day) having been consecrated on the previous Sunday. The principal vestments that are worn by the priests are the *stœcharion* (alb), the *epimanikia* (maniple), the *epitrachelion* (stole), and the *phœnolion* (chasuble); in addition to these, the bishops wear the *omophorion* (pall); but both in form and ornamentation these differ in many respects from the corresponding Western vestments. The every-day dress of ecclesiastics is a tall, flat-topped cap, and a cassock of some sober colour, frequently dark-blue, over which is worn a flowing black robe. Besides, or instead of, bells, an instrument called the *semantron* is used for summoning the congregation to service. This is sometimes of iron, resembling a piece of the tire of a wheel; but more commonly it is a long flat board, narrow in the centre, so that it may be grasped by one hand, while it is struck with a wooden mallet by the other.

CHAPTER IV.

THE CHURCH, THE STATE, AND THE PEOPLE.

Union of Church and State in the Eastern Empire—Questions of doctrine—Reasons for the Union—Influence of the Union upon the State— Effect upon the Church—Judicial power of the bishops—Comparison with the Western Church—Popular character of the Greek Church—Origin of this—Influence of orthodoxy—Formation of Modern Greek nationality—The clergy and the people—Charitable institutions—Attitude towards slavery

IN the Eastern empire the union of Church and State has been exhibited on the largest scale that the Christian world has ever seen. From the beginning to the end of the empire, from the foundation of Constantinople to its capture by the Turks, this union continued to exist; indeed, it may be said, in a sense, even to have survived the empire, for some of the privileges and some of the restrictions which attach to an established Church have been continued to the Greek Church under the Mahometan rule. The central point on which this system turned, the bond by which this union was maintained, was the person of the emperor. In Constantine's time Christianity was not the established religion of the empire, but a privileged religion to which the emperor belonged. The laws by which the Church was regulated, though they were enforced by the civil arm, were at first made independently of the

Union of Church and State

state. Its members were guaranteed freedom from persecution, and the prospect presented itself that their religion would soon become the religion of the court, perhaps also that of the empire; but this depended on the relation in which they stood to the emperor. It was Theodosius the Great who established Christianity, and by him the Church in the eastern empire was united with the imperial administration; but from the time of Constantine the emperor was supreme in ecclesiastical as well as in civil matters. The right to occupy this position was claimed by his successors, and was acknowledged as belonging to them; and throughout Byzantine history this authority was exercised in an increasingly despotic manner.

This supremacy did not in the first instance imply any interference with matters of doctrine. Constantine regarded his own province as lying outside the Church. But the power of convening general councils, which he and subsequent emperors possessed, placed in their hands an authority which might be extensively exercised in regulating the decisions of those who had the right to determine such questions. Nor was their influence long restricted within these limits. The position of Constantine himself in the Nicene Council was so exceptional, owing to his being at once a convert to Christianity and the master of the world, that we cannot argue from the part which he took in its deliberations to a claim on his part to the right of interference; but it seems plain that his persuasions, to say the least, considerably affected its decisions. Other indirect influences, also, soon made themselves felt. Some of the higher clergy were deterred

Questions of doctrine

from opposition by the fear of the imperial displeasure; others were drawn into subserviency by the hope of advancement; others again joined themselves to one or other of the powerful court parties, and these became doctrinal parties, and took their share in theological disputes. A further advance was made in the course of the Monophysite controversy. In 476 the usurper Basiliscus issued an encyclical letter condemning the decrees of the Council of Chalcedon, which was to be signed by all the bishops on pain of being deposed from their office; and when his opponent, the Emperor Zeno, was reinstated in power, and attempted to heal the breach between the orthodox and Monophysite parties, his famous *henoticon,* or *concordat,* was set forth on imperial authority. But in the hands of a rigid centraliser like Justinian, the liberty of judgment which the bishops originally possessed was still further restricted, and dogmatic controversies were settled by imperial decrees, such as that which was known by the name of the edict *De tribus capitulis* (544). Throughout a great part of the Byzantine period the emperors claimed to be supreme in matters of belief, as much as in matters of discipline. The claim was not uncontested, but the reason why so much latitude was generally conceded to them, even when force was not brought to bear, was this—that the emperors and their subjects were, as a rule, at one in this matter. The title by which the emperor styled himself was ἐν Χριστῷ πιστὸς Βασιλεὺς τῶν Ῥωμαίων—an equivalent of our 'Defender of the Faith.' Besides this, the majority of the emperors were sincerely interested in ecclesiastical subjects, and not a few were well versed in theology. Thus they were, and were regarded as being, persons identified with the Church, and capable of entering into the questions which it regarded as all-important; and as orthodoxy became a passion with the Byzantine laity, a link was thus formed to unite the people with their rulers. It was only when some emperors of the dynasty of the Palæologi endeavoured to force the alien doctrines of the Roman Church on their subjects as the condition of obtaining help from the West, that this bond was broken. Before that time, the position of the emperor as head of the Church presented no difficulty, because he was recognised as orthodox.

It was natural that the Roman emperors, when they adopted Christianity, should wish to exercise a control over it, because so powerful an agency, existing outside the range of the civil government, might prove itself extremely dangerous. The evidence of this had been given on former occasions, when jealousy of this great independent organisation had been the chief cause of the persecutions. In all the important cities of the East, Christian congregations were found whose members were united by ties of brotherhood, and were accustomed to act together for common objects, and were ready to assist one another in time of need. These churches, again, were in constant communication with one another, and from their uniform system of government and management, and the attraction exercised by common beliefs, and hopes, and fears, constituted a power, which, if employed for political purposes, might be found more influential than the State itself. Even the exalted character and loftiness of purpose that were conspicuous in many of their

Reasons for the union

chief men, were elements fraught with danger, because their possessors were thus qualified to be leaders, and were gifted with that enthusiasm which in all ages has been the dread of ordinary politicians. But from the time that this widely extended society became allied with the civil government, the risk of a collision between them was averted. The bishops, who might have been the foremost champions in a great rebellion, became dependent on the emperor's authority and willing agents of the administration; and the head of the State, though he was still, by virtue of his office, the representative of the old pagan religion of Rome, could claim the allegiance of his Christian subjects as being the head of their Church.

Influence of the union upon the State

In the early period of its history the Church developed itself independently from within, and was not interfered with, except in the form of antagonism, by any disturbing influence from without. But, on the other hand, it had not as yet exercised its full influence over society; by moulding the thoughts and motives of individuals, it had leavened the State to a certain degree, but the civil institutions remained outside its range. This was changed when Christianity became the recognised religion. The Church and the State then stood side by side, mutually affecting one another; and thus it was open to the Church to elevate and purify the State. The Church's influence soon made itself felt in a variety of ways. As early as Constantine's time the punishment of crucifixion was abolished; immoral practices, like infanticide, and the exhibition of gladiatorial shows, were discouraged, the latter of these being forbidden in

Constantinople; and in order to improve the relation of the sexes, severe laws were passed against adultery, and restrictions were placed on the facility of divorce. Further, the bishops were empowered, in the name of religion, to intercede with governors, and even with the emperor, in behalf of the unfortunate and the oppressed. And gradually they obtained the right of exercising a sort of moral superintendence over the discharge of their official duties by the judges, and others, who belonged to their communities. The supervision of the prisons, in particular, was entrusted to them; and, whereas in the first instance their power of interference was limited to exhortations addressed to the judges who superintended them, in Justinian's reign the bishops were commissioned by law to visit the prisons on two days of each week, in order to inquire into, and, if necessary, report upon, the treatment of the prisoners. In all these and many other ways, the influence of the State in controlling and improving society was advanced by its alliance with the Church.

At the same time the Church itself was not less leavened by its union with an alien power. Its leaders at the period when the connection was formed did not realise what the consequences would be. They were overjoyed at their deliverance, and the deliverance of their flocks, from the fear of persecutions, such as those of which they had a vivid remembrance; and they were dazzled, independently of worldly considerations, by the possibilities which this alliance opened out for the spread of the Gospel. They did not perceive that the Church might be lowered by

Effect upon the Church

being made subject to an autocratic will, and that it could no longer be, what it had hitherto been, an independent, self-governing community. Thus, too, worldly attractions were introduced, the tendency of which was to impair the motives by which Christians had been influenced. In the year 321 Constantine enacted a law allowing the Church to receive legacies, a thing which was not permitted without the leave of the State. This measure, of which advantage was taken on a large scale, increased the prosperity of the Christian communities; but it also added to the class of self-seeking ecclesiastics. Above all, the temptation henceforth existed to invite the secular arm to assist in maintaining true doctrines and repressing error. To do so was to abandon one of the leading maxims of Christianity, that the Gospel was to be propagated by its own moral and spiritual power, and not by force. The result was in a high degree injurious both to the Church and the State. By this means large bodies of Christians, as we shall hereafter see, were alienated, and an impulse was given to their withdrawal from the orthodox Church, while the empire, owing to the ill-will that was thus caused, suffered the loss of important provinces.

One of the most powerful causes in introducing a secular element into the administration of the Church, *Judicial power of the bishops* was the exercise of a judicial power by the bishops. From the earliest period it was the custom, in accordance with St. Paul's injunction on the subject, that disputes between Christians should not be referred to the heathen tribunals, but should be settled within their own communities. In the course of time, when the episcopal system of government was fully developed, it became, as was natural, one of the functions of the bishop to decide these disputes. But as the reference of such questions to this tribunal was a voluntary matter on the part of those concerned, it was only so far as they agreed to submit to it that its decisions were valid. In Constantine's time, however, such transactions came to have a legal force. By him the bishop's judgment was made binding, without the power of appeal, when once the parties in a suit had referred it to him: and this judicial authority was still further increased by Theodosius, when he rendered orthodox Christianity the established religion of the empire. The power thus given might be exercised in a salutary manner for the purpose of repressing litigation and inculcating unanimity, but it also involved the bishops in a large amount of secular business, and withdrew them from their purely spiritual functions. This system was reinstituted with great shrewdness, though for a very different purpose, by Mahomet II. after the fall of Constantinople. That skilful politician perceived the advantages which would arise from using the higher clergy as his agents in reconciling the laity to the Ottoman domination. With this view he invested the Greek patriarch, and the bishops in the different provinces as his subordinates, with extensive judicial powers for the decision of civil as well as ecclesiastical causes, together with the permission to enforce a sentence by excommunication. Of these facilities for obtaining a settlement of disputed questions within the limits of their own nationality, the Greeks from the first largely availed themselves, owing, in a great degree, to the corrupt administration of justice by the Turkish tribunals. Thus, from being in the first instance arbitrators, the bishops came to be recognised magistrates of the empire; and, while they benefited their co-religionists by their protection, they themselves fell into the position of Ottoman officials. Besides this, it has always been a part of the Turkish statecraft to employ the Greeks as an instrument for governing the other nationalities of the empire. With this object they were placed in the position of the most favoured race, and governors, both ecclesiastical and civil, were appointed from among them to hold sway in provinces whose Christian inhabitants belonged to a different stock. Thus the Turks put in practice the maxim 'Divide and conquer' which has proved so serviceable to them in dealing both with their own *rayahs* and with the nations of Western Europe, and the Greeks became the object of jealousy and dislike to the other Christian subjects of the Porte.

The position of the Eastern Church in all these respects is best understood by comparison with what happened in the West. From the time at which persecutions ceased, the bishop of Rome was only a nominal subject of whatever power was dominant in Italy. His sovereign usually resided at a distance from Rome, and, whether he were a Western emperor or a Gothic king at Ravenna, or an Eastern emperor at Constantinople, allegiance was more easily claimed than exacted. An ecclesiastical ruler in this position, having manifold interests depending upon him throughout his vast patriarchate of the West, and being appealed to in numerous cases where temporal

Comparison with the Western Church

and spiritual questions were closely interwoven, could hardly escape from ultimately becoming a potentate; and his primacy as bishop of the imperial city might easily be interpreted into a supremacy over the whole Church, derived from St. Peter as the chief of the apostles. But in the Eastern Church it was impossible that any such thing should happen. Constantinople, as a Christian city, had no history behind it; and its bishops, being the head of a new patriarchate, could not put forward pretensions based on primitive inherent right. Side by side with it there were other and more ancient patriarchates at Antioch and Alexandria, the existence of which was sufficient to disprove any such claim; and the bishop of Constantinople, however great his position might be, was still a subject of the Byzantine emperor. It is true that in the time of Constantine's successors the Church gave evidence of its independent spirit in resisting an Arian emperor like Constantius, or a pagan emperor like Julian; and at various periods of its history its rulers preferred deposition or imprisonment to compliance with unrighteous acts on the part of the chief of the state. But, after these early days, we meet with no patriarch like St. Athanasius or like Nicon in Russia, who showed himself willing to resist the civil head, and capable of doing so. The dignity of the patriarchate of Constantinople waxed and waned according to the corresponding state of the empire, whereas the Papacy arose on the ruins of temporal states and to a great extent in defiance of their power. Thus it was denied to the Eastern Church to play the conspicuous part in the history of the world, and to achieve the great successes, which have fallen to the lot of her Western sister; but, at the same time, she was saved by her position from advancing claims incompatible with the independence of Christendom, and from incurring the scandals which have disgraced the Church of Rome. There was nothing seen in that communion like the employment of excommunication by ambitious pontiffs, until their fulminations were disregarded and at last brought into ridicule; still less was there anything like their use of the power of interdict, by which a whole people was afflicted and denied the comforts of religion because of some quarrel in which they were not directly interested. No patriarch of Constantinople has been reduced to obtaining money on a large scale by scandalous means, such as the sale of indulgences; nor has there been seen in Eastern Christianity such a thing as the employment of an armed force by one who claimed to represent the Prince of Peace.

When we turn from these questions of the union of Church and State to the relation of the Church in Eastern Europe to the people, the feature which most attracts attention is its popular character. Notwithstanding the unattractive nature of its services, which, as has been already remarked, have neither the elevating influence of instrumental music nor the awakening power of preaching to recommend them, its places of worship are regularly attended, and dissent is almost unknown. The congregations, too, unlike what is found in any religious bodies in the West, are mainly composed of men, and not of women and children; and the laity are recognised as being directly concerned in whatever affects the

Popular character of the Greek Church

Church, and can be counted on as being interested in its affairs and zealous in its support. There is, moreover, no false shame among them about openly professing religion. It is not regarded as a subject which a man should avoid, and his feelings about which should be studiously concealed from his neighbours, but as a matter of common sympathy, which no one would think of ignoring. In this way it enters into the most ordinary occurrences of life. During the whole of the Easter season the address Χριστὸς ἀνέστη, together with the reply ἀληθῶς ἀνέστη, take the place of 'good day' and all other familiar salutations. The enjoyment of a holiday is regularly associated with a religious service, which inaugurates the day's festivities. In remote districts the public worship may be said to partake of a domestic character, for the chief of the village elders, or the layman who can read best, leads the responses from a well-worn service-book, while others correct him whenever he is at fault. In its observances, its associations, and its influences, the Church is throughout the Church of the people. At the present day much of this is due, no doubt, to the power which the Greek Church has exercised in maintaining Greek nationality, so that the two are indissolubly allied and almost identified. Still this strong affection of the people for their Church, even where the practice of their lives is not regulated according to its precepts, is in great measure a feeling inherited from very ancient times, so that it is well worth while to trace its origin and history.

Before the time of Constantine, Christianity had produced a marked impression on Greek society. During a period of nearly six centuries from the time of Alexander the Great, that people had gradually degenerated, so that, though the outline of their character was the same as in their best days, the colours had faded. But in the latter half of the third century of our era finer qualities and more vigorous elements begin to reappear, and are conspicuously seen in the successful resistance which the cities of Greece offered to repeated invasions of the Goths at this period. The cause of this change is to be found in the influence exercised on the Greeks by the Christian religion. This had long been working among them in secret, and its power was the greater because it had advanced from below upward, and had permeated to a great extent the lower and middle classes. It not merely pervaded every relation of life, but penetrated also to the motives and springs of action. It improved the moral condition of the Greeks by elevating their views of life, by quickening the conscience, and by infusing earnestness into the character; and it renovated their social condition by pointing out to them their duties to one another, by encouraging corporate feeling, and in particular by purifying the domestic relations through its influence on the female sex. At the same time the habit of meeting for the administration of their communities accustomed the Christians to discussion and action in common; and, in consequence of this, oratory revived among the Greeks, and new vigour was infused into their municipal institutions. Synods of the Church now took the place of Amphictyonic and other assemblies of former days, as places where subjects of public interest were debated. It is not too much to say, that the

Its origin

Eastern Empire was saved from the fate which overtook that of the West by the unanimity inspired by Christianity. So closely was the cause of the Greek nation already bound up with that of the Christian Church!

The alliance which was thus commenced was still further cemented in the time of Constantine's successors. At this period, while the Roman empire was still nominally pagan, and the nobility of Rome were avowedly so, the Roman emperors had adopted the Arian tenets, and showed marked favour to the clergy of that party. But the Greeks were as little disposed to respect the theological opinions of the heads of the state, as they were to sympathise with the traditional superstitions of their conquerors; and in consequence of this they clung more closely than ever to the orthodox Church, which was in direct antagonism to both these parties. By gradual stages orthodoxy came to take the place of nationality in the Eastern empire. The people called themselves Romans, and the name Hellen was regarded as equivalent to 'pagan'; but meanwhile the orthodox creed and the Greek language had formed the nation. It is difficult to overestimate the intensity of the theological spirit which at last pervaded the whole population. It reached its climax in the reign of Constantine Pogonatus (668), when the imperial troops in Asia Minor rose in sedition, and having marched towards the capital, and encamped on the Asiatic shore of the Bosphorus, demanded that the emperor should admit his two brothers to an equal share in the public administration, in order that the Holy Trinity in heaven, which governs the spiritual world, might be represented by a human trinity, to govern the political empire of the Christians. One of the forms of acclamation by which a Byzantine emperor was wont to be saluted by the populace, was, 'Equal to an apostle' (ἰσαπόστολος). At a later period religion was the element of unity which combined all races and all interests. To be orthodox was the same thing as being a member of the Eastern Church, and that again was equivalent to being a loyal subject of the empire. But from the time of the Comneni onwards, when the administration fell more and more into the hands of the Greeks, and Greek ideas and influences generally prevailed, the Orthodox Church came to be regarded as the Greek Church. Hence many races, especially in Asia Minor, are now called, and call themselves, Greek, who have no claim to that title beyond that of being members of the Eastern communion.

It was also, to a great extent, the influence of the Church that produced that fusion of races within the limits of Greece Proper, which has consti-tuted the Modern Greek nationality. We have already seen (p. 20), how during the Middle Ages large numbers of Slavonian colonists overspread that country, especially after the depopulation caused by the plague of A.D. 747. The conversion of this people to Christianity, and their consequent adoption into the Orthodox Church, gradually obliterated the distinction between them and their Greek neighbours, and caused the two races to amalgamate into one. In the working out of this process the influence of superior civilisation carried the day, and the result was the Hellenizing of the Slavonians. At the present day no

<small>Formation of modern Greek nationality</small>

trace remains, either of their language, or of their separate nationality.

To these causes of the popularity of the Eastern Church must be added the intimate connection that existed between the clergy and the people. In the earliest period such a connection was only natural, because the clergy were the representatives of the fraternal Christian communities. But from the time of Constantine onwards, a distinction requires to be drawn between the higher and the lower clergy. As soon as the bishops were recognised as an order in the state, and came to have administrative authority, a power was at work, which tended to sever them from the people at large. For some time, indeed, the operation of this was only partial, and the heads of the Church were able and willing to protect their flocks against the despotism of the imperial authority, and the unjust exactions of local governors; but this beneficial influence steadily diminished in the course of succeeding centuries, and after the separation of the Eastern Church from the Western, the subserviency of the higher clergy to the state, and the conservatism of their ideas, discouraged all attempts at progress on the part of the people. But with the parochial clergy the case was different. From living among the people they were intimately acquainted with them, and shared their feelings, for they suffered equally with them from the oppressive taxation, the neglect of the provinces, and the other evil results of the statecraft of the Eastern empire (see p. 5). Thus, as early as the time of Arcadius and Honorius, when the division of the Roman empire caused the influence of Greek nationality to be more definitely felt in the East, a close connection begins to manifest itself between the lower clergy and the people; and when Justinian seized the revenues of the free cities, and deprived them of their most valuable privileges, it was the clergy who saved the population from lapsing into utter barbarism. As being the most powerful class in the community, they henceforth took the lead in all public business in the provinces. When the schools and the physicians were robbed of the funds destined for their maintenance, they lent their help to support them; and they aided the charitable institutions, and reinvigorated the communal and municipal organisation of the people. The growth of the alliance thus formed between the clergy and the laity is not easy to trace in detail; but still it is a definite fact of history, and Finlay, the impartial historian of the Eastern and Byzantine empires, frequently dwells upon it as determining the course of events. The Church was now the only agency left that could lift up its voice against despotism, or remedy the evils which it caused.

The charitable institutions which have just been mentioned were themselves originally founded either

Charitable institutions by, or through the influence of, the Church. Such were the hospitals (νοσοκομεῖα), the orphanages (ὀρφανοτροφεῖα), the institutions for the support of helpless aged persons (γηροκομεῖα), the almshouses (πτωχοτροφεῖα), and the establishments for the reception of strangers (ξενῶνες.) St. Basil founded a number of almshouses with hospitals attached to them. Justinian and Theodora established a penitentiary for fallen women (μετάνοια). The emperor Isaac Angelus (A.D. 1185) provided a hospital, and a hostelry for the entertainment of a hundred travellers free of charge. Many similar institutions are recorded as having been erected, throughout the whole course of the history, both by emperors and private individuals. In Constantinople, during the Byzantine period we find that a public officer, called the Orphanotrophos, or 'minister of charitable institutions,' existed for the supervision of these; a fact which speaks well both for the civilisation of the Empire, and for the influence which Christianity had exercised upon it.

The position of slaves, also, was greatly improved in the Eastern Empire by the agency of the Church. Attitude towards slavery. This is a question which must always attract the attention of those who desire to form a just estimate of the condition of society in antiquity, because of the number of souls that are represented by that class. By Constantine's legislative enactments the emancipation of slaves was facilitated. Places of Christian worship obtained the right of asylum, so that slaves could find protection there, for the time, against the anger of their masters, and the clergy had an opportunity of subsequently interceding for them. At first this privilege belonged to the churches only by traditional usage; but in the reign of Theodosius II. (431) a law was passed, which forbade, on pain of death, the forcible removal of anyone who had taken refuge in a sacred building. Gradually the employment of slaves came to be regarded in religious circles as a thing to be tolerated rather than approved. Theodore Studita, who may be taken as a representative of the strictest religious views of the ninth century, says on this subject, 'A monk ought not to possess a slave, either for his own service, or for the service of his monastery, or for the culture of its lands; for a slave is a man made after the image of God.' But he adds, 'this, like marriage, is only allowable in those living a secular life.' The extinction of slavery in the Eastern Empire, it should be observed, was not due to Christianity, for, although the Fathers of the Church had raised their voices against it, yet that religion had recognised slavery as an institution, however much it might endeavour to mitigate its evils; nor yet was it owing to the advance of civilisation, for culture among the Greeks was intimately connected with the employment of slaves. It was rather produced by an alteration that took place in the condition of certain classes, which annihilated the distinction between the freeman and the slave. When the oppressiveness of taxation had destroyed the wealthy proprietors, and, in order to prevent the land from falling out of cultivation and thus diminishing the revenue, the cultivators of the land were tied to the soil, the poorer class of freemen began to sink down into the condition of serfs. On the other hand, the slaves who were employed in agriculture became, for the same reason, an object of solicitude to the legislature, and their proprietors were forbidden to alienate them. They thus acquired a recognised position, not far removed from serfdom; and when all the lower class were reduced to the same state of poverty, the difference in the political status of the two orders came to be obliterated. This process of amalgamation, as might be expected, was a very gradual one, and extended over several centuries.

CHAPTER V.

THE ORTHODOX CHURCH AND THE HERETICAL CHURCHES.

Causes of separation—Churches of Syria and Egypt national—Suspicion and persecution—The Nestorians—Their missions—Their present state—The Jacobites—Their later history—The Egyptian or Coptic Church—Its decline—The Abyssinian Church—The Armenians—Their history—Their influence—The Monothelite controversy—Martin I. and Maximus—Sixth General Council—The Maronites—The Paulicians—Their leaders—Their persecutions—The Bogomilians—Their treatment by Alexius Comnenus.

Churches of Syria and Egypt national

THE history of the formation of the national, or so-called heretical, churches of the East is closely interwoven with political questions. First among these was the relation of the Greeks to the other races of the East. During the period which intervened between Alexander the Great and Constantine, the countries of south-eastern Europe and of Western Asia as far as the Taurus range were almost completely Hellenised; but beyond that limit the same thing had not happened. In Syria and Egypt the Hellenic influence was mainly confined to the great cities, and the national life, though repressed by the irresistible force of the Roman government, still possessed great vitality. This was increased by the foundation of Constantinople, which formed a new focus of Greek civilisation and influence, and thus attracted to itself similar elements which had existed elsewhere, so that from that time onward Antioch and Alexandria were less imbued with the Hellenic spirit, and became more definitely national centres. But when the Roman empire was parted and became two heads, no provision was made for the Oriental peoples: they were attached to the eastern branch of the empire, and thus became politically subservient to the Greeks. From this arose a strong feeling of antagonism to the ruling race, which needed only a slight cause to fan it into a flame; and such a cause—in default of other outlets, which were closed by the strong hand of despotism—was found from time to time in theological questions, which the speculative tendency of the Eastern mind was constantly disposed to raise. Thus Syria and Egypt were the native regions of Nestorianism and Monophysitism. Nestorius, it is true, was patriarch of Constantinople at the time when he broached his heresy of the two persons in Christ; but he had only just been transferred thither from Antioch in Syria, and at the council of Ephesus, where he was condemned, his views were supported by a large contingent of Syrian bishops. Similarly, the Monophysite tenets were eagerly maintained by the Egyptian church, the leading motive for this support being the idea that those who opposed them were attacking the doctrine of their own Cyril of Alexandria, who had been the great antagonist of Nestorius; and the condemnation and deposition of Dioscorus, the successor of Cyril in his see, and the strongest supporter of Eutyches, inaugurated the separation of that church from the rest of Christendom.

The idea that nationality was influential in causing the schisms which thus arose, is at once suggested by the fact, that neither the Nestorian nor the Monophysite doctrines, from which they started, gained any hold either in the Greek or the Latin church.

A further cause of alienation existed in the suspicious feelings with which every national movement was regarded by the central government. To those whose primary aim was to consolidate the heterogeneous elements of which the Roman empire was composed, the assertion of nationality appeared to be a step towards rebellion. Hence the provincial churches became the object of jealous observation. Before Constantine's time, Christianity had been mostly confined to the middle and lower classes, and had consequently been closely allied with the people in the various provinces, and had assumed local usage; the Scriptures also had been translated into various languages of the East, and the services were performed in the native tongues. But from the time when that emperor formed a political alliance with the Church, the clergy in the provinces rendered themselves liable to be accused of heresy whenever they identified themselves with any national movement in ecclesiastical matters. The ill-will that was thus aroused was greatly aggravated by the policy of persecuting heretics. As early as Constantine's reign the secular arm undertook to repress views which were contrary to those of the orthodox Church. Indeed, that emperor's edict for suppressing the meetings of heretics, which is given in his Life by Eusebius, breathes the spirit of the most violent intolerance; and in an evil hour the rulers of the Church availed themselves of that unhallowed aid. The natural result was the growth of disaffection wherever doctrines were held which had either been pronounced unorthodox by the Church at large, or were suspected of being so. This was brought to a head in the time of Justinian, in whom religious bigotry and political despotism were combined to a greater degree than in any of his predecessors. His endeavours to enforce unity of belief thoroughly alienated the eastern provinces of the empire, and prepared the way for future invaders. The name of Melchite—a term of Syriac origin, invented by the Jacobites, and signifying Imperialist—was now applied by the provincials to the adherents of the orthodox Church, as having their doctrines determined for them by a temporal sovereign. The want of earnest allegiance thus arising enabled the Persians to penetrate into the heart of the empire, and after they were finally repulsed by Heraclius, secured an easy victory in Syria and Egypt to the Saracens. So completely at last did the religious point of view dominate every other, that at the present day the names by which the descendants of these provincials are known —Copt, Jacobite, Maronite, &c.—convey rather the idea of religion than that of nationality.

The earliest in date of these separatist churches was that of the Nestorians, who adopted the views which were condemned at the Council of Ephesus (A.D. 431). Within the limits of the Roman empire, however, this sect was rapidly extirpated by persecution; and even in the patriarchate of Antioch, where, as we have seen, the tenets of Nestorius at first found greatest favour, it had disappeared as early as the

<small>The Nestorians</small>

time of Justinian. But another field lay open to it in the Persian kingdom of the Sassanidæ, and in this it ultimately struck its roots deeply. The Chaldæan church, which at the beginning of the fifth century was in a flourishing condition, had been founded by missionaries from Syria; its primate, or Catholicos, was dependent on the patriarch of Antioch, and in respect of language and discipline it was closely connected with the Syrian church. It is not surprising, therefore, to find that some of its members lent a ready ear to the Nestorian doctrines. This was especially the case with the church-teachers of the famous seminary at Edessa in Mesopotamia; and when they were dispersed, owing to the tyrannical proceedings of Rabulas, the bishop of that city, who was a strong adherent of Cyril of Alexandria, they diffused these tenets throughout the length and breadth of Persia. One of their number, Barsumas, who was bishop of the city of Nisibis from 435 to 489, by his long and active labours contributed most of all to the establishment of the Nestorian church in Persia. He persuaded the king Pherozes (Firuz) that the antagonism of his own sect to the doctrine of the established church of the Roman empire would prove a safeguard for Persia, because it would remove any temptation on the part of the Christians in his empire to conspire with his enemies. The suggestion harmonised with the traditional views of the Sassanidæ, who had often prohibited correspondence between the Chaldæan clergy and their brethren in Syria; and from that time Nestorianism became the only form of Christianity tolerated in Persia. If we can trust the statement of Abulpharagius, the historian of the thirteenth century—who, however, was a Jacobite and therefore liable to be prejudiced in the matter—this decision was followed by a fearful massacre of all those who remained faithful to the older church, and Barsumas was not guiltless of promoting the persecution. The Catholicos of Chaldæa now threw off his dependence on Antioch, and assumed the title of Patriarch of Babylon. The school of Edessa, which in 489 was again broken up by the Greek emperor, Zeno, was transferred to Nisibis, and in that place continued for several centuries to be an important centre of theological learning, and especially of biblical studies. In the succeeding period multitudes of those who were persecuted for their religious opinions by Justinian and his successors took refuge in Persia, and swelled the numbers of the Nestorians.

The characteristic, which beyond all others distinguished the Chaldæan church, was its missionary zeal. In this respect it far outstripped all the other Eastern communions. Gibbon has examined the authorities for these missions with his usual cautious criticism, and has described them with less than his usual coldness, and implies no doubt of their historic truth. In the sixth century the Nestorians had established churches from the Persian Gulf to the Caspian Sea, and had preached the Gospel to the Medes, the Bactrians, the Huns, and the Indians, and as far as the coast of Malabar and the island of Ceylon. At a later period, starting from Balk and Samarcand, they spread Christianity among the nomad Tartar tribes in the remote valleys of the Imaus; and the inscription of Siganfu, which was discovered in China, and the genuineness of which is considered to be above suspicion, describes the fortunes of the Nestorian church in that country from the first mission, A.D. 636, to the year in which that monument was set up, A.D. 781. In the ninth century, during the rule of the caliphs at Bagdad, the patriarch removed to that city, and at this period twenty-five metropolitans were subject to him, of whom those who lived within a moderate distance met him in yearly synod, while the rest were bound once in six years to send a confession of their faith and their obedience to him. The number of souls that were embraced in the Nestorian church, together with the Jacobites, who were a smaller body, were computed to outnumber the Greek and Roman communions. Dr. Neale says, 'It may be doubted whether Innocent III. possessed more spiritual power than the patriarch in the city of the Caliphs.'

From the eleventh century onwards the prosperity of the Chaldæan church declined, owing to the terrible persecutions to which its members were exposed. Foremost among these was the attack of Timour the Tartar, who almost exterminated them. Within the present century their diminished numbers have been still further thinned by frightful massacres inflicted by the Kurds. Their headquarters now are a remote and rugged valley in the mountains of Kurdistan, on the banks of the Greater Zab, the river which Xenophon has immortalised in his narrative of the Retreat of the Ten Thousand. Here in the village of Kochannes is the simple residence of the patriarch, whose office is hereditary, and who lives in very primitive style. Beyond the boundary which separates Turkey from Persia to the southward of Mount Ararat, a similar community is settled on the shores of Lake Urumia.

Their present state

A still larger colony is to be found at Mosul, and others exist at Diarbekir, and elsewhere in the neighbourhood of the Tigris. Some of these have joined the Church of Rome, but the majority still maintain the belief of their fathers; though in a people whose faith is so simple, and whose intelligence is almost incapable of dealing with exact theological distinctions, it would be difficult, except in words, to discover the taint of heresy. Their total number is estimated at less than 18,000 souls. Of their widely extended missions only one fragment now remains, in the Christians of St. Thomas on the Malabar coast of India. This interesting community, though cut off by long intervening spaces of country from the rest of Christendom, continued to maintain their religion and their civilisation; and their bishops, despite all dangers by sea and land, were ordained at Mosul by the Nestorian patriarch. Our own Alfred is reported to have sent an embassy to them; but they were first revealed to the Western world by the Portuguese, who in the fifteenth century established themselves at Goa, and endeavoured to bring this ancient church under the supremacy of the Pope. But while they succeeded in cutting them off from communication with their patriarch, they inspired them with a detestation of Rome; and the result was that in despair they threw themselves into the arms of the Jacobites, to whose communion they still belong. Their prelates have been ever since obtained from the representatives of that body either in Alexandria or in Diarbekir.

The fourth general council, that of Chalcedon (A.D. 451), at which the doctrine of those who maintained the existence of a single nature in Christ was condemned, was much more fruitful in producing separation than the Council of Ephesus which preceded it had been. In consequence of it, three important national churches, those of Syria, Egypt, and Armenia, ultimately broke away from the Catholic Church. We should notice, however, the difference of view which prevailed among these with regard to the disputed tenet. The Armenians embraced the Eutychian view, that the divinity is the sole nature in Christ;. while the Egyptians held to the doctrine, which is specially termed Monophysite, that the divinity and humanity make up one compound nature in Christ. Syria, now no longer Nestorian, fluctuated between the two forms of opinion, and after at first adopting the Eutychian tenet, was drawn into that of the Monophysites, chiefly by the influence of Severus, patriarch of Antioch (513). Let us follow the fortunes of the last-named church. During the first half of the sixth century the Monophysite party in Syria was threatened with becoming gradually extinct, owing to the deficiency of clergy, of which the Emperor Justinian had found means to deprive them, when a man arose among them, who was distinguished for indefatigable zeal in the cause to which he devoted himself, and who did more than anyone else towards preserving and extending his communion. This was the monk James, who is usually known as Jacobus Baradæus—Al Baradai, 'the man in rags'—which name he received, it is said, from the circumstance of his going about as a beggar. He belonged to the monastery of Phasitla, in the district of Nisibis, and was ordained by certain imprisoned bishops to be the metropolitan of their church. Travelling hither and thither with great rapidity in the face of many dangers, he visited the Syrian and neighbouring provinces, ordained clergy for his party, and gave them a patriarch of Antioch as their superior: by this means he called down upon himself the indignation of the orthodox clergy and the emperor, and orders were given to seize him, but his beggar's disguise secured him from capture. In this manner he continued his labours with great success for thirty-three years, until his death in A.D. 578. It was probably from him that the sect obtained the name of the Jacobites.

The Jacobite patriarchs of Antioch, however, were unable to reside in that city while it remained in the power of the emperors, and consequently *Their later history* settled themselves at Amida on the Tigris, now Diarbekir, at which place they still have their headquarters. During the middle ages the Syrian Christians were widely spread throughout Asia, though to a less extent than the Nestorians, and considerable learning existed among them. Their most distinguished scholar was Abulpharagius, whose annals are the only mediæval history of the Asiatic church which we possess; he was born in 1226, and held the office of Mafrian of the East, a sort of Jacobite vice-patriarch. At the present day their communities are for the most part confined to the neighbourhood of the Euphrates and Tigris, and they amount to less than 200,000 souls. Though they have so long been removed from their primitive home, they have by no means forgotten their origin. Their ecclesiastical language is Syriac, though Arabic and even Turkish are sometimes substituted for it. Their patriarch always takes the name of Ignatius; and though this custom arose at the end of the sixteenth century, there can be little doubt that the name is derived from that of the saint who was the first bishop of Antioch.

The importance of the Egyptian church on account of its theological learning and the influence of its monastic system, and the stubborn temper of the Egyptian people, rendered it a matter of the first importance how they would receive the decrees of Chalcedon. Unfortunately, the condemnation of the Monophysite views appeared to them a reaffirmation of the errors of Nestorius; and the deposition of their patriarch Dioscorus, a hot-headed and violent man who deserved no sympathy, caused them to regard him as a martyr to the truth. His successor, Proterius, was an adherent of the opposite tenets; and in consequence of his nomination the Monophysites formed a party of their own, and violent struggles ensued for many years between the two factions. The *henoticon* or *concordat* of the Emperor Zeno in 482, which was intended to serve as a basis for peace by enforcing mutual toleration and ignoring as far as possible the disputed points, only brought out to view more clearly the antagonism that prevailed between them. But it was the heavy hand of Justinian which caused the final schism. His nominee for the office of patriarch, Apollinaris (551), entered Alexandria with a guard of soldiers, and after proceeding to the cathedral and mounting the throne, divested himself of his military garb, and displayed himself to the people as the head of their church. When they attacked him with curses and a volley of stones, he replied by ordering his soldiers to charge, and, in the massacre which followed, a large number of the citizens perished. Apollinaris maintained his position for eighteen years; but meanwhile the Monophysites had appointed a rival patriarch, and as their party had all along been the more numerous, their church became more and more the church of the nation. When persecution was renewed in the time of Heraclius, their patriarch Benjamin was forced to escape from Alexandria into the desert, but we are told that in his flight he was encouraged by a voice which bade him expect at the end of ten years the aid of a foreign nation, who, like the Egyptians themselves, were circumcised. This nation was the Arabs (640).

The history of the Coptic church under Mussulman domination is a weary tale of long oppression and steady decline. At the present day the patriarch resides at Cairo, and has thirteen or fourteen bishops under him. This church is deeply sunk in ignorance, but retains more primitive customs than any other communion, such as the kiss of peace, which is interchanged throughout the congregation, and the practice of conferring ordination, not by imposition of hands, but by the act of breathing. On many grounds, independently of its sufferings, it has strong claims on our sympathy. Its people are the descendants of one of the most wonderful nations of antiquity—the Egyptians. The language which is used in its services, though unintelligible to the congregations, is the same, however much debased, which Moses heard at the court of Pharaoh, and through which he became learned in all the wisdom of the Egyptians. And, as the Melchite or orthodox church in Egypt is practically extinct, it is the only representative of the church of St. Athanasius.

Its decline

THE HERETICAL CHURCHES 83

One offshoot of the Egyptian church remains to be mentioned—the Ethiopian or Abyssinian church. This was founded from Alexandria in the fourth century, and adopted the same views on the Monophysite controversy as were taken by the Coptic church. When Nubia, which intervenes between Egypt and Abyssinia, ceased to be a Christian country, owing to the destruction of its church by the Mahometans, the Abyssinian church was cut off from communication with the rest of Christendom, though it still maintained the succession of its primates by obtaining their consecration from Alexandria. Thus it continued until the sixteenth century, when, like the Christians of St. Thomas in India, it was visited by the Portuguese. In the wake of that people the Jesuit missionaries followed, and at last, in 1626, the reigning monarch, Segued, renounced his connection with the Egyptian church and swore allegiance to the see of Rome. His people rebelled in vain; but his son and successor, Basilides, expelled the intruders and re-established the faith of his forefathers, which has continued to the present day to be the religion of the nation. They remain an almost unique specimen of a semi-barbarous Christian people. Their worship is strangely mixed with Jewish customs; dancing forms part of their ritual, as it did among the Jews; the Sabbath is still observed as well as the Lord's Day; circumcision is practised; and they believe that they possess the ark of the covenant, which was miraculously transported to them. But, notwithstanding their superstition and the separation of religion from morality that is found among them, the most intelligent traveller who has visited their country bears witness that Abyssinia 'compared with other nations of Africa unquestionably holds a high station. She is superior in arts and in agriculture, in laws, religion, and social condition to all the benighted children of the sun.'

The Armenians have inhabited from time immemorial the lofty table-land of Western Asia, which intervenes between the Mediterranean, the Black Sea, and the Caspian, and in which the Tigris, the Euphrates, and the Araxes take their rise. Their church is the oldest of all national churches. They were converted by St. Gregory, called 'The Illuminator,' who was a relative of Dertad or Tiridates, their prince, and had been forced to leave the country at the same time with him, and settled at Cæsareia in Cappadocia, where he was initiated into the Christian faith. When they returned, both prince and people embraced the Gospel through the preaching of Gregory (A.D. 276), and thus presented the first instance of an entire nation becoming Christian. The persecutions they subsequently suffered, especially at the hands of the Persian monarchs, endeared the Church to the people, and it has been identified with them and bound up with their national existence throughout their long history. It is generally admitted that the heresy which has been imputed to them exists in name only, and not in reality. By an accident they were unrepresented at Chalcedon, and, owing to the poverty of their language in words serviceable for the purposes of theology, they had at that time but one word for Nature and Person, in consequence of which they misunderstood the decision of that council. Their ecclesiastical writers express the orthodox doctrine

The Armenians

with sufficient clearness. Their liturgies, too, contain nothing that is unorthodox; but this is true also of the liturgies of all the separatist churches that have been mentioned. It was not until eighty-four years had elapsed that they finally adopted Eutychianism, and an anathema was pronounced on the Chalcedonian decrees (536). This decision was welcome to the Persian ruler Chosroes, who now possessed a large part of their country, and rejoiced that this portion of his subjects should be estranged from their brethen in the Roman empire.

We have seen that the Monophysite tenets of the Armenians differed from those of the Jacobites; and, as <small>Their history</small> a matter of fact, the two communions have remained separate from one another, and are so at the present day, even where their churches exist in the same city. But for this alienation there was a stronger reason than divergence of creed. It arose at a very early period from the jealousy of the Armenians towards the Syrian clergy on account of their overweening influence in the south-west part of Armenia. In fact, before the Armenian alphabet was invented by St. Mezrop—who for that reason is justly numbered among their foremost saints—at the beginning of the fifth century, only Syrian bibles were in use in Armenia; and, in the part just mentioned, the bishops, who were Syrians, wrote and officiated in their own tongue, and at last they aspired to the Armenian patriarchate itself. After St. Mezrop had translated the Scriptures into the Armenian language, their church obtained a standing-ground independent both of the Syrians and the Greeks. Subsequently to the fall of the Sassanidæ in the seventh century, Armenia was disputed for by the Eastern empire and the Saracens; but from 859 to 1045 it was ruled by a native dynasty of vigorous princes—the Bagratidæ. This was brought to an end by the suspicious policy of the Byzantine emperors, who, as has been already mentioned (p. 22), overthrew this kingdom, and thus admitted the Seljouk Turks into Asia Minor. After this Armenia passed into the hands of various Mahometan powers, until at length the greater part of it was incorporated in the Ottoman empire. The last great calamity which fell upon it happened in 1605, when Shah Abbas of Persia removed 12,000 families from their homes and settled them near Ispahan. The districts which lie to the north of Ararat have gradually passed into the hands of Russia. Within the borders of that country, not far from the foot of the great mountain, lies Etchmiadzin, the patriarch of which place is the head of the Armenian church. To his jurisdiction the great bulk of the nation is still subject, though a certain number, not inconsiderable, have joined the Roman communion, and are known as united Armenians.

The Armenian character is naturally a powerful one, and the race is distinguished, in its political and social life, by industry, perseverance, and long-suffering endurance. Their intellect, though slow in movement, possesses great depth and sobriety. The calamities of the nation have become in one sense the cause of its greatness, for the enforced emigration which was brought about by invasion and persecution has dispersed them widely, and consequently extended their influence. Those of the upper class are known throughout Turkey as leading bankers and merchants, and their

<small>Their influence</small>

shrewdness and aptitude for business are proverbial. They are also to be found engaged in trade in most of the capitals of Europe, and throughout the length and breadth of Asia, including India. Their nationality and their church can hardly fail to take an important part in determining the future of the East.

The councils of Ephesus and Chalcedon, which resulted in the withdrawal from the Catholic church of Monothelite the Christian bodies hitherto mentioned, and controversy the discussions which preceded them, have received but a passing notice in these pages, because they belong rather to the general history of the Church. But the next controversy which calls for our attention— the Monothelite—requires a somewhat fuller treatment, because of its intimate connection with the policy of the empire. The person who originated it was the Emperor Heraclius. That famous conqueror, in the course of his campaigns against Persia, had perceived the political importance of reconciling the Monophysite sects to the Church, and thus restoring their allegiance to the imperial government. He had also had interviews with some of their bishops, and in the course of these was led to the conclusion that a common ground of agreement for the orthodox church and the seceders might be found in the expression 'One divinely human mode of working and willing in Christ.' This formulary was approved both by Sergius, the patriarch of Constantinople, and by the Roman bishop, Honorius; though the latter, reckoning the question as one of the unprofitable subtleties which endanger the interests of piety, deprecated the use of any definite statement on the subject. From various quarters, however, objections to this new doctrine began to make themselves heard; and, in order to silence these, Heraclius, in the year 638, put forth his *Ecthesis*, a dogmatic edict, which forbade all discussion of the question of the single or double operation of the will in Christ, while it expressed itself favourably to the former view. But the controversy thus started was not to be suppressed in this manner, and the emperor met the fate of those who endeavour to reconcile two parties by force, and to impose a rule of faith on others. A strong opposition arose to the Monothelite tenets, the principal leader of the party being Maximus, an acute thinker and learned theologian, who had previously held the office of first private secretary in the imperial court, but resigned that position in order to advocate what seemed to him the orthodox belief.

Heraclius died in 641, but Constans, who succeeded him as emperor after a brief interval, followed in his footsteps in attempting to check the rising controversy. For this purpose he revoked the *Ecthesis*, and published in its place an edict of his own, which was called the *Type* (648). In this the theological question was almost entirely ignored; but it was ordained that the Church should abide by the doctrine as it stood before the discussion commenced, and severe penalties were instituted for the punishment of those who refused to abide by this decree. But meanwhile the bishops of Rome had warmly adopted the side opposed to Monothelitism, and now the existing pope, Martin I., without consulting the emperor, summoned a council, which from its being held within the precincts of the Lateran palace, was called the Lateran Council, and established the doctrine of two wills, at the same time condemning the opposite doctrine and its advocates. Thereupon was seen a spectacle revolting to the feelings of Christendom. The Bishop of Rome was still a subject of the Eastern empire, and this proceeding on his part was regarded as an act of rebellion. Orders were therefore given to seize him and transport him for trial to Constantinople. The aged man, who for several months previously had been suffering from sickness, was suddenly removed from the palace by the exarch Calliopas, and put on shipboard; and after receiving shameful treatment on the voyage, in the course of which he was left for a year on the island of Naxos, he at last reached the Byzantine capital. There he was kept in prison for three months before his case was heard; and after his trial he would have been condemned to death had it not been for the intercession of the patriarch Paul, who was himself lying on his deathbed. He was banished to the city of Cherson in the Crimea, where, after having borne his sufferings with great fortitude and resignation, he died in 655, two years after he had quitted Rome. An attempt was then made to persuade Maximus, who had throughout been the soul of the opposition to the Imperial decrees, to consent to the compromise of the *Type*; but in vain. When all negotiations had failed, he was subjected to even more barbarous treatment than the pope. He was publicly scourged, his tongue was cut out, and his right hand was cut off; and he also died in exile shortly after, in consequence of the injuries he had received.

By these violent measures the emperor succeeded in crushing his antagonists, and not only was the *Type* accepted, but Monothelite views for a time became predominant in the Eastern Church. From this cause **Sixth General Council** a schism arose between the East and the West, for the Roman see continued to manifest zeal in maintaining the doctrine of two wills. All communication between the churches was for a time suspended; and still more hostile measures would have been resorted to, had it not been for Constantine Pogonatus, who in 668 had succeeded to the throne. He was anxiously desirous that the peace of the Church should be restored; and with this object, while he professed himself unqualified to determine a point of doctrine, he wrote to the pope, inviting him to send representatives to a council, at which the question in dispute might be freely investigated and finally decided. To this proposal Pope Agatho agreed, and accordingly in the year 680 the sixth œcumenical council assembled in Constantinople. There, after numerous sessions, in the course of which the Eastern bishops professed themselves satisfied with the arguments adduced by the other side, the tenets of the Monothelites were condemned, and the doctrine was established, that there are in Christ two wills and two natural modes of working, united without schism, and without confusion, as well as without change; so that no conflict ever existed between them, but the human will was invariably subject to the divine and almighty will.

The opinion which was thus expelled from the Church continued to form part of the creed of one race, **The Maronites** which exists at the present day. These are the Maronites, who constitute the Christian population of the Lebanon. Their founder, John

Maron, was a monk who lived in this district towards the end of the seventh century; and when Macarius, the Monothelite patriarch of Antioch, was deposed by the Trullan council, Maron was consecrated by some bishops who adopted the proscribed tenets, and took upon himself the functions of a patriarch. In this character he was recognised, first by his monastery, and afterwards by the inhabitants of the neighbouring country, who from that time formed a separate Monothelite church. Owing to the rugged character of the mountains they inhabit, they have succeeded in maintaining their nationality—for the creed formed a nation—notwithstanding the various conquerors who have occupied Syria. In the twelfth century, however, through the influence of the Crusaders, they unanimously embraced the communion of Rome; and they are now described as perhaps the most ultramontane people on the face of the earth, though they retain certain peculiar observances of their own. Their connection with that church has produced some literary fruits, for, from the Maronite college at Rome, in the eighteenth century, proceeded the Assemani, whose learned compilations have been utilised by writers on Oriental subjects from the time of Gibbon onwards. The patriarch resides in the convent of Kenobin, close to the group of cedars which are the last remnant of what was once the famous forest of Lebanon. Subject to him are eight bishops, one of whom resides in Cyprus, in which island there are many Maronites. The terrible massacre inflicted on this people by their neighbours in the Lebanon, the Druses, is within the memory of the present generation.

The heretical sect of which we have next to speak, did not separate from the Church, like those bodies of Christians which have hitherto been mentioned, but existed from the first as an independent communion. These were the Paulicians, who arose in the latter half of the seventh century in the regions bordering on the Euphrates, which intervene between Asia Minor and Mesopotamia. They professed to base their religious system on the writings of St. Paul; and this is probably the origin of their name—a view which is corroborated by the circumstance that their leaders were wont to adopt names derived from the disciples and companions of that apostle, such as Silvanus, Titus, and Tychicus. St. Peter they regarded as a Judaising apostle, and they rejected his epistles, as being irreconcilable with the Pauline doctrines. While they reverenced the four Gospels, they gave the preference to that of St. Luke, as having been written under the influence of St. Paul; and, after that, they esteemed most highly the gospel of St. John—no doubt, because many of its expressions might be interpreted in accordance with their own mystical views. In their strong desire to restore what they conceived to be apostolical simplicity and spiritual worship, they opposed, not only the offering of reverence to images, but the use of the cross and the observance of the sacraments. They called their places of worship oratories ($\pi\rho o\sigma\varepsilon v\chi a\iota$), and eliminated every element of sacerdotalism, so that their teachers were not distinguished from other persons either by their dress or by any other outward sign. The only ceremony which they allowed was that of prostration before the book of the gospels. With these views they combined principles derived from Gnosticism, the influence of which phase of religion had survived in this remote district. They believed in dualism, and, with that repugnance to matter which is characteristic of the Gnostic systems, they referred the creation of the sensible world to the evil principle, which they represented as the Demiurge. The redemption which was wrought for mankind by Christ was their deliverance from the dominion of this power, which could not be effected merely by the divine light of the knowledge of God falling on the soul, while it was imprisoned in the body. Though they avoided the extreme error of the Docetæ, who regarded the body of Christ as a phantom, they could not allow that he had any contact with human flesh; and thus they maintained that he brought with him from heaven a body of higher substance, and with this passed through his Virgin mother as through a channel. It followed from this, that the sufferings of Christ were excluded from any part in the work of redemption. As they derived Judaism from the Demiurge, they rejected altogether the scriptures of the Old Testament. It is further noticeable with regard to the Paulicians—and the same thing is found not unfrequently in the history of theosophic sects—that they justified the use of deceptive arts, when questioned with regard to their tenets, so that on some occasions they escaped persecution by the employment of equivocal expressions. One of their leaders, when under examination, professed his belief in the Catholic Church, the Mother of God, and the Sacraments, accepting those terms, not in a literal, but in a symbolical, sense.

The founder of this sect, who was called Constantine, but afterwards took the name of Silvanus, was born near Samosata on the banks of the Euphrates. He was educated in a Gnostic sect, and either had not read the New Testament scriptures at all, or had done so very imperfectly, till a deacon, who was returning home from captivity, probably among the Saracens, and was hospitably entertained in his house, left him as a present a complete copy of them. Being deeply impressed by the doctrines which he found there, and engrafting them on the views in which he was brought up, he felt himself called to inaugurate a religious reformation, and with this object he laboured with great activity for twenty-seven years. But the increase of his sect attracted the attention of the Imperial Government, and in the year 684 the Emperor Constantine Pogonatus sent an officer of his household, called Simeon, into those regions, with authority to suppress by force these heretical views. The story that follows bears a marked resemblance to the conversion of St. Paul. At the command of Simeon, Constanstine was stoned to death by some of his renegade disciples; but the majority of his followers firmly adhered to their faith, and Simeon himself, while endeavouring to bring them over to the doctrines of the Church, was struck with the Christian sincerity which they displayed, and thus became attracted by their opinions. These impressions ripened in his mind after his return to Constantinople, and at the end of three years he once more sought the headquarters of the sect, and assuming the name of Titus became their leader. In consequence of his influence the party still further increased, until, in 690, a neighbouring bishop again requested the

Their leaders

government to interfere, and, in the course of the enquiry that followed, Simeon and many others died at the stake. For a century from this time the Paulician body was rent by divisions; but, towards the commencement of the ninth century, another reformer, Sergius, arose in Asia Minor, to which country many had migrated from fear of the Saracens. His method of teaching was more definitely controversial than that of his predecessors, for he used first to present to his hearers the practical doctrines of Christianity, and then to contrast them with the condition of the dominant church. He traversed every part of Asia Minor, confirming the Paulician communities, and spreading their doctrines, including the Gnostic dualism which from the first had been embodied with them; and so great was the effect of his preaching, that even monks, nuns, and clergy are said to have willingly listened to him. But at last he seems to have been carried away by spiritual pride, for he spoke of himself in extravagant terms, and appropriated titles which belong to Christ alone—the porter, the good shepherd, the light of the house of God. His labours fell in the reign of Nicephorus I., who advocated a tolerant ecclesiastical policy; but when persecution recommenced under the successors of that emperor, Sergius and his followers withdrew into the territory of the Saracens, where they were favourably received as enemies of the empire. Ultimately he was assassinated by a zealot for church doctrine, in the year 835.

The persecutions of the Paulicians fill some of the darkest pages of Byzantine history. Again and again their extirpation was attempted, but with no result beyond that of forcing them to change their abode, and sometimes even with disaster to the imperial troops. After the most violent of these attacks in the reign of Theodora, who finally restored the worship of images in the East, Karbeas, one of the principal officers on the staff of the general commanding that district, hearing that his father had been crucified for his adherence to the doctrines of the Paulicians, fled to the Saracens (845), and under their auspices, fortified himself with a large body of Paulicians in Tephrice, a strong position among the spurs of Anti-Taurus, from which he ravaged the neighbouring country. He was succeeded by his son-in-law Chrysocheir, who gathered round him so many fugitives, that Basi the Macedonian, after fruitlessly attempting negotiations with him, found himself obliged seriously to undertake the conquest of the place (871). With a view to this, he first captured the cities in the neighbourhood of the Euphrates, which afforded aid to the Paulicians, and at last defeated the inhabitants of Tephrice in a battle, in which Chrysocheir himself was slain. After the lapse of a century, John Zimisces transported a number of those who remained in Asia to Thrace, in order to reinforce a colony of them who had been planted there in the days of Constantine Copronymus; they were thus removed from the temptation of leaguing with the Saracens, and their warlike spirit rendered them serviceable for defending the northern frontier of the empire. There they continued to dwell, in the neighbourhood of Philippopolis, and we afterwards hear of them as serving in the armies of Alexius Comnenus.

Their persecutions

It is to these Paulician colonies in Thrace that we

can trace the origin of another sect, which arose among the Bulgarians, and spread from them into the neighbouring parts of the empire—the Bogomilians. Their founder, Jeremiah, who was otherwise called Bogomil—a Slavonic name, signifying the Friend of God—lived in Bulgaria in the middle of the tenth century, while that country was still independent of the Byzantine power. His system was a modification of the Paulician doctrines, retaining their dualism, but assimilating them more closely to Christianity. His followers called themselves simply Christians, and were distinguished by their strict morality, their composed demeanour and their ascetic life. Their strength lay in their opposition to the formalism that prevailed in the Church, and in their satisfying a longing which was felt for a purer form of religion. They celebrated the memories of the iconoclastic emperors. They had neither churches nor services: Satan, they said, dwelt first at the temple at Jerusalem, and afterwards in St. Sophia's at Constantinople. Their teachers went from place to place instructing and confirming their communities; and prayer, which among the Greek portion of the sect was observed as often as twelve times in the twenty-four hours, was performed either in the open country or in private houses. They were divided into two classes, the 'simple believers' and the 'perfect,' who aimed at maintaining a higher spiritual level. The number of the latter was small, for their life was as severe as that of an anchorite. Owing to their feeling of antagonism towards the flesh as representing the element of matter, the 'perfect' might not marry, and abstained from animal food and from wine. They lived in poverty, renounced all family ties, dressed in black, and spoke little. Though they devoted themselves to instructing the young and visiting the sick, they were required to take their share in manual labour. All who belonged to this order, whether men or women, might preach. They refused to take an oath, and would not engage in war. At the head of this communion was a bishop, and under him was an order of apostles, and another of deacons. A portion of their property was devoted to the service of the church, and was employed, partly in maintaining their poor and sick bretheren, and partly in paying the expenses of their preachers. The members of the sect generally were noted for their industry, but they were not allowed to accumulate more than was necessary for the support of their families. They observed the practice of confession, which took place monthly in the presence of the 'perfect,' but without the mention of individual sins. All, in order to be saved, had to be admitted on their deathbeds into the number of the 'perfect.' The 'simple believers' had the right of divorcing their wives—a custom, which naturally became a cloak for great licentiousness.

It will readily be understood that, from the time when the Bulgarians were finally subjugated by Basil II. in 1018, the Bogomilians were regarded with the greatest suspicion by the authorities, both civil and ecclesiastical, of the empire. Alexius Comnenus was conspicuous in his attempts to convert them, both by argument and by force. His treatment of their leader, Basilius, was worthy of his hypocritical character. Having discovered by means of torture applied to a member of the sect the position which he held—for,

Treatment by Alexius Comnenus

owing to the unostentatious behaviour of this body, it was not easy to identify its adherents—he summoned him into his presence, and invited him, in a friendly manner, to explain his opinions to him, and to state the arguments by which he had laboured to correct the vain superstitions of the clergy. The Bogomilian leader—whose demeanour was respectful, and whose shrunken features gave him the air of an ascetic—being thus encouraged, declared his grounds of objection to the established Church, and fully expounded his views. At the conclusion of the interview the emperor drew aside a curtain and revealed the imperial secretary, by whom his words had been committed to writing, together with the patriarch and other dignitaries of Church and State. His condemnation as a heretic followed, and as he refused to recant his opinions, he was condemned to be burnt at the stake. His execution was delayed for eight years, and every form of solicitation was brought to bear upon him; but he resisted all these, and ultimately suffered with great fortitude. In order to counteract these tenets, Alexius founded the city of Alexiopolis, as a rival to Philippopolis, to serve as a head-quarters for converted heretics. They had taken deep root, however, among the South Slavonic peoples; and the diffusion of this belief, and the antagonism of its adherents to dominant churches wherever found, go far to account for the ease with which the Ottomans conquered the lands of the Balkan peninsula in the fourteenth and fifteenth centuries. The further spread of these views, with various modifications, into Western Europe, and their development into the Catharist and Albigensian systems of belief, exercised an important influence on the Latin church.

CHAPTER VI.

THE ICONOCLASTIC CONTROVERSY.

The principles at stake in it — Growth of image-worship — The emperor Leo III.—His decree against images—Pope Gregory II.—St. John Damascene—Constantine Copronymus—Treatment of the monks—The Empress Irene—Tarasius patriarch—Second council of Nicæa—Fate of Constantine VI.—Leo the Armenian—Theodore Studita—Death of Leo—Michael the Stammerer—Theophilus—Restoration of images—Effects of the controversy on society — Attitude of the West—Statues and pictures—Hymnology of the period—Rules of composition—The leading hymn-writers—Specimen and translation.

THE iconoclastic controversy is the most remarkable episode in the history of the Byzantine church. It continued, with one interval, for a century and a half, and this period was a highly critical one for the Eastern empire, and witnessed an extraordinary development of its power and prosperity. The principles which were represented by the two sides in the dispute, though they have made themselves felt also in other ages of the Church, have never been developed with the same intensity. On the one hand was the desire to approach God in worship as directly as possible, without the intervention of any subsidiary or intermediate agency; on the other was the longing to interpret that which is beyond human comprehension by aids of various kinds, and to help the spiritual part

Principles at stake

of man by appeals to the senses. The ultimate development of the two principles may be seen respectively in the rigid, unimaginative monotheism of Mahometanism, and in some of the more extravagantly anthropomorphic forms of religion. The same influences were at work at a later period in the Protestant reformation on the Continent, and in the Puritan movement in England; but such historical parallels are apt to be misleading, because of the extraneous elements, doctrinal and political, which each particular controversy involved. The Byzantine struggle is rendered especially intricate by its close connection with politics, in which respect the ordinary relations of parties were inverted; for whereas usually the church was the subservient instrument of the state, or at least acted in concert with it, on this occasion the aims of the two were frequently antagonistic to one another. Hence it came to pass that, since one of the motives by which the iconoclast emperors were swayed in carrying on the contest, was undoubtedly the desire of concentrating still further their despotic power, the monks, and those of the clergy who took a prominent part in the support of image-worship, became almost unintentionally the champions of freedom. On a first view, there is something extremely repellent both in the barbarous ferocity of the image-breakers, and in the fanatical superstition of the image-worshippers. But it is of great importance, in order to form a right judgment of the spirit of the period, that we should endeavour to disentangle the good principles which were at work in the midst of this mass of confusion and corruption. By doing so we shall discover that the one party were animated with a genuine zeal for reformation, and a desire for purer forms of worship; and that the others, in whom the religious life of the time is most conspicuously seen, were possessed by fervent spirituality, and readiness to suffer for what they considered to be a righteous cause. That which will ultimately emerge to view as the really ignoble and anti-Christian feature of the period is the cringing and time-serving spirit of a large portion of the higher clergy, who were ready to sacrifice self-respect, consistency, and straightforwardness, not to mention the interests of the Church, to the desire of retaining the favour of the rulers and their own positions.

In the early ages of the Church, the use of images was unknown. Owing to the employment of art in heathen worship, the Christians regarded it with suspicion, and that not merely because of its previous associations, but as being dangerous to spiritual religion. Thus, Clement of Alexandria says, when speaking on this subject, 'We must not adhere to the sensuous, but we must rise to the spiritual. The familiarity of daily sight lowers the dignity of the divine, and to wish to honour a spiritual being by means of earthly matter is to degrade it by sensuousness.' Gradually the representation of Christian emblems, such as the fish, the dove, and the Good Shepherd, were introduced, first into private houses, and afterwards into churches. But when Christianity became the dominant creed in Constantine's reign, and devout persons were able, without fear of attack, to devote a portion of their wealth to the adornment of their places of worship, a great change took place; art came to be recognised as the handmaid of religion, and the sacred buildings were

Growth of image-worship

elaborately ornamented with pictures of scripture subjects, and after a time with statues also, representing the Saints and Christ himself. In Oriental Christendom, where a livelier imagination and more ardent temperament prevailed, the growth of this practice, and of observances connected with it, was much more rapid than in the soberer Church of the West. Before long the custom of prostration before the images was introduced, and miraculous cures were attributed to their agency. Some were reputed not to have been made by human hands. The lower classes ceased to distinguish between the image itself and the person designated by it as the object of worship; and by the beginning of the eighth century, religion in the Eastern Church had been overlaid by a mass of superstition owing to this cause, and the spiritual element in it was greatly obscured in the minds of the people. But for this very reason, any attempt to remedy the evil might easily impair the popular faith itself, with which this parasitic growth was so closely entwined; and it was sure to meet with a widespread resistance, because the subject of the controversy was not connected with recondite questions of doctrine, like those which had preceded it, but was intelligible to all.

The man who undertook to grapple with this abuse was the Emperor Leo III., the Isaurian. Though a rude, unlettered soldier, he was among the ablest of the Byzantine monarchs. He found the empire on the verge of extinction, and left it the most powerful state in Christendom. By his defence of Constantinople against Moslemah, he saved his own kingdom from being destroyed, and Europe from being

Leo III.

overrun, by the Saracens. By reconstituting the military system, reorganizing the taxation, and codifying the laws of the empire, he placed himself in the first rank of reformers. He cannot, therefore, rightly be regarded either as a brutal tyrant or as a reckless meddler. What was his motive for interfering in religious matters—whether he was chiefly instigated by conviction or by policy—it is not easy to determine. That he was zealous for the extension of the Church, and intolerant in his method of propagating the faith, was seen in the early part of his reign, when he forced the Jews to receive baptism, and compelled the Montanists to conform to the established religion. Before he became emperor, he held the office of general of the Anatolic Theme, and being there brought into contact with Mahometans and heretics, may have become anxious to remove the stigma of idolatry which they attached to the Church. His principal adviser in the matter, it is to be observed—Constantine, the bishop of Nacolia, in Phrygia—came from those regions. As he was so thorough-going in his reforms, he may also have been anxious to strengthen the state by invigorating the religious sentiment of the people. And further, it may have been from the first a part of his centralising policy to render the Church more completely subservient to himself. Finally, as he spoke of himself as called, like Hezekiah, to banish idolatry, which had been growing for centuries, his leading motive may have been the desire to extirpate a corrupt system. It is, moreover, difficult to determine whether Leo at the commencement of the attack was supported by the feeling of a large number of the intelligent citizens. In the course of the controversy, many of the more enlightened adopted his view; but the body which formed throughout the strength of the movement was the army. The forces of the empire were now largely recruited from the Armenians, the Paulicians, and other sects, which were hostile to the Church and its observances. Afterwards they supported the same side with still greater enthusiasm, because of their devotion to the emperors, who had so often led them to victory in the field.

The commencement of the attack was made in 726, the tenth year of Leo's reign. It has generally been <small>Decree against images</small> thought that the emperor proceeded gradually in the matter, and at first only ordered that the images in churches should be raised higher, so as to be out of reach of the adoration of the people. But this does not seem to have been the case. The original edict decreed the destruction of these objects, and such as were exposed in public places were removed; but owing to the opposition of the patriarch Germanus it did not take effect in churches, except where the bishops were favourable to the proceeding. A rebellion of the inhabitants of Greece in the following year, the primary cause of which was the administrative reforms of Leo, was fanned into a flame by this decree, and the imperial fleet in the Cyclades proceeded to attack Constantinople, but was completely defeated. A violent eruption of the volcano of Thera (Santorin) which took place at the same time, was regarded by the people as a manifestation of divine wrath against the authors of sacrilege. In 730 Germanus, who was more than ninety years of age, was again called upon to join in an edict against images, and as his arguments in their favour availed nothing with the emperor, he resigned his office; and his secretary Anastasius, who was in favour of the measure, was appointed patriarch in his place. The work of destruction now commenced in earnest; the statues were everywhere removed, and the pictures on the walls were whitewashed over, and though numerous outbreaks occurred, and some executions took place before it was accomplished, yet on the whole the opposition was not formidable. The act which caused the greatest indignation was the removal of the magnificent image of Christ, which surmounted the bronze gateway of the imperial palace, and was the object of great reverence. In order to take down this statue and burn it, a soldier of the guard had mounted a ladder, when a number of women assembled at the spot to beg that it might be spared; but, instead of listening to them, the soldier struck his axe into the face of the image. Infuriated by this, which appeared to them to be an insult offered to the Saviour himself, they dragged the ladder from under his feet and killed him. The emperor avenged his agent by executing some, and exiling others, of the offenders; and set up in the place of the statue a plain cross, with an inscription explaining the significance of the change.

In the defence of images there stood forth two champions, the one in the West, the other in the East; and the points of view from which they respectively regarded them illustrate the different feelings of the two churches on the subject. The former of these was Pope Gregory II., who at first strongly remonstrated with the emperor on his edict, and afterwards, when he endeavoured to enforce its observance in Italy, encouraged his people to disregard the order, and

<small>Pope Gregory II.</small>

defied his nominal sovereign in violent and even insulting language. At last he excommunicated his nominee, the patriarch Anastasius. But he advocated the retention of images on the practical ground of their utility in instructing the young and ignorant, and as being an incentive to devotion. Far more exalted and more subtly defined was the position attributed to them by the other advocate, who spoke from the distant East.

St. John Damascene. This was John of Damascus, otherwise known as St. John Damascene, the last of the Fathers of the Greek Church. This learned and acute theologian, who in many ways was superior to the age in which he lived, at one time filled a civil post of some importance under the Caliphs who now ruled in Syria, but afterwards retired to the monastery of St. Saba, in the wilderness of Engedi, the strange position of which, overhanging a deep gorge that leads down to the Dead Sea, is still the wonder of the traveller. As he lived in the dominion of the Saracens he was beyond the reach of the emperor's arm, and now undertook the cause of his suffering co-religionists. In three powerful addresses he set forth his arguments for image worship. Some of these follow the familiar lines of defence, that these objects were memorials of the mysteries of the faith, and that in the adoration of them the spiritual was reached through the medium of the material. But beyond this he made it plain that, to his mind, and the minds of those who thought with him, the worship of images was closely connected with the doctrine of the Incarnation, the earthly material having been once for all sanctified when the Son of God took human flesh, and being thenceforth worthy of all honour. From this we may learn, both how it came to pass that the most religious men of the age became enthusiasts for what was in itself superstitious, and also what was the cardinal point of difference between them and their opponents. For, while the one side regarded figures of Christ as a degradation of a heavenly being, to the other they were a practical confession of his true humanity, and any disregard of them appeared in the light of a denial of the Incarnation. At last when it was found that the emperor persevered in his attack, the iconoclasts were anathematised by the orthodox congregations in all the Mahometan countries outside the empire. Both John and Gregory protested throughout against the interference of the state with the church in this matter, as being beyond its province; and, owing to the close connection which existed between the clergy and the people, they were generally regarded as the assertors of liberty and of the right of private judgment in opposition to despotism.

Leo III. died in 741, and was succeeded by his son Constantine, called Copronymus from the circumstance of his having defiled the font at his baptism. This prince, who inherited his father's strength of will, and a large portion of his ability, was, like him, a rude soldier, and was characteristically said to prefer the odour of the stable to the perfumes of his palaces. His temper was hard and merciless, and he regarded opposition to his arbitrary will in the light of rebellion. He was fanatical in his iconoclasm, though to him, in all probability, the question turned as much on the right of the emperor to govern the church, as on the merits and demerits of image-worship. His natural violence was further stimulated by the rebellion of his brother-in-law, Artavasdus, which occurred at the commencement of his reign, and was favoured by the image-worshippers. When the usurper was dethroned in 744, he began to form plans for carrying out his ecclesiastical policy, but it was not until ten years later that he was able to put them into execution. He then determined to convoke a general council, which might finally sanction the doctrines of the iconoclasts, and in the year 754 an assembly of three hundred and thirty-eight bishops was convened at Constantinople. The subservient prelates, few of whom probably were decided iconoclasts, not only condemned the use of statues and pictures in unmeasured terms, but even proscribed the godless art of painting. In pursuance of their decrees the laws already in existence were more vigorously enforced, the possession of images by private persons was prohibited, and illuminations representing sacred subjects were ordered to be removed from the ecclesiastical books.

The enforcement of these ordinances called forth a violent opposition. The monks especially refused to give up the objects of their veneration, and the most cruel measures were resorted to in order to compel them. Three hundred and forty-two persons of this order, collected from different districts of the empire, who refused to submit to the council, were thrown into prison, and mercilessly scourged; some among them were blinded, while others had their noses or ears or hands cut off. Some of those who were held in the highest veneration by the people suffered at this time. Andrew, a hermit, named the Kalybite from the

<small>Treatment of the monks</small>

grotto in which he dwelt, entering the emperor's presence, shouted to him, 'If thou art a Christian, why dost thou persecute Christians?' He was thereupon tried for refusing to obey the emperor's edicts, and being condemned to death, was scourged in the hippodrome and executed. Another hermit, Stephen, the most prominent advocate of images in the empire, when imprisoned for contumacy at Constantinople, was the object of so much attention, that Constantine exclaimed, in a moment of vexation, 'It seems, in truth, that this monk is really emperor, and I am nothing in the empire!' These words, like those of Henry II. with regard to Becket, caused Stephen's death. Some officers of the guard, who overheard them, dragged him from his prison and cruelly murdered him, after which his body was dragged through the streets. So far was the emperor carried in his detestation of monachism, that he would have been glad to exterminate the order altogether. Some monasteries were confiscated, with all their estates and property. Multitudes of monks took refuge in the West, or in the dominions of the neighbouring barbarians. After this we cannot be surprised that the historians of the time have imputed all manner of vices to him. These statements we may safely reject, and his memory is sufficiently branded by the stigma of cruelty. But he is said to have been gentle in his domestic relations; as a general he was distinguished; and during his reign the empire enjoyed great prosperity.

By this policy, carried out during a reign of more than thirty years, Constantine V. believed that he had extinguished the worship of images. But meanwhile he had planted in the bosom of his own family a seed, from which their restoration was destined to arise. He had married his son, Leo, to Irene, an Athenian lady of great beauty and accomplishments, and she was a devoted supporter of images. At the time of her marriage, indeed, she had been made to swear that she would renounce these, but the sanctity of an oath did not restrain her from accomplishing the end which she desired. Leo IV., who ascended the throne in 775, maintained his father's policy, but owing to the weak state of his health he was less energetic in his administration. The monks, who during the previous reign had been forced to conceal themselves, now once more appeared in public, and were received as confessors with joy and enthusiasm. When, however, an attempt was made by persons about the court, with the connivance of Irene, to introduce images into the palace, this was discovered by the emperor, who punished with imprisonment those who had taken part in the combination. But his early death in 780 changed the aspect of things. Irene now became regent for her son Constantine, who was only ten years old, and prepared to carry into execution her cherished design. At first it was necessary to proceed with caution, because of the feelings of the army, which, as we have seen, was usually the stronghold of iconoclasm, and the disaffection of which might have been fatal to her position. She, therefore, contented herself with allowing the laws against images to fall into disuse, and promoting monks to the higher offices in the Church; and then waited for an opportunity of taking more decisive measures.

The Empress Irene

The opportunity was not long in coming. The patriarch Paul, an aged man and a lover of peace, induced by an attack of sickness, in the year 783 suddenly resigned his office, and retired to a monastery. He had been appointed by an iconoclast emperor, and himself adhered to those views, but the gentleness of his disposition prevented him from being a strong partisan. But when the empress visited him in his cloister, and enquired the reason of this unexpected step, he declared that he repented of his hostility to image-worship, because it had cut off the church of Constantinople from communion with the rest of the Christian world. He had retired to a monastery, he said, for the purpose of doing penance; and he recommended—possibly at the suggestion of others—that, in order to heal the schism, a general council of the Church should be held, to decide the disputed question. Shortly after this he died. It was now a matter of the first importance who should be appointed in his place; and as most of the existing bishops were nominees of the iconoclasts, the choice of the empress fell on the imperial secretary, Tarasius, who bore a character for profound religion, and had given evidence of ability. In order to secure a large number of adherents to this appointment an assembly of the people was summoned, and in pursuance of a prearranged plan, the name of Tarasius was proposed, and received with acclamation. At first Tarasius professed his unwillingness to accept the office on account of the difficulties involved in presiding over a church which had been anathematised by the rest of Christendom; and when the empress solicited him further, he only agreed on the condition that a council, such as his predecessor had suggested, should be called together.

Tarasius patriarch

Measures were at once taken to carry this proposal into effect, and messengers were dispatched to Rome, to persuade the pope to send representatives. Hadrian at first demurred, owing to the irregularity of the appointment of a layman to the patriarchal see, but ultimately consented, in consideration of the exigencies of the times. With the view, also, of making the proposed council seem truly œcumenical and superior to the council of iconoclasts, the patriarchs of Antioch, Jerusalem, and Alexandria were requested to send delegates; but, as Syria and Egypt were now in the hands of the Saracens, difficulties arose in the way of this, and the persons who appeared as delegates from those countries were in reality unauthorised.

The seventh general council of the Church was summoned to meet in Constantinople; but when it was convened in that city the assembly was dispersed by the violence of the soldiery, and it became necessary to adjourn it and to find a safer place for its deliberations. Accordingly it was postponed for a year and was transferred to Nicæa, a city which was venerable from the traditions of the previous council, and was removed from the turbulent factions of the capital. There, in September 787, it met, to the number of about 350 members, and whereas at Constantinople many of the bishops still maintained their hostility to images, they had found reason in the interval to change their views. The opening of it was marked by a degrading spectacle—in the recantation of a number of the prelates who had been prominent iconoclasts; these came forward and expressed their contrition for their errors, and, notwithstanding some murmurs from the opposite side, were absolved by the patriarch Tarasius and publicly readmitted into the Church. The business of the council was completed in seven sessions, and the use of statues, pictures, and other objects representing sacred subjects and persons was authorised. In order formally to ratify this decision an image was brought into the assembly and kissed by all the members. It should, however, be observed that idolatrous worship was formally discountenanced. 'Bowing to an image,' so ran the decree, 'which is simply the token of love and reverence, ought by no means to be confounded with the adoration which is due to God alone.' At the conclusion of the proceedings the whole conclave repaired to Constantinople. There the final session was held in the imperial palace of Magnaura in the presence of Irene herself and her son Constantine VI., both of whom subscribed its acts. The scene is represented in a Greek manuscript, now in the Vatican, and the young emperor (the empress is omitted) is the most conspicuous personage. In the foreground is a prostrate figure, which seems to represent the spirit of iconoclasm that was now overthrown.

Thus the party favourable to images triumphed, and a quarter of a century elapsed before any attempt was made to reverse the decision. But in the meantime a terrible tragedy was enacted, which throws a lurid light on the character of Irene. In her mind the ruling passion was ambition, and, in order to gratify that, she proved that she was capable of sacrificing the most sacred feelings of human nature. When Constantine came of age a struggle arose between him and his mother, the one desiring to assume his rightful authority,

Fate of Constantine VI.

the other to retain the power that she possessed. Both the court and the army were divided into two factions, and after a long period of intrigue they came to open hostilities. Gradually the severity of Constantine alienated from him the imperial guards, and his divorcing his first wife Maria, in order to marry Theodota, one of his mother's maids of honour, gave deep offence to the monks. Irene seized the opportunity, and by her orders her son was carried off from the Asiatic side of the Bosphorus and conducted to the palace, where his eyes were put out. The unnatural mother only retained the throne for five years after this time. Whereas she had previously shown great address in conducting the administration, and great capacity for business, she now became negligent, and abandoned the management of public affairs to others. In consequence of this a conspiracy was formed against her by the courtiers, and she was dethroned and exiled to the island of Lemnos, where she died shortly after almost forgotten.

The second period of the iconoclastic controversy was of shorter duration than the first, but resembled it in two characteristic points—it was introduced by a soldier from the eastern frontier of the empire, and was brought to an end by the influence of a woman. The party opposed to images had been so powerful up to the time when Irene by her adroit negotiations achieved its discomfiture, that we cannot feel surprised if it did not finally acquiesce in its defeat; and Leo the Armenian, who renewed the struggle shortly after he was raised to the throne in 813, came from the bosom of the army, which retained its attachment to the memory of the iconoclast emperors. As early as

Leo the Armenian

the time of his coronation Leo had excited suspicions by evading the custom, which was regularly observed on such occasions, of presenting the patriarch with a written profession of orthodox belief; but he did not proceed further until he had repulsed the Bulgarians, whose forces had advanced within dangerous proximity to the capital. He then engaged the patriarch, Nicephorus, in a discussion on the merits of the question, and requested him to agree that such images as were within reach of the adoration of the people should be removed. Meanwhile the soldiers took the matter into their own hands, and assaulted the statue of Christ over the bronze gate of the palace, which Leo the Isaurian had removed, but which had been replaced by Irene; this the emperor ordered once more to be taken down, on the pretext of preserving it from desecration. Yet for a long time he refrained from any stringent measures; indeed he professed himself anxious to act as a mediator between the two parties; but at length the intemperate and seditious language of the monks on the one side, and the violence of the military on the other, forced him to interfere, and in his exasperation he assumed the character of a persecutor. Nicephorus was deposed; those who refused to keep silence on the subject were dealt with as rebels and brutally treated; and at last the use of images was strictly prohibited, and the books used in the schools were so compiled as to infuse an abhorrence of them into the minds of the young. This state of things continued until the end of Leo's reign in 820.

The leading advocate of images at this time was Theodore Studita, as John Damascene had been in the previous period. In this remarkable man, who was head of the monastery of Studium at Constantinople, a lofty religious spirit and genuine piety were strangely combined with bigotry in the assertion of his views. We have already noticed his protest against the employment of slaves (p. 70). He raised his voice also, in a spirit of toleration foreign to all parties in that age, against the persecution of the Paulicians, saying that it was right, not to punish, but to instruct, the ignorant. He denounced, as a betrayal of truth, the accommodation (οἰκονομία)—that is, mental reservation and equivocation—which many of the clergy employed in professing their opinions, in order to escape persecution. When the patriarch Tarasius did not venture to oppose the marriage of Constantine VI. with Theodota after his divorce, Theodore inveighed against it as an adulterous connection, and neither flattery, nor threats, nor exile could induce him to connive at the act. His hymns, which remain to us, are full of spiritual fervour. All eyes were now turned towards him as the leader of the monastic party. He was an old man, but was unflinching in his resolve. He carried the pictures which had been removed from the churches in solemn procession through the streets of the city, to give them a safe asylum in his monastery. For this act of defiance he was banished to Asia Minor, but he continued by his letters to inflame the zeal of his adherents. At last, when the fury of the emperor burst upon the monks, he was shamefully ill-used, and on one occasion was left half-dead under the lashes of the scourge. All this he bore with the patience of a martyr, testifying that in his endurance

Theodore Studita

of suffering he saw the grace of God freely bestowed without any merit of his own. But both in this and the succeeding reign he, more than any other person, hindered the reconciliation of parties and the restoration of peace to the Church. He firmly opposed the spirit of compromise, which began to make itself felt, and denounced his opponents as heretics, with whom he would hold no communication.

That Leo V. for his part was no irreligious opponent of the Church is clearly shown in the story of his death, which is at the same time one of the most dramatic incidents in Byzantine history. The honest reforms that he instituted, in purifying the administration of justice and readjusting the taxation—in which respects he is acknowleded to have been a useful sovereign—had rendered him unpopular with his courtiers; and a conspiracy was formed against him, and was headed by his most intimate friend, Michael the Amorian, otherwise called the Stammerer, who was carried away by the ambition of mounting the throne. The plot was discovered, and Michael, after being tried in a court of justice, was condemned to death. The sentence would have been immediately carried out, but it was Christmas Eve, and the empress implored her husband to defer the execution until the holy season was passed. He consented, though with a strong presentiment of danger, since he was aware of the extent of the conspiracy. During the night, being unable to sleep, he visited the cell of his prisoner, when he found the door open, and the criminal lying in profound slumber on his jailor's bed. Though his suspicions were aroused, he took no immediate precautions. But the purple

Death of Leo

buskins of the emperor had been recognised by a slave who was concealed under the bed; and when Michael was informed by him of what had passed, he sent word to the other principal conspirators, that, unless they at once effected his deliverance, he would reveal their names. On Christmas morning it was the custom to reinforce the choir of the chapel in the palace with additional singers, in order to increase the imposing effect of the service; and among these, and disguised in their dress, under which weapons were concealed, a number of the conspirators effected their entrance. They knew the emperor would be present, because of his religious habits, and his fondness for displaying his deep sonorous voice in the choir. At first, however, he was with difficulty recognised, because he had enveloped his person in a fur mantle, and wore a thick bonnet on his head, to keep off the raw cold of the morning. When he was identified, and an attack was made upon him, he snatched up a crucifix, and with that defended himself, until the hand which held it was cut off. He then fell before the altar, where his body was hewn in pieces. His rival was immediately brought forth from the prison, and proclaimed emperor with the fetters still upon his limbs.

If the image-worshippers thought that Michael, from opposition to the policy of his predecessor, would favour their side, they were mistaken. His one aim was to restore and preserve tranquillity in the empire, and with this object he endeavoured to establish the principle that everyone should be at liberty to act without molestation according to his convictions. Such a view gave no satisfaction to persons like Theodore

[margin: Michael the Stammerer]

Studita, who anathematised all who differed from them; but it was acceptable to a more moderate party that was now growing up, in whose judgment a distinction might be drawn between the weak, who need sensible aids to devotion, and the mature, for whom Scripture teaching suffices. Pictures which were in elevated positions were now allowed to remain, and considerable latitude was permitted to the monks within the walls of their monasteries, though they were forbidden to preach publicly on the subject. But this system was discarded by Michael's son and successor Theophilus, who was the last, and one of the most determined, of the iconoclasts. He was a highly cultivated man, having been educated by John the Grammarian, who was a distinguished scholar, and on account of his attainments had been employed on several important embassies. Theophilus, therefore, was better qualified than others to estimate the principles that were at stake, but his capricious temper rendered him liable to be swayed by passion. In his civil administration he was distinguished by his rigid justice, and the stories which got abroad of the somewhat whimsical manner in which he paraded this, caused him to be regarded in later Byzantine times as a representative of that virtue. His taste made him a lover of poetry, music, and architecture, and churches as well as palaces were erected by his orders. But in ecclesiastical matters he was a bigot, and his violence was only partially restrained by the influence of John, whom he appointed patriarch, and who, though an iconoclast, was large-minded and tolerant in his opinions. The persecution of the monks and clergy was now recommenced; hundreds were thrown into prison, and

Theophilus

others, who were ejected from their convents, perished from destitution. One of them, called Theodore, was afterwards known by the surname of Graptos, because he was branded in the forehead by the emperor's orders. The making of images was proscribed, and the sacred vessels, ornamented with figures, were desecrated and sold in the public markets.

But we are approaching the conclusion of the weary strife. As on the previous occasion, so now, it ended in the restoration of images, and the chief actor in the scene was the empress of an iconoclastic monarch. The story of Theophilus' selection of a wife, by which event the change was ultimately rendered possible, is of a part with his capricious conduct in other matters. The most beautiful maidens in Constantinople were assembled, that he might choose his bride from among them. The fairest of these was Eikasia; and when the emperor paused in front of her, holding a golden apple in his hand, he exclaimed musingly, with an allusion to the Fall, 'Of how much evil hath woman been the cause?' The lady, with too ready wit, replied, with an allusion to the Virgin Mother, 'And of how much good?' The emperor was offended by her forwardness, and passing on, bestowed the apple on the more modest Theodora. The new empress was one of a family of image-worshippers, and in course of time her children were initiated into the same practice, as one of them with innocent garrulity revealed to the emperor, by telling him of the pretty toys which their grandmother gave them to kiss. On the death of Theophilus, Theodora became regent for her youthful son Michael; and Manuel, her uncle, was one of those appointed to assist her in

Restoration of images

the administration. A dangerous illness, by which Manuel was attacked, hastened the impending change. Several monks visited his bedside, and assured him that God would spare his life if he promised to devote himself to the restoration of images. He promised, and recovered; and thenceforward he set to work earnestly to fulfil his vow. The patriarch John was deposed, and Methodius, a supporter of the opposite faction, was appointed in his place. But the empress was tenderly attached to her husband's memory, and declined to take any further steps until she was assured that the sin which he had incurred by his iconoclasm was forgiven. This assurance the clergy professed themselves unable to give; but at last Theodora declared that on his death-bed he had expressed his repentance, and had kissed an image which she presented to him. This testimony was pronounced satisfactory, and his absolution in the sight of God was promised. The last obstacle was thus removed, for every rank of society had learnt to detest the controversy and the domestic strife which it engendered. On the first Sunday in Lent in the year 842 the long-banished pictures were introduced with solemn pomp into the church of St. Sophia, and that day has ever since been observed in the Greek Church as the festival of Orthodoxy.

It is instructive to notice the effects which this contest produced on Byzantine society. During the earlier period its influence was bracing, as was shown by the renewed vigour which pervaded the empire; both sides were thoroughly in earnest, and among the image-worshippers a strong religious zeal, among the iconoclasts an element of Puritan energy,

Effects on society

was evolved. Hence at this time the prosperity of the empire was very remarkable. Finlay, who is distinguished as a historian by the attention which he has bestowed on the state of the people, does not hesitate to say: 'That the moral condition of the people of the Byzantine empire under the iconoclast emperors was superior to that of any equal number of the human race in any preceding period, can hardly be doubted. The bulk of society occupied a higher social position in the time of Constantine Copronymus than of Pericles; the masses had gained more by the decrease of slavery and the extension of free labour than the privileged citizens had lost. Public opinion, though occupied on meaner objects, had a more extended basis, and embraced a larger class.' But in the later stages of the struggle, when the people at large were weary of the strife, and the contest was felt to be in reality one between church and state, the prevalent hypocrisy—in the capital at all events—generated disrespect for religion, and this was followed by widespread immorality. Theodora's son, the emperor Michael, who was known as the Drunkard on account of his intemperate habits, was a type of his age. Not only did he indulge in scandalous debaucheries, and appear as a charioteer in the hippodrome, but he burlesqued religion, and caricatured the ceremonies of the Church, parading the streets in masquerade with a company of mock priests, and with a buffoon arrayed in the patriarchal robes. Yet his love of festivals rendered him popular, and his ribaldry passed without protest from the people of Constantinople.

In Western Europe the controversy was regarded with somewhat varied feelings. The papacy supported without reserve the party of the image-worshippers; and the events that followed were of the first importance to the Holy See, for the alienation arising from iconoclasm was an influential cause of the loss of the exarchate to the Eastern empire, and from this resulted the appeal to Pepin to deliver Italy from the Lombards, and his subsequent donation to the popes of the old Byzantine province, whereby the foundation of their temporal power was laid. But among the nations north of the Alps, and especially among the Franks, a different tone of feeling prevailed. By them images were regarded as memorials and suggestive objects, and nothing more; and the synod of Frankfort (794), which was convened by Charles the Great, while it blamed the iconoclasts, protested against the superstition of the Greeks, as embodied in the decrees of the council of Nicæa. Charles himself entered the lists, and in the work entitled 'The Four Caroline Books,' set forth his views to that effect. At a later period, when Michael the Stammerer sent an explanation of his opinions on iconoclasm both to pope Paschal I. and to Louis the Pious, the latter of these held a synod at Paris in 825, which, in drawing up a reply which might be sent to the Greek emperor, covertly condemned the image-worship patronised by the Roman see. It is also to be noticed that, owing to the persecutions that were set on foot in the Eastern empire, numbers of Greeks at this time migrated into South Italy, in order to exercise their cherished worship with greater freedom. At the present day rock-hewn hermitages, and churches covered with Byzantine frescoes, remain in remote parts of that country as a memorial of this period, being the work

Attitude of the West

either of those colonists themselves or of their descendants.

The subsequent history of the use of images in the Eastern Church presents a curious anomaly. At the present day, while the Latin Church advocates the veneration both of statues and pictures, the orthodox communion proscribes the former while it retains the latter. To an Oriental Christian a statue introduced into a place of worship is as repulsive as to a Mahometan, and the crucifix is disallowed for the same reason. This is a distinct departure from the principles laid down by the Seventh General Council. The change must have been brought about very gradually; so much so that no trace remains to us of the steps by which it came to pass. Dean Milman has suggested an explanation in the following passage:—

<small>Statues and pictures</small>

'To the keener perception of the Greeks there may have arisen a feeling that, in its more rigid and solid form, the image was more near to the idol. At the same time the art of sculpture and casting in bronze was probably more degenerate and out of use. At all events, it was too slow and laborious to supply the demand of triumphant zeal in the restoration of the persecuted images. There was, therefore, a tacit compromise; nothing appeared but painting, mosaics, engraving on cups and chalices, embroidery on vestments. The renunciation of sculpture grew into a rigid, passionate aversion.'

When this had taken place, a traditional mode of representation grew up, in accordance with which sacred subjects should be painted. This was stereotyped by a remarkable book, which was compiled at an unknown but early period—the 'Guide to Painting,' of Dionysius of Agrapha, which contains rules, very often of a minute description, for the treatment of these subjects, specifying the position and attitudes of the figures, the expression of the faces, and the backgrounds and accompaniments. This manual is regularly in use at the present day, and explains the singular uniformity of design in the paintings, both ancient and modern, of the Greek Church.

An account of the iconoclastic controversy would be imperfect, which did not contain some notice of Byzantine hymnology, because the principal authors of this species of composition flourished at that time, and the extraordinary development which the art then received was connected with the fervour excited by that movement. The great majority of the hymn-writers were on the side favourable to images, but we hear also of the Emperor Theophilus as composing hymns which were sung in churches. For a full discussion of the nature of this elaborate form of sacred poetry—of the different kinds of hymns and odes, their metrical and rhythmical laws, and the music to which they were sung—as well as for an account of what is known of the authors themselves, together with a large collection of specimens of the compositions, the reader is referred to the admirable work of Christ and Paranicas, *Anthologia Græca Carminum Christianorum*. A brief, but useful summary of the main points connected with the question will be found in Mr. Hatherly's edition of Dr. Neale's 'Hymns of the Eastern Church.' All that can be attempted here is to mention very briefly the chief writers, and the characteristics of these religious poems.

[margin: Hymnology of the period]

The translation that is given below, and the first lines that are quoted, are taken from Dr. Neale, whose felicity in maintaining the spirit of the originals and reproducing it in an English form has been already referred to.

The hymns that were used in public worship in the Greek Church were composed, not, like the sacred poems of Synesius and Gregory Nazianzen, in classical metre regulated by quantity, but in rhythmical measure according to accent. It is true that, even as late as the time of John Damascene, a few were written according to the old classical system; but as the pronunciation of Greek was at this period determined by accent alone, they were regarded as artificial, and unsuited for popular use. Up to the beginning of the eighth century these hymns were simple, independent odes; but about that period, and therefore shortly before the commencement of the iconoclastic movement, the system of *canons* was introduced, which gave an opening for grander treatment. A canon is usually made up of eight or nine odes (nine was the proper number, but, for reasons which we cannot here discuss, the second ode was usually omitted), and each ode consists of a number of stanzas; these stanzas correspond to one another in the rhythm of their verses, though not always exactly in the number of syllables. By this means, as in a symphony, a great subject could be more effectively worked out. At the same time less elaborate hymns were still composed. The period which preceded this change may be called that of the *rise* of Greek hymnology, the century that followed it that of its *perfection*, while the ages which succeeded the close of that era mark its *decline*. Its decadence was caused, partly

<small>Rules of composition</small>

by the dying out of the enthusiasm from which its inspiration was drawn, and partly by the attempt to write canons in honour of saints of whose history next to nothing was known, the result of which was the introduction of intolerable verbiage.

The most eminent composers of hymns during the first of these periods were Sergius, patriarch of Constan-
<small>The leading hymn-writers</small> tinople (610–641), the same who supported the emperor Heraclius in his Monothelite views; his contemporary Sophronius, who was patriarch of Jerusalem; Anatolius, and Romanus. Unfortunately the dates of both the two last-named are doubtful. Anatolius, to whom we owe the evening hymn—

> The day is past and over;
> All thanks, O Lord, to Thee!

has been thought to be the same as the patriarch of Constantinople of that name at the time of the Council of Chalcedon, but the identification is very doubtfully established. Again, Romanus is said to have lived in the reign of Anastatius; but whether Anastatius I. (491–518) or Anastatius II. (713–716) is meant, is not certain; though, as the latter of these two emperors was only four years on the throne, it seems more probable that the earlier period is meant. As many as ninety of his poems exist unpublished in the library of the monastery of St. John at Patmos, and Dr. Krumbacher, who has lately examined these, pronounces him to be the greatest Christian hymn-writer. Among those who wrote in the second, and most important, period there are several whose names have already occurred in this chapter, as Germanus, John Damascene, Tarasius,

Theodore Studita, and Methodius. Andrew of Crete (660–732), the author of the hymn—

> Christian! dost thou see them
> On the holy ground?

is famous as having been the first writer of canons, and especially as having composed the Great Canon, a long penitential hymn which is used in Lent. But in respect of this species of composition the palm must be conceded to John Damascene, and his rival and companion Cosmas surnamed ὁ μελῳδὸς, who was, like him, an inmate of the convent of St. Saba. The two fine Easter hymns—

> The Day of Resurrection!
> Earth, tell it out abroad;

and

> Come, ye faithful, raise the strain
> Of triumphant gladness;

are by the former of these writers. The composer of greatest repute in the third period was Joseph of the Studium, who lived in the middle of the ninth century; but the English hymns that are derived from him—as 'O happy band of pilgrims,' 'Stars of the morning,' and 'Let our choir new anthems raise,'—are rather centos than translations. The art of hymn-writing continued to be practised in the Greek Church down to the year 1376, but the compositions of the decline have little merit.

The specimen that follows is the original of the hymn, 'Come, ye faithful,' which is the first ode of a canon: the reader will notice the rhythmical correspondence of the stanzas, when recited according to accent. In Dr. Neale's translation the fourth

Specimen and translation

stanza has been altered in order to introduce the doxology.

Ἄισωμεν πάντες λαοὶ | τῷ ἐκ πικρᾶς δουλείας
 Φαραὼ τὸν Ἰσραὴλ ἀπαλλάξαντι
καὶ ἐν βυθῷ θαλάσσης | ποδὶ ἀβρύχως ὁδηγήσαντι
ᾠδὴν ἐπινίκιον, | ὅτι δεδόξασται.

Σήμερον ἔαρ ψυχῶν, | ὅτι Χριστὸς ἐκ τάφου
 ὥσπερ ἥλιος ἐκλάμψας τριήμερος
τὸν ζοφερὸν χειμῶνα | ἀπήλασε τῆς ἁμαρτίας ἡμῶν·
αὐτὸν ἀνυμνήσωμεν, | ὅτι δεδόξασται.

Ἡ βασιλὶς τῶν ὡρῶν | τῇ λαμπροφόρῳ ἡμέρᾳ
 ἡμερῶν τε βασιλίδι φανότατα
δορυφοροῦσα τέρπει | τὸν ἔκκριτον τῆς ἐκκλησίας λαόν,
ἀπαύστως ἀνυμνοῦσα | τὸν ἀναστάντα Χριστόν.

Πύλαι θανάτου, Χριστὲ, | οὐδὲ τοῦ τάφου σφραγῖδες,
 οὐδὲ κλεῖθρα τῶν θυρῶν σοι ἀντέστησαν.
ἀλλ' ἀναστὰς ἐπέστης | τοῖς φίλοις σου, εἰρήνην, δέσποτα,
δωρούμενος τὴν πάντα | νοῦν ὑπερέχουσαν.

> Come, ye faithful, raise the strain
> Of triumphant gladness ;
> God hath brought His Israel
> Into joy from sadness ;
> Loosed from Pharaoh's bitter yoke,
> Jacob's sons and daughters ;
> Led them, with unmoistened foot,
> Through the Red Sea waters.
>
> 'Tis the spring of souls to-day :
> Christ hath burst His prison,
> And from three days' sleep in death
> As a sun hath risen ;

All the winter of our sins,
    Long and dark, is flying
From His light, to Whom we give
    Laud and praise undying.

Now the Queen of seasons, bright
    With the Day of splendour,
With the royal Feast of feasts,
    Comes its joy to render;
Comes to glad Jerusalem,
    Who, with true affection,
Welcomes in unwearied strains
    Jesu's Resurrection.

Alleluia now we cry
    To our King Immortal,
Who triumphant burst the bars
    Of the tomb's dark portal;
Alleluia, with the Son
    God the Father praising;
Alleluia yet again
    To the Spirit raising.

CHAPTER VII.

THE MISSIONARY EFFORTS OF THE EASTERN CHURCH.

Conversion of the Slavs—Cyril and Methodius—Mission to the Khazars—St. Clement's remains—The Moravians—Visit to Rome—Methodius archbishop—The Bulgarians—Conversion of Bogoris—He hesitates between Rome and Constantinople—Clement of Ochrida and his work—Subsequent fortunes of the Bulgarian Church—The Russians—Early conversions—Vladimir—Embassy to Constantinople—Baptism of Vladimir—Peaceful conversion of the people.

IF the missionary spirit is the best evidence of vitality in a church, it certainly was not wanting in the Eastern Church during the ninth and tenth centuries of our era. This period witnessed the conversion to Christianity of the principal Slavonic peoples, whereby they are both linked with Constantinople, and bound together by those associations of creed, as well as race, which form so important a factor in the European politics of the present day. The Moravians, the Bulgarians, and the Russians were now brought within the fold of the Church; and the way was prepared for that vast extension of the Greek communion by which it has spread, not only throughout the Balkan peninsula and the lands to the north of it, but wherever Russian influence is found—as far as the White Sea on the one side, and Kamtchatka on the other, and into the

Conversion of the Slavs

heart of Central Asia. The leaders in this great work were the two brothers, Cyril and Methodius, who, in consequence of this, have since been known as the Apostles of the Slavonians. What Mezrop did for the Armenians, what Ulfilas did for the Goths, was accomplished for that race by Cyril in the invention of a Slavonic alphabet, which from this cause is still known by the name of the Cyrillic. The same teacher, by his translation of the Scriptures into their tongue, provided them with a literary language, thereby producing the same result which Luther's Bible subsequently effected for Germany, and Dante's *Divina Commedia* for Italy. It is no matter for surprise that, throughout the whole of this great branch of the human race—even amongst the Russians, who owed their Christianity to another source—the names of these two brothers should occupy the foremost place in the calendar of Saints. It is not less significant that their names are not even mentioned by the Byzantine historians.

Cyril and Methodius were born about the year 826, at Thessalonica, in the neighbourhood of which city Slavonic tribes were even then settled. Cyril, or rather Constantine, for the name by which he is familiarly known was given him by Pope Hadrian II. at the time of his consecration as bishop shortly before his death, was the younger of the two; but, owing to his superior talents, which were fully recognised by his brother, he began from an early age to assume the more prominent position. At seven years old he had a dream that his father desired him to take in marriage the fairest maiden in Constantinople, and that the object of his choice was Wisdom ($\Sigma o\phi\iota a$). He

Cyril and Methodius

was afterwards educated at the capital, one of his instructors being the future patriarch Photius, and so great ability did he show in mastering all the sciences of the time that the emperor Theophilus, whose attention he attracted, caused one of his own sons to be brought up along with him. After he was grown up the grand logothete Theoctistus offered him his god-daughter to wife, and held out to him at the same time the prospect of high employment in the state; but Cyril refused, saying that he desired to devote himself to the pursuit of knowledge and to the service of God. He was then ordained priest, and received the appointment of librarian to the patriarch, but being seized with a desire for the monastic life, which his brother Methodius had already embraced, he retired to a convent on the shores of the Sea of Marmora. From this he was summoned to occupy the chair of philosophy at Constantinople, an office which he discharged with distinction, so that the title of Philosopher became attached to his name.

But it was not long before he was called to the work of converting the heathen. The Tauric Chersonese (now the Crimea) was inhabited at this time by the Khazars, a Turanian tribe of so great importance, that in the previous century Leo the Isaurian had married his son Constantine Copronymus to a princess of that race, and the emperor Leo IV., who was the offspring of that marriage, was known as Leo the Khazar. These people were pagans, but their ancient faith was being assailed by Jewish and Mahometan missionaries, so that their ruler or khan, in despair of arriving at the truth, sent an embassy to the Greek emperor Michael, requesting him to furnish them with a teacher who was capable of refuting the others' arguments and of converting his people to Christianity. The emperor's choice fell upon Cyril, and for this purpose he set out in the company of his brother Methodius for the town of Cherson (near the site of the modern Sebastopol), which was administered by a Byzantine governor. There they resided for some time, in order to make themselves acquainted with the language of the Khazars, and then proceeded to the headquarters of the khan. They were received with honour, and, after Cyril had held disputations with the advocates of the other creeds and confuted them, he preached the Gospel to the people. The khan himself and a part of the nation were converted, but the impression made does not seem to have been lasting. A traveller who passed through their country sixty years later mentions that they were then divided between pagans, who constituted the minority, Mahometans, Jews, and Christians.

During the residence of the two brothers at Cherson, however, an event occurred, which exercised a considerable influence on their future history. This was the discovery of the remains of St. Clement of Rome. According to the tale given in the 'Clementine Epitome,' this Saint was banished to this place by Trajan, and, in consequence of the numerous conversions which he made, was thrown into the sea by the heathen, with an anchor round his neck. Gradually it came to be believed that his body was miraculously preserved in a submarine tomb, and that at certain times it was possible to make pilgrimages to it. This legend, we may observe in passing, obtained a wide currency, and was the reason

St. Clement's remains

why St. Clement was adopted as the representative of the sea-kings, and hence became the patron saint of Denmark and Norway—a *culte*, of which a familiar evidence remains in the parish of St. Clement *Danes* in London, the emblem of which is an anchor. However, the story of Cyril and Methodius informs us that Cyril, after fasting and prayer, descended into the sea, which retired before him, and having found the body, brought it up with him, and conveyed it to Constantinople. Afterwards, both when they proceeded to Moravia, and when they visited Rome, the possession of this sacred relic, which they carried with them, caused them to be received with especial honour. The head of the saint was brought at a later period to Kieff in Russia, where we are told that in the year 1146 it was placed on the head of the Metropolitan of Russia as a form of consecration.

It was after the return of the two brothers to Constantinople that their thoughts were turned towards Moravia, which was destined to be the great field of their labours. The circumstances which led to their mission were the following. The Moravians, who were a Slavonic race, occupied at this time a wider area than is represented by the modern Moravia, for they extended, not only from the confines of Bohemia to the Carpathians, but also far away to the south, even beyond the Danube. Their religion, as pagans, was a sort of primitive nature-worship, and as some of their early myths implied reflection on such subjects as the unity of God and the immortality of the soul, it was natural that they should look favourably on a higher form of belief, which would offer them a solution of

[marginal note: The Moravians]

these questions. Already, by the agency of German missionaries, Christianity had found its way into various parts of the tribe; but it was felt that its influence was closely connected with the extension of the sovereignty of the emperor of the West, and threatened the existence of their nationality. Accordingly their prince Rastislav or Rastiz, somewhere about the year 862 requested the emperor of Constantinople to send them one who, in addition to other qualifications, should be able to teach them to read the Scriptures in their native language. For this office no one was found as fit as Cyril, especially on account of his knowledge of the Slavonic tongue, with which he seems to have been acquainted from the days of his early residence in Thessalonica. He now set to work to invent a Slavonic alphabet, and to translate the Gospels into that language. When this was, in part at least, accomplished, he set out with his brother from Constantinople, and after residing for some time in Bulgaria, through which country they had to pass on their way, and preaching Christianity there, they reached their destination towards the end of 863. Their first care was to instruct the most intelligent of the young people of the country in the use of the alphabet and the reading of the Bible, and they translated the breviary into the vulgar tongue. Then, in the words of the Slavonic legend, the ears of the deaf were opened, and the tongue of the dumb was loosed.

These proceedings did not pass without protest. The Western clergy, as might be expected, regarded the ap-
<small>Visit to Rome</small> pearance of missionaries from the Greek Church as an intrusion on their rightful province, and such an innovation as the use of an unauthorised

language in the services of the Church, offered a ready handle for attack. The view was now generally accepted, that there were only three sacred languages, Greek, Latin, and Hebrew; and when we consider that long after this time Dante passed through a severe struggle before making up his mind to compose his epic in the vulgar tongue, we perceive the greatness of Cyril in rising superior to such prejudices. The pope, Nicholas I., was now requested to interfere; and in obedience to his summons, Cyril and Methodius set out for Rome, but did not reach that city until after his death occurred, at the end of 867. His successor, Hadrian II., received them with marked favour, and approved both their translation of the Scriptures, and their use of the Slavonic language in the services. The importance of the occasion is marked by an incident which appears in the legendary narrative. When the pope and the conclave were deliberating on this question, their doubts were silenced by a supernatural voice, suddenly heard in the midst of them, exclaiming, 'Let everything that hath breath praise the Lord.'

Cyril was now consecrated bishop by Hadrian, but he did not long survive the event, for little more than a year had elapsed since his arrival in the Holy City when he died, at the early age of forty-two, and was buried in the basilica of his patron, St. Clement. After this, another Slavonic prince, Kocel, who ruled in Pannonia, begged the pope that Methodius might be sent to confirm his people in the faith; and consequently he returned as archbishop of Moravia and Pannonia, with the right of general

<small>Methodius archbishop</small>

superintendence of all the Slavonic countries. But his fortunes for the rest of his life were destined to be chequered. He lost the aid of his former supporter Rastislav, who was taken prisoner and blinded by Louis the German, and his successor, Swatopluk, accorded him but a treacherous support. The neighbouring bishops of Passau and Salzburg refused to acknowledge that he had any spiritual rights in Pannonia, and, according to one account, they procured his banishment to a monastery in Germany, where he was detained for two years and a half. Pope Hadrian also died in 872, and his successor, John VIII., was less well-informed as to the state of things in Moravia. Nevertheless the preaching of Methodius produced a great effect, and he gathered around him a number of disciples, some of whom, especially Clement and Naum, took an important part in the evangelisation of Bulgaria. His fame also spread into Bohemia, and the prince of that country, Borivoï, was baptized, and the foundations were laid of that Bohemian church, which is now among the foremost in its reverence for the apostles of the Slavonians. But at last the persistency of his enemies prevailed, and he was once more summoned to Rome in 879, to answer to the charge, not only of using the vulgar tongue in the services of the Church, but also of heresy, because he omitted the clause *Filioque* from the creed. Pope John, however, gave judgment in his favour on both these points, and confirmed him in his office as metropolitan. But the troubles of Methodius' life were not yet ended, for on his return he found a rival prelate introduced in his place, and Swatopluk used all his endeavours to promote the use of Latin, and to discourage that of the native language. But, whatever opposition he might meet with from the prince and the clergy, he was loyally supported by the people. He died peacefully in the year 885, after seeing the Gospel firmly planted among the south Slavonic races.

About the same time that the Moravians received Christianity, another important people, the Bulgarians, were converted. After the extinction of the Avars, this nation, who had long been in subjection to them, had founded an important monarchy in the ancient Moesia at the end of the seventh century; and this, for a period of nearly 350 years, was a standing menace to the Byzantine empire. When first they appeared in Europe, they were a Turanian or Hunnish tribe; but before the time of which we are speaking they had imperceptibly changed their nationality and their language, for by intermingling with the more numerous Slavonian tribes of the countries in which they settled, they became, to all intents and purposes, a Slavonic race. A large number of them seem to have emigrated into Western Macedonia before the ninth century, and there, in all probability, received a further infusion of Slavonic blood. Owing to the neighbourhood of Constantinople also, and the trade between that city and the German and Scandinavian peoples, which passed through their country, they became a commercial nation, and advanced in the arts of life. From motives of policy, therefore, as well as from religious zeal, the Byzantine emperors would naturally desire the conversion of so powerful a people in close proximity to them.

The Bulgarians

In the first instance, Christianity was introduced into Bulgaria by means of Greek captives taken in war. As early as the year 813, we are told, in an irruption of the Bulgarians into the empire, a number of the inhabitants were carried off, and amongst them a bishop, who formed the companions of his captivity into a church, and endeavoured with their assistance to propagate the true faith. Little impression, however, was made on the people at large, until a more favourable opening presented itself in the following manner. The sister of their king, Bogoris or Boris, had been taken prisoner by the Greeks in early youth, and had been educated as a Christian at Constantinople. In the course of time she was restored to her country, and thereupon she devoted herself to the object of converting her brother to the religion she had adopted. At first her efforts met with little success, because Bogoris was in fear of a rebellion in case of his deserting the faith of his ancestors; but at length his heart was softened by reason of a famine which sorely afflicted the country, and he became susceptible to religious influences. The story which follows, though it rests on very slender foundations, deserves to be introduced, because it is found in all ecclesiastical histories. The sister, having observed the fondness of the prince for painting, sent for a monk and artist, called Methodius, who in many accounts is identified with the brother of Cyril. Bogoris commissioned him to paint a hunting scene on a wall of one of his palaces; but instead of this, he painted a representation of the Last Judgment, which produced such an effect on the mind of the monarch, that he determined to embrace Christianity. This story, which is also related in connection with the conversion of the Russian Vladimir, is rejected by the latest Slavonic

Conversion of Bogoris

scholars; and even the account of the return of the sister from Constantinople is open to grave doubts. It appears also that ere this Bogoris had been in communication with the German emperor with regard to his adoption of the Christian faith, from which we may gather that he was greatly swayed by political motives. Thus much is certain, that at the conclusion of a war with the Byzantine empire in 864, Bogoris became a Christian, and received the name of Michael from the emperor Michael III., who undertook to be his sponsor. On this occasion a tract of country on the southern side of the Balkan range was ceded to the Bulgarians, and was called by them Zagora. By the Greeks it was pretended that the cession was made as a baptismal donation. The residence of Cyril and Methodius in Bulgaria, which has been mentioned as having taken place when they were on their way to Moravia, must have occurred shortly before this time.

The Bulgarian prince now proceeded to force the acceptance of Christianity on his people. The result of this step was a violent rebellion; but when Bogoris marched out to meet his revolted subjects, with only forty-eight attendants, wearing the cross on his breast, they were panic-stricken and took to flight. The monarch's revenge proved how little of the spirit of Christianity he had imbibed, for, while he spared the common people, he put all the rebellious nobles, together with their families, to death. After this, no further resistance was made to the introduction of the new creed. The Greek clergy, however, took little pains to provide for the spiritual wants of the people, and Bogoris himself was alienated by their refusal to allow his kingdom

[margin: Rome or Constantinople?]

to possess a bishop of its own. He was thus led to turn his thoughts westward, and to enter into negotiations with the see of Rome. His ambassadors were favourably received by Pope Nicholas I., and replies were sent by him to a hundred and six questions about which his advice was asked for the guidance of the new converts in their Christian life. The good sense of the Western bishop which these evince, and his power of understanding the religious needs of a semi-barbarous people, form a characteristic contrast to the point of view of the Eastern patriarch Photius, who, when writing a letter of exhortation to Bogoris after his conversion, combines practical advice with the discussion of minute questions of controversial theology. However, owing to the suspicious temper of the prince, or it may be to the exorbitant claims of the Roman pontiff, no agreement could be arrived at with regard to the person who should be appointed bishop in Bulgaria; and consequently, when Basil the Macedonian ascended the throne (A.D. 867), Bogoris once more opened negotiations with Constantinople. An archbishop was now sent from that city, and ten episcopal sees were established in the country. Thenceforward friendly relations sprang up between the Greeks and Bulgarians, and on all solemn occasions the place of honour next after the Greek patriarch was conceded to the archbishop of Bulgaria.

We may now revert to the disciples of Methodius. After the death of that apostle his leading associates were persecuted in Moravia, and being forced to escape from that country, took refuge in Bulgaria, where they were welcomed by Bogoris, who still occupied the throne (886). Their zeal, when

Clement of Ochrida

transferred to this new sphere of action, was very effectual in propagating Christianity among the Bulgarians, especially in Western Macedonia, which became the great field of their labours. Of one of their number, Clement, an interesting biography has come down to us, composed by one of his pupils, who is thought by Neander to have been the well-known archbishop Theophylact; but this is a mistake, for that writer did not flourish till considerably later (*circ.* 1077). Its value consists in the light which it throws on the manner of life and mode of working of these missionaries, and it tends to raise them greatly in our estimation. Clement was a native of Achrida (now Ochrida), on the lake of the same name (in classical times the Lacus Lychnitis) on the confines of Western Macedonia and Albania, and in this city he founded a monastery. There he forwarded the improvement of the people, not only by giving oral instruction, but also by composing simple homilies in the Bulgarian language for the use of the priests, by introducing the fine arts and building beautiful churches, and by improving horticulture through the importation of new fruit-trees. In order to train up a body of teachers, he gathered round him a large number of young men, on whose Christian instruction he bestowed particular attention; but he also himself took pains to teach the children. The large-minded views and the strong element of personal sympathy which appear in this account amply justify the enthusiastic affection with which his biographer speaks of him. He had now returned to the Eastern communion, and before his death in the year 916 he became bishop of Belitza, the first episcopal see established in those parts.

In the metropolitan church at Ochrida there exists at the present day an ancient wooden statue of St. Clement of Rome, which probably dates from this period, and recalls the connection of Cyril and Methodius with the memory of that saint—from whom, also, it is not improbable that Clement of Ochrida received his name It is now kept concealed from view, and, as being a statue, is regarded as an illicit object, but has been spared on account of its venerable antiquity. The memory of one of Clement's fellow-missionaries, St. Naum, is perpetuated by a monastery which is called after him, at the southern end of the lake of Ochrida.

A word may here be added as to the subsequent fortunes of the Bulgarian church. In the year 923, at *Subsequent fortunes* the end of a war between the Greeks and the Bulgarians, a treaty was concluded between the emperor Romanus I. and the Bulgarian monarch Samuel. One of the stipulations contained in this was that the independence of the Bulgarian church should be publicly recognised, and that the archbishop of Dorostylon should be officially acknowledged as patriarch of Bulgaria, both by the emperor and by the patriarch of Constantinople. Fifty years later, when Bulgaria was conquered by John Zimisces (972), the patriarchal dignity in that country was for a time abolished; but it was revived again before the end of that century, when the Bulgarian chief Samuel transferred his seat of government to Ochrida (p. 19), and made that place the head-quarters of the patriarchate. Even after the overthrow of the Bulgarian kingdom by Basil II. in 1018 the Bulgarian church was allowed to retain its independence, only the title of its head was changed from Patriarch to Archbishop. This prelate, however, was appointed by the emperor, and Greeks were usually nominated to the see, so that Ochrida became the headquarters of a Greek *propaganda*. But it was not until 1767 that this arrangement was cancelled. In that year the last independent archbishop of Ochrida was forced by the Porte to resign, and the see was incorporated in the patriarchate of Constantinople. Still, these events in their national history were not forgotten by the people, and at last within our own time they have regained their ancient rights. In 1860 an agitation commenced on the part of the Bulgarian church to free itself from the jurisdiction of the patriarch of Constantinople, and this was carried to a successful issue, so that in 1870 a separate Bulgarian exarchate was officially recognised by the Porte. Thus the ecclesiastical independence of that people became an accomplished fact before their political freedom, but up to this time the Bulgarian church has been treated as excommunicate by that of Constantinople.

The last, and in its results by far the most important, conquest of the Byzantine church was the conversion of the Russians. The Greeks first became acquainted with this nation, as they had with the Bulgarians, by means of hostilities. Shortly after Ruric, the Scandinavian founder of the royal dynasty of Russia, had established himself as sovereign in that country, two of his companions, Oskold and Dir, became princes of Kieff on the banks of the Dnieper. Before long they made themselves masters of the whole course of that river, and came into collision with the Byzantine settlements on the shores of the Black Sea. In this

The Russians

way they heard of the wealth of Constantinople, and, no plan being too bold for such adventurers, conceived the idea of making themselves masters of, or at least of plundering, the strongest city in the world. In the year 865, and in the reign of Michael III., the inhabitants of that place were astonished by the appearance in its neighbourhood of a fleet of two hundred small vessels, containing armed men, which passed down the Bosphorus. As the citizens were unaccustomed to have the horrors of war thus brought before their very eyes, a profound impression was produced on them by this spectacle; but in reality these freebooters were not formidable opponents, when met by trained soldiers and systematic warfare. A force sufficient to put them to flight was easily mustered, and their vessels were destroyed by the rising of a sudden storm, which was attributed to the influence of a garment of the Virgin, which the emperor removed from one of the churches and dipped in the sea.

Oskold and Dir, who were the leaders of this expedition, and were taken captives, are regarded as the first *Early conversions* of the Russians who embraced the Gospel; and it is probably to this event that Photius, who was patriarch at this time, refers, when in a circular letter, issued in 866, he describes the Russian nation as beginning to exchange heathenism for Christianity. By commercial intercourse, also, and by the employment of the Varangians, as the Scandinavian mercenaries were called, in the body-guard of the Byzantine emperors, the seeds of the true faith were scattered among that people, so that as early as 891, in a catalogue of dioceses subject to the patriarch of Constantinople, the metropolitan see

* L 2

of Russia is mentioned. Anyhow, fifty years later, on the occasion of a treaty of peace being concluded between the prince Igor and the Greek emperor, we hear of a church of the prophet Elias as existing at Kieff, and also that, whereas the pagans employed in the Russian army swore by the Slavonic divinity Perun, the baptized Russians took an oath by the God of the Christians. It was probably through this Christian community at Kieff that the doctrines of the Gospel, and its superiority to other forms of religion, came to the knowledge of the widowed princess Olga, who governed Russia during the minority of her son Swatoslav. Being inspired with the desire of embracing that faith, she undertook a voyage to Constantinople for that purpose, and there received baptism at the hands of the patriarch Polyeuctes, while the emperor Constantine Porphyrogenitus, who has left a detailed account of the ceremonies connected with her reception, became her godfather. At the font she received the name of Helena, after the sainted mother of Constantine the Great; and Nestor, the old Russian annalist, describes how the patriarch on that occasion foretold to the princess the blessings which would descend through her means on future generations of Russians.

The results of Olga's conversion were not destined immediately to appear. Her son Swatoslav was a fierce warrior—indeed, his campaigns on the Danube, first against the Bulgarians and afterwards against the empire, and his final defeat by John Zimisces, form an important chapter in Byzantine history. Such a disposition was ill suited to accept the precepts of Christianity, and he refused to listen to his mother's

Vladimir

persuasions, though his affection for her caused him to tolerate her religion, and to allow those who agreed with her to profess their faith openly. He also entrusted his son Vladimir to her care while he was himself absent on his distant expeditions; and though the youth grew up a pagan, yet the instruction and the example of the pious Olga seem not to have been lost upon him. The story of his conversion, the details of which seem to be historical, is one of the strangest of such narratives. We are told that the emissaries of various religions—Bulgarian Mussulmans from the Volga, Jews from among the Khazars, and representatives of the Western Church from Germany—endeavoured to win him to their views. He listened to them in turn, and for various reasons rejected them all. The Mahometans practised circumcision, and forbade the use of wine. The Jews, when questioned about their home, confessed that it had been destroyed; Vladimir would not accept the creed of those whom God had dispersed among the nations for their sins. The Christianity of the West seemed strange to him, it was beyond his ken. 'Return home,' he said to the German missionaries; 'our ancestors did not receive this religion from you.' At last there appeared a 'philosopher' or monk from Greece. With him the Russian prince conferred at greater length, and expounded to him the views of those who had already solicited him. The philosopher replied to these, and then proceeded to expound the principles of the Christian faith as believed by his church. Then follows the story—which we have already noticed as being introduced, though with less historical authority, into the account of the conversion of Bogoris—of the production of a picture of the Last Judgment, and of its being shown to Vladimir. When the prince perceived the different lot of the righteous and the wicked, he was deeply affected, and exclaimed, 'Blessed are these on the right hand, but woe to those on the left.' Thereupon the missionary urged him to be baptized, in order that he might secure his salvation; but Vladimir still hesitated, and deferred his decision, though he dismissed his instructor with rich presents. In the following year he consulted with his nobles on the subject, and by their advice determined to send chosen men to the countries where the various religions were professed, in order that they might view them on the spot and report upon them.

Envoys were accordingly despatched for this purpose, and after making enquiries concerning the other creeds, they finally arrived at Constantinople.

Embassy to Constantinople

The occasion was a momentous one, for it involved the future of the Russian Church and nation; and the circumstances were worthy of it. The powerful emperor Basil II. was on the throne, and he determined that the strangers should be received in the most impressive manner. 'Let them see,' he said, 'the glory of our God.' The place into which they were ushered, the cathedral of St. Sophia, was at that time the grandest of all Christian temples. There all the pomp of the ceremonial of the Eastern Church was displayed, and choristers with white wings, resembling angels—whether this was symbolical representation or pious fraud we need not too closely enquire—mingled in the procession of clergy. The patriarch, clad in his most splendid vestments, celebrated the Liturgy in their presence, and the brilliancy of the lights, the harmonious chanting, the solemnity of the scene, and the presence of what seemed to them to be heavenly visitors, produced a profound impression upon them. They returned to their own country Christians already in heart, and when they reported their mission to the prince, they made the following declaration with regard to the Greek religion: 'When we stood in the temple we knew not where we were, for there is nothing else like it upon earth; there, in truth, God has his dwelling with men; and we can never forget the beauty we saw there. No one who has once tasted sweets, will afterwards take that which is bitter, nor can we any longer abide in heathenism.'

But Vladimir, who still was thoroughly pagan at heart, determined to win his new religion sword in hand. With this view he fitted out an expedition, and attacked the city of Cherson, which was in the dominion of the Byzantine empire. The place made a stubborn resistance, and at last Vladimir made a vow that, if he was successful in capturing it, he would be baptized. He achieved his object, but, before fulfilling his vow, he sent to Constantinople to demand of the emperor the hand of his sister Anna in marriage. The princess sacrificed herself to this barbarous alliance for the propagation of the faith, and on her arrival at Cherson, in the company of a body of clergy, she persuaded her future husband to hasten his baptism. To this he consented; and as he came up from the water, after the rite had been administered to him by the bishop of Cherson, he exclaimed, 'To-day I have become acquainted

Baptism of Vladimir

with the true God.' He now caused a church to be erected in the place which was the scene of his conversion, and dedicated it to St. Basil, after which he returned to Kieff, bearing with him, as a sacred relic, the head of St. Clement of Rome, the finding of whose remains by Cyril has been already mentioned. The extirpation of heathenism, and its replacement by Christianity, were now proceeded with in earnest. The great wooden idol of Perun, the god of thunder, was dragged from its place to the Dnieper, and pushed down the stream of that river until it finally disappeared in the rapids. Having accomplished this without resistance, and being supported by the good-will of the nobles of his company, Vladimir then proclaimed that whosoever on the morrow should not repair to the river, whether rich or poor, he should hold him for his enemy. In answer to his call the citizens of Kieff, with their wives and children, flocked to the Dnieper, and there were baptized by the Greek clergy. 'Some stood in the water up to their necks,' says Nestor the historian, 'others up to their breasts, holding their young children in their arms; the priests read the prayers from the shore, naming at once whole companies by the same name.' The prince himself stood on the bank in a transport of joy at the sight, commending his people to God, and praying that He would confirm him and them in the faith. (A.D. 980).

The remarkable feature in the conversion of the Russian people is the rapidity and ease with which it *Peaceful conversion of the people* was effected. Its progress was marked by no violent resistance and no shedding of blood. One reason of this may have been the difference of creed between the Slavonic Russians and their Scandinavian rulers, which facilitated the toleration of another religion. But it also seems highly probable that a knowledge of Christianity, and a prepossession in its favour, were already widely spread among the people at large, and that the conversion of the ruler served as a signal which was readily welcomed by others. Vladimir wisely followed up the movement which he had set on foot, by establishing Christian schools at Kieff, and by introducing the Cyrillic alphabet and the Cyrillic translation of the Scriptures. The same system was carried out by his successor, Yaroslav, and during his reign numerous churches and monasteries were founded, and the Byzantine system of canon law was introduced. But, notwithstanding that the church in Russia was thus placed on a more or less independent footing, its connection with Constantinople was of long duration. For the first three centuries of its history its metropolitans were, with hardly an exception, Greeks, and the accomplishments and address which these natives of the South brought with them enabled them to take a high position in the country. The great Petchersky Monastery, which became the model of all the future monasteries of Russia, was founded by a Russian hermit, who had received his first impulse towards the monastic life on Mount Athos; and the rules which were adopted there were those of the monastery of the Studium at Constantinople. The mode of conducting the services, the arrangement of the churches, the styles of architecture and painting in Russia, are unmistakably those of the Byzantine church. At the present day, when the Russian church is under a separate jurisdiction from that of Constantinople, though in friendly communion with it, the two are closely bound together by a spiritual link, and the Greek origin of all that is ecclesiastical in Russia is at once perceptible.

CHAPTER VIII.

THE MONASTIC SYSTEM OF THE EASTERN CHURCH.

Permanence of the system—Mount Athos—Eastern monastic life—Contrast with the West—Phases of monastic life—Hermits and Stylites—System of St. Basil—Love of tranquillity—The Hesychasts—Incidental uses of the monasteries—Their unfavourable side—Strange monastic abodes.

No feature in the organisation of the Eastern Church has been more permanent or has been less affected by change than its monastic system. The existing monasteries, even where their buildings have been restored, present their original appearance, owing to the conservative spirit which has prevailed in their reconstruction; the pictures, with which the walls of their churches and refectories are covered, correspond exactly to their early prototypes; and the mode of life, and even the tone of thought of their inmates, is completely that of the middle ages. It is, therefore, possible in this case to commence the study of the past by regarding the present, and to examine the institution in the form in which it now appears, before proceeding to enquire into the steps by which it arose. For that purpose the monasteries of Mount Athos furnish us with the most complete example. During a period of a thousand years that sanctuary has been the stronghold of monasticism in the East, and has been regarded as a centre and bulwark of Orthodox Christianity. As a place of pilgrimage it reckons only second to Jerusalem, and the festival of the Transfiguration, which is celebrated on the summit of the mountain on August 6, is attended by numerous devotees from Russia. Throughout Greece and Turkey it is known as a home of the fine arts, and painters of religious subjects who are educated there are extensively employed in those countries. And to the student of history it presents an epitome of the system, because all the various phases of Eastern monastic life still exist there.

The peninsula which is occupied by this monastic community, and which is the easternmost of the three that stretch like a trident from the coast of Macedonia into the north of the Ægean, is forty miles in length and, on an average, about four miles broad. It is intersected by a steep mountain ridge, from which lateral valleys and deep gorges run down to the coast on either hand; and at the southern end it throws up a vast conical peak, 6,400 feet high, the base of which is washed on three sides by the sea. The whole of this area, with the exception of the bare marble peak, is covered with magnificent natural vegetation, though at intervals appear farms and monastic buildings with bright patches of cultivated land about them, which have been reclaimed by the hands of the monks. The monasteries, twenty in number, are built at intervals throughout the peninsula, chiefly in the neighbourhood of the seashore; but, besides these, numerous smaller communities are settled on the moun-

Mount Athos

tain slopes. Each monastery is surrounded by a massive
wall of defence, over which, as seen from outside, appear
the domes of one or more Byzantine churches, a tall
tower, which was used in more troublous times to
watch for the approach of corsairs, and the spiry forms
of several cypresses. Within extreme irregularity prevails, the only detached buildings, as a rule, being
the central church and the refectory ($\tau\rho\acute{a}\pi\varepsilon\zeta a$), while all
around stand wooden cloisters, staircases, chapels, and
vine-covered trellises one above another at every angle.
More picturesque structures it is difficult to conceive.
The number of monks varies greatly in the different
monasteries, the smallest being twenty-five, the largest
three hundred. The whole number on the Holy Moun-
tain, as the peninsula is called ($\tau\grave{o}$ "$A\gamma\iota o\nu$ "$O\rho o\varsigma$), is
believed to be about three thousand; but in addition
to them there is a fluctuating population of seculars
($\kappa o\sigma\mu\iota\kappa o\acute{\iota}$), who are employed as servants and farm-
labourers, and these may amount to as many more.
No woman may set foot in the peninsula, and, in order
to render the rule as absolute as possible, all female
animals also are excluded. In other Greek monasteries
the latter part of this regulation is not observed, but
the principle seems to have been recognised at an early
period. Theodore Studita, the abbot of the Studium
monastery in the ninth century, thus enjoins his brethren
in one of his letters: 'You, who have renounced all
communion with the female sex, ought not to employ a
female animal for labour.'

 The life of these monks, or *caloyers*, as they are called
($\kappa a\lambda\acute{o}\gamma\varepsilon\rho o\varsigma$, ' a good old man '), whatever view may be
taken of its serviceableness, is in accordance with the

primitive idea of monasticism. The objects which it has in view, are retirement from the world and its temptations, entire devotion to the service of God in religious exercises, and mortification of the flesh. Six or seven hours of every day, and more on Sundays, are occupied by the church services; and on some of the greater festivals, the almost incredible time of from sixteen to twenty hours is spent in church. The life is one of the sternest bodily self-denial. Very few of the monks ever touch meat, and on fast days they take only one meal, which is generally composed of bread, vegetables, and water. In addition to this, they never get an unbroken night's rest, as the first service commences between 1 and 2 A.M. There are different grades of sanctity among them. The majority of the monks assume the Lesser Habit (τὸ μικρὸν σχῆμα), but a few aspire to wear the Great Habit (τὸ μέγα σχῆμα), which is a kind of breastplate or stomacher of a woollen material, worked with a cross and other devices, and is the sign of the highest monastic austerity. In the stricter convents the monks generally communicate once a fortnight, and this is unusually often according to the practice of the Greek Church in this matter. Only a small proportion of them are clergy, and the clerical office is in no way connected with the monastic profession. Even in the large establishments it is not usual to find more than ten or twelve of the community in Holy Orders, and in the smaller ones there are but just enough to carry on the services. The rule that they follow is that of St. Basil, and this is observed almost universally throughout the Eastern communion.

Eastern monastic life

From this it will be seen that there is nothing in the

Greek Church which corresponds to the distinction of monastic Orders in the West, or to that assumption of various functions which has rendered those Orders such important agencies in advancing Latin Christianity. Thus it is in regard of learning. Though from the way in which the books have been used and marked in the libraries on Athos, there is evidence that there have been students among the monks, yet this was no part of the system; and at the present time the libraries are rarely opened, and the monks do not pretend to make study a part of their occupation. The learned Benedictine Order has found no counterpart in the East. Nor, again, have they devoted themselves to teaching or the propagation of the faith, like the preaching Orders of the Latin Church. Here, too, there are exceptions, for Cyril and Methodius, and others who distinguished themselves by their missionary labours, were monks; and of late years the Bulgarian monastery of Chilandari on Athos has set on foot a system of sending a number of ordained monks into Bulgaria, on a sort of home mission, to assist the parish priests in extensive districts; but such employments are an accidental outgrowth from the monastic life. The theory of that life is this—that these bodies serve as an example of holiness, since they contain a number of men devoted to piety and religion; that they maintain intact the old customs and principles; that their constant prayers are a support to the Church; and, above all, that their members are placed in a favourable position for securing their own salvation. To use the words with which some of them endeavoured to persuade a western traveller to sojourn among them:

Contrast with the West

'Forsake the world and join us; with us you will find your happiness. Here you will enjoy soft breezes, and the greatest of all blessings—freedom and inward peace. For he alone is free who has overcome the world, and has his abode in the laboratory of all virtues (ἐργαστήριον πασῶν ἀρετῶν) on Mount Athos.' Thus, in respect of the monastic life, we trace the same contrast between the Eastern and the Western Church, which we have already noticed in so many other points—the one is more contemplative, the other more practical.

Originally all these communities were *coenobite*— that is to say, its members had a common stock and common table, and were governed by one abbot or hegumen, who was elected for life. But in the course of time another system grew up, which about half the monasteries on the Holy Mountain have now adopted—the *idiorrhythmic*, where 'every man is a rule to himself.' Where this prevails, the constitution is a sort of republic, the government being in the hands of two superiors annually elected; and the inmates generally take their meals in their own cells, and both in regard of laying by money and the disposal of their time are in a position of comparative freedom. But besides the regular convents, other and simpler forms of monastic life are found on Athos. First of all there are the hermits, who dwell in perfect solitude, practising the sternest asceticism. These have their abode either in caves by the seashore, or in rude habitations, with perhaps a chapel attached to them, and their food is brought to them from some neighbouring monastery. The attraction which is still exercised by the eremitic life is proved by some of the in-

Phases of monastic life

habitants of the convents retiring by preference from time to time to these solitudes. Again, in the retreats (καθίσματα) we find small associations of monks living together in retirement, and supporting themselves by their common labours; and when a number of these retreats are assembled round a central church, a skete (ἀσκητήριον) is formed, which in some cases differs from a monastery only in not possessing an independent constitution. It is in the sketes and retreats that Eastern monachism presents its most favourable aspect, on account of the simplicity of the life, and the industry of their inmates, who are occupied either in working in the fields, or in making monastic garments and similar employments. The affairs of the entire community on Mount Athos are superintended by the Holy Synod, a governing body to which each of the twenty monasteries sends a representative; and one of these, according to a fixed annual cycle, holds the position of president and is called 'the First Man of Athos,'—an office which has existed ever since the tenth century.

From this sketch of eastern monastic life, as it is found at the present day in its most typical example, we may proceed to enquire into the steps by which it grew up, and the development of its various phases. The hermit life, which was its earliest stage, originated, as is well known, with St. Antony in Egypt, and the leading motive which induced men to embrace it was the desire to escape from the profligate life that prevailed during the third and fourth centuries of our era in the great cities of the Roman empire, and especially at Alexandria. When once an impulse had thus been given to the pursuit of solitude and self-

Hermits and Stylites

mortification, thousands of earnest Christians withdrew into the deserts, in order to pass their lives at a distance from the abodes of men. In the course of time the numbers became so great that it was necessary to introduce some order among them, and so, early in the fourth century, a form of cœnobite life was instituted by Pachomius, who established an ascetic community on the island of Tabennæ in the Nile. But though this organised system was generally adopted for the future, the purely eremitic theory was not wholly abandoned, but spread into other countries, and assumed new and strange forms. Conspicuous among these extravagant devotees were the Stylites, who passed their lives on the summits of lofty pillars. The most famous of this class, Simeon Stylites, lived in Syria in the first half of the fifth century, and so great was the influence that he exercised through his reputation for sanctity, that thousands of the nomad Arabs are said to have been baptized in consequence of his exhortations. The religious point of view of such a character, the deep abhorrence of self which was the cause of his mortifications, the longing for a higher life, the temptation to spiritual pride, and the impression produced on the multitude, are delineated with great sympathetic insight by Tennyson in his poem on the subject. During the middle ages hermits—and among them Stylites and Dendrites, as those were called who inhabited high trees —were very numerous in the Byzantine church. Morbid and unhealthy as was the spirit which prompted them, they possessed a great power over the minds of men, as we have seen in the course of the iconoclastic controversy. Their fearlessness procured them a hearing, and their unworldliness brought their words home to the hearts of those who turned away from others. In the pictures on the walls of the monastic churches the hermits represent the highest type of the religious life.

The cœnobite system, which was inaugurated by Pachomius in Egypt, was more completely organised, and fixed as the monastic rule of the Church of Constantinople, by St. Basil. The early Egyptian cœnobia (λαῦραι, as they were called, from their 'lanes' or irregular clusters of cells) correspond more nearly, in respect of their simpler regulations, to the sketes of later times. St. Basil seems to have been impressed with the evils attendant on the hermit life, for he writes on that subject in the following terms: 'The eremitic life conflicts with the essential character of Christian love, since here each individual is concerned only for what pertains to his own good; while the essence of Christian love prompts each to seek, not alone what serves for his own advantage, but also the good of others. Neither will such a person find it easy to come to the knowledge of his failings and deficiencies; since he has no one to correct him with love and gentleness. What is written in Ecclesiastes (iv. 10) applies to the case of such a person: "Woe to him that is alone when he falleth, for he hath not another to help him up." In a society many can work together, so as to fulfil the divine commands on different sides. But he who lives alone is ever confined to one single work; and while this is being done other works must be neglected.' The principle here stated, though of course strongly opposed by the hermits, met with a wide

System of St. Basil

acceptance, and before long monasteries with a rule of common life became numerous in the Eastern Church. After a time the establishment or endowment of such an institution was regarded as meritorious, and wealthy persons, or such as held high office in the state, erected sumptuous conventual buildings in pleasant localities as an act of piety, and in some cases with the further object of providing places of retirement for themselves, in which they might end their days in peace in the midst of religious associations. The sides of lofty mountains, from their seclusion and the salubrity of their atmosphere, were especially resorted to, and the Bithynian Olympus, and the Trojan Ida, as well as Athos, were thickly planted with the dwelling-places of such communities. To such lengths did this custom run, that we find Nicephorus Phocas in the tenth century issuing an order to prevent donations being made to the monasteries, but this was speedily allowed to fall into abeyance. The emperors of the dynasty of Comnenus, finding that the monks were a support to them in fostering that opposition to the Latin Church and Western ideas which was a part of their policy, showered their favours upon them, and the Athos communities were at this time made independent of the patriarch of Constantinople. Even the century that preceded the capture of the city, though it brought disaster to the Greeks elsewhere, was a period of prosperity to these societies. It seemed almost as if the emperors and leading men, conscious of the increasing weakness of their position, were disposed to make over a part of their possessions to what seemed to them the safer keeping of the monks.

The secret of the attractiveness of this life is to be found in the love of tranquillity (ἡσυχία), which is characteristic of the Oriental mind. Ask any Greek monk at the present day, and he will assign this as his reason for embracing the monastic profession. In the middle ages even princesses who were endowed with personal beauty and wealth, are known to have preferred the retirement of the cloister to the pleasures and excitements of the palace. Hence the monasteries were often spoken of as places of contemplation (φροντιστήρια), and the monks were called, and applied to themselves the name of, philosophers. It is not surprising, therefore, that this state of mind gave birth at various times to different forms of mysticism. The most remarkable phase of this is found in the tenets of those monks on Mount Athos, who from this cause received the name of Hesychasts (ἡσυχάζοντες) or Quietists. By these it was maintained that, after long abstinence and contemplation, they could see in the middle of their belly, which was the seat of the soul, the light which appeared to the Disciples at the transfiguration of Christ, and that this light was part of the essence of God himself, and therefore immortal and eternal. This view was combated by a Calabrian monk called Barlaam, and the discussion which followed gave occasion for four councils, and involved emperors and patriarchs in its confusion, Gregory Palamas being the leader of the monks' party, on which side also the Emperor Cantacuzene was found, while Nicephorus Gregoras supported Barlaam and their other opponents. The dispute, which continued for ten years (1341-51), ended in the discomfiture and condemnation of the sceptic, and the establishment of the doctrine of the uncreated light of Tabor. It was believed also, and apparently not without reason, that the faith of many of the monks of Athos was impregnated with tenets resembling those of the Bogomilians—a class of views to which extravagant asceticism has always proved favourable. The suspicion went so far that in 1351 a formal investigation was set on foot against the First Man, Nephon, before the bishops of Salonica and Erisso; and though they decided that he had done nothing more than receive beggars and needy strangers of that sect, yet for a time the monks were brought into considerable disrepute.

In order to estimate rightly the importance of these monasteries, it is necessary that we should consider the purposes which they incidentally served, in addition to what was recognised as their traditional system. In the first place, they were the training-places of the higher clergy. In consequence of the mischievous rule which required that the bishops should be celibate, while the parochial clergy were married, the prelates had usually to be taken from the ranks of the monks; and when these were banished from their sees or deposed—a thing which, owing to the prevalence of intrigue and other causes, has been, and is, of not uncommon occurrence in the Greek Church—they were usually required to take up their abode once more in a monastery. Unsuccessful pretenders to the throne, also, and persons on whom any suspicion of sinister designs might fall, were frequently immured in such a place of confinement, if their lives were spared; while several emperors, for instance Cantacuzene, retired thither of their own free will; and others, impressed with the idea that the monastic habit was a passport to heaven, assumed it shortly before their death. At certain periods learned men—whether theologians, such as John Damascene and Theodore Studita, or men of general culture, like Michael Psellus the Younger (*circ.* 1050) —resided within their walls; indeed, in the ninth century the monastery was the centre of intellectual life in the empire. Since many of their inmates devoted their leisure to calligraphy, it was greatly owing to them that so many transcripts of the classical writers, as well as of the Fathers of the Church, were made. The arts of painting and of carving in wood and ivory were practised there; and also that of illuminating manuscripts, of which so many fine specimens still remain in the libraries of Europe. Still more important is the service which these institutions have rendered in every age by taking thought for those for whom society at large does not provide. Lunatics are often housed within their walls, and retreats are established for lepers in their vicinity. They have served as refuges for the persecuted, and for those perplexed by the distractions and confusions of the world. It is not too much to say that thousands have been saved from suicide by their means.

But the unfavourable side of monasticism is not less conspicuously seen in these communities. They have always been strongholds of superstition and intolerance. The worship of relics and miraculous pictures, and the legends connected with them, have been fostered especially within their walls. When controversies arose, the monks were always found on the side opposed to moderation and enlightenment. Whatever view they espoused, they were the fiercest of partisans,

<small>Their unfavourable side</small>

for the range of their mental vision was limited, and they lacked the conciliatory spirit which the experience of life is apt to engender. In respect of their standard of morals, indeed, they never reached the demoralisation of the West. Yet Eustathius, the good and learned archbishop of Thessalonica in the twelfth century, denounces in no measured terms the corruption of the monastic life in his age. Some of the monks he accuses of affecting severity and pretending to see visions, merely for the purpose of obtaining veneration and presents from the multitude; others, he says, were malefactors who had adopted this calling in order to escape the punishment of their crimes; while others, again, turned their attention to money-making, and grew rich as cattle-dealers and wool-merchants. The ancient books in the libraries were being sold, and impediments were thrown in the way of men of literary attainments when they wished to join their societies. It was in consequence of abuses such as these that, a century later, in the reign of Andronicus II., the patriarch Athanasius, who was a stern reformer, introduced a number of stringent ordinances, whereby to regulate the conduct of the monks. All habits that savoured of worldliness—all luxuriousness of living, and frequent appearance in public, especially in the marketplaces—were now strictly repressed. But the reformation that was thus instituted lasted only during the term of office of its originator, and the real cure for the evil was provided by the Ottoman conquest, which reduced all classes among the Greeks to the same state of subjection. Yet the inherent fault of the system remained, in the want of definite occupation, and the absence of elevating influences such as education. A large proportion of the Greek monks at the present day are either ignorant peasants, or are drawn from a class not much higher in the social scale. In any country, and under the most favourable circumstances, the process of bringing together a number of such persons into a community, with no domestic ties to influence them, and with a certain allowance of time at their command, would not tend to produce spirituality, and is capable of fostering a large amount of evil. And this is the condition of the Eastern monasteries at the present day.

In the Liturgy of St. Basil there occurs a prayer for 'those that are in deserts and mountains, and in dens and caves of the earth.' In its primary acceptation the clause may have been intended to apply, as the original passage in the Epistle to the Hebrews does, to persons escaping from persecution; but it is difficult not to fancy that it may have referred also to those who betook themselves to remote places in order to cultivate without interruption the religious life. Certainly, some of the positions which were selected for monastic abodes during the middle ages, whether with a view to greater asceticism, or for the sake of security in troublous times, or even, as it might seem, from a predilection for a wild and romantic place of residence, can be fitly described in these terms. The tufa rocks that flank the valley of Gueremeh in Cappadocia, in the neighbourhood of the city of Cæsareia, St. Basil's own see, have been hollowed into innumerable chambers, which were once the abode of monks. The place is now deserted, and not a trace of its history remains; but the cells and sepulchral vaults of this Byzantine

Strange monastic abodes

Pompeii are still visible, and rock-hewn refectories, with benches and tables cut in the solid stone, and subterranean churches still bright with frescoes of sacred subjects. The largest convent in the Peloponnese, that of Megaspelæon, occupies, as its name implies, a vast cavern, which was the original abode of the monks; now a lofty wall has been erected in front of its mouth, and resting partly on this, and partly on the rock behind, stand the picturesque wooden dwellings of its present occupants. Still more strange is the position of the monastery of Sumelas at the back of Trebizond, which is built in a cave in the very middle of a perpendicular face of cliff nearly a thousand feet in height, and is only accessible by a wooden staircase from the side. The buildings, which are crowded together within this natural hollow, date from the year 1360, when it was rebuilt and endowed by the Emperor Alexius Comnenus III. of Trebizond. Most wonderful of all are the monasteries of Meteora in the north-west of Thessaly, which occupy the summits of a number of columnar masses of rock, and are reached either by ladders attached to the cliffs, or by a rope and net, with which these fishers of men draw up their visitors to their aërial abodes. One of these, that of St. Stephen, was founded by the Emperor Cantacuzene in the middle of the fourteenth century.

CHAPTER IX.

THE SEPARATION OF THE GREEK AND LATIN CHURCHES.

Early tendency to divergence—Political differences between the Greek emperors and the popes—Ecclesiastical differences between the two patriarchates—Papal claims of supremacy—Ignatius and Photius—Counter-excommunications of the two churches—Doctrinal differences—The *Filioque* clause—The question of *azyma*—Renewal of the strife by Michael Cerularius—The final schism—Effect of the crusades—Attempts at reunion—Council of Lyons—Council of Ferrara—Removed to Florence—Repudiated by the Greeks.

THE separation of the Eastern and Western Churches, which finally took place in the year 1054, was due to the operation of influences which had been at work for several centuries before. We have already seen (p. 33) how from very early times a tendency to divergence existed, arising from the tone of thought of the dominant races in the two, the more speculative Greeks being chiefly occupied with purely theological questions, while the more practical Roman mind devoted itself rather to subjects connected with the nature and destiny of man. In differences such as these there was nothing irreconcilable; the members of both communions professed the same forms of belief, rested their faith on the same Divine Persons, were guided by the same standard of morals, and were

Early tendency to divergence

animated by the same hopes and fears; and they were bound by the first principles of their religion to maintain unity with one another. But in societies, as in individuals, inherent diversity of character is liable to be intensified by time, and thus counteracts the natural bonds of sympathy, and prevents the two sides from seeing one another's point of view. In this way it co-operates with, and aggravates the force of, other causes of disunion, which adverse circumstances may generate. Such causes there were in the present instance—political, ecclesiastical, and theological; and the nature of these it may be well for us to consider, before proceeding to narrate the history of the disruption.

The office of bishop of Rome assumed to some extent a political character as early as the time of the first Christian emperors. By them this prelate was constituted a sort of secretary of state for Christian affairs, and was employed as a central authority for communicating with the bishops in the provinces, so that after a while he acted as minister of religion and public instruction. As the civil and military power of the Western Empire declined, the extent of this authority increased; and by the time when Italy was annexed to the Empire of the East in the reign of Justinian, the popes had become the political chiefs of Roman society. Nominally, indeed, they were subject to the exarch of Ravenna, as vicegerent of the emperor at Constantinople, but in reality the inhabitants of Western Europe were more disposed to look to the spiritual potentate in the imperial city as representing the traditions of ancient Rome. The political rivalry that was thus engendered was sharpened

Political differences

by the traditional jealousy of Rome and Constantinople, which had existed ever since the new capital had been erected on the shores of the Bosphorus. Then followed struggles for administrative superiority between the popes and the exarchs, culminating in the shameful maltreatment and banishment of Martin I. by the Emperor Constans (p. 89)—an event which the see of Rome could never forget. The attempt to enforce iconoclasm in Central Italy, as we have seen, was influential in causing the loss of that province to the Empire; and even after the Byzantine rule had ceased there, the controversy about images tended to keep alive the antagonism, because although that question was once and again settled in favour of the maintenance of images, yet many of the emperors, in whose persons the power of the East was embodied, were foremost in advocating their destruction. Indeed, from first to last, owing to the close connection of church and state in the Byzantine empire, the unpopularity of the latter in Western Europe was shared by the former. To this must be added the contempt for one another's character which had arisen among the adherents of the two churches, for the Easterns had learnt to regard the people of the West as ignorant and barbarous, and were esteemed by them in turn as mendacious and unmanly.

In ecclesiastical matters also the differences were of long standing. These related to questions of jurisdiction between the two patriarchates. Up to the eighth century, the patriarchate of the West included a number of provinces on the eastern side of the Adriatic—Illyricum, Dacia, Macedonia, and Greece. But Leo the Isaurian, who probably foresaw that Italy

<small>Ecclesiastical differences</small>

would ere long cease to form part of his dominions, and was unwilling that these important territories should owe spiritual allegiance to one who was not his subject, altered this arrangement, and transferred the jurisdiction over them to the patriarch of Constantinople. Against this measure the bishops of Rome did not fail to protest, and demands for their restoration were made up to the time of the final schism. A further ecclesiastical question, which in part depended on this, was that of the supremacy over the Church of the Bulgarians. We have already noticed in connection with the conversion of that people (p. 143), how the prince Bogoris swayed to and fro in his inclinations between the two churches, and how he ultimately gave his allegiance to that of the East; but the controversy did not end there. According to the ancient territorial arrangement, the Danubian provinces were made subject to the archbishopric of Thessalonica, and that city was included within the Western patriarchate; and on this ground Bulgaria was claimed by the Roman see, as falling within that area. The matter was several times pressed on the attention of the Greek Church, especially on the occasion of the council held at Constantinople in 879, but in vain. The eastern prelates replied evasively, saying that to determine the boundaries of dioceses was a matter which belonged to the sovereign. The emperor, for his part, had good reason for not yielding, for by so doing he would not only have admitted into a neighbouring country an agency which would soon have been employed for political purposes to his disadvantage, but would have justified the assumption on which the demand rested, viz., that the pope had a right to claim the provinces which his predecessors had lost. Thus this point of difference also remained open, as a source of irritation between the two Churches.

But behind these questions another of far greater magnitude was coming into view, that of the papal supremacy. From being in the first instance the head of the Christian Church in the old imperial city, and afterwards patriarch of the West, and *primus inter pares* in relation to the other spiritual heads of Christendom, the bishop of Rome had gradually claimed, on the strength of his occupying the *cathedra Petri*, a position which approximated more and more to that of supremacy over the whole Church. This claim had never been admitted in the East, but the appeals which were made from Constantinople to his judgment and authority, both at the time of the iconoclastic controversy and subsequently, lent some countenance to its validity. But the great advance was made in the pontificate of Nicholas I. (858–867), who promulgated, or at least recognised, the False Decretals. This famous compilation, which is now universally acknowledged to be spurious, and can be shown to be the work of that period, contains, among other documents, letters and decrees of the early bishops of Rome, in which the organisation and discipline of the Church from the earliest time are set forth, and the whole system is shown to have depended on the supremacy of the popes. The newly discovered collection was recognised as genuine by Nicholas, and was accepted by the Western Church. The effect of this was at once to formulate all the claims which had before been vaguely asserted, and to give them the authority of unbroken tradition. The result to Christen-

Papal claims of supremacy

dom at large was in the highest degree momentous. It was impossible for future popes to recede from them, and equally impossible for other churches, which valued their independence, to acknowledge them. The last attempt on the part of the Eastern Church to arrange a compromise in this matter was made by the emperor Basil II., a potentate who both by his conquests and the vigour of his administration might rightly claim to negotiate with others on equal terms. By him it was proposed (A.D. 1024) that the Eastern Church should recognise the honorary primacy of the Western patriarch, and that he in turn should acknowledge the internal independence of the Eastern Church. These terms were rejected, and from that moment it was clear that the separation of the two branches of Christendom was only a question of time.

Already in the papacy of Nicholas I. a rupture had occurred in connection with the dispute between the rival patriarchs of Constantinople, Ignatius and Photius. The former of these prelates, who was son of the emperor Michael I., and a man of high character and a devout opponent of iconoclasm, was appointed, through the influence of Theodora, the restorer of images, in the reign of her son Michael the Drunkard. But the uncle of the emperor, the Cæsar Bardas, who was a man of flagrantly immoral life, had divorced his own wife, and was living publicly with his son's widow. For this incestuous connection Ignatius repelled him from the Communion. Fired with indignation at this insult, the Cæsar determined to ruin both the patriarch and his patroness, the empress-mother, and with this view persuaded the emperor to free himself from the trammels of his mother's influence by forcing her to take monastic vows. To this step Ignatius would not consent, because it was forbidden by the laws of the Church that any should enter on the monastic life except of their own free will. In consequence of his resistance a charge of treasonable correspondence was invented against him, and when he refused to resign his office he was deposed (857). Photius, who was chosen to succeed him, was the most learned man of his age, and like his rival, unblemished in character and a supporter of images, but boundless in ambition. He was a layman at the time of his appointment, but in six days he passed through the inferior orders which led up to the patriarchate. Still, the party that remained faithful to Ignatius numbered many adherents, and therefore Photius thought it well to enlist the support of the bishop of Rome on his side. An embassy was therefore sent to inform Pope Nicholas that the late patriarch had voluntarily retired, and that Photius had been lawfully chosen, and had undertaken the office with great reluctance. In answer to this appeal the pope despatched two legates to Constantinople, and Ignatius was summoned to appear before a council at which they were present. He was condemned, but appealed to the pope in person. On the return of the legates to Rome it was discovered that they had received bribes, and thereupon Nicholas, whose judgment, however imperious, was ever on the side of the oppressed, called together a synod of the Roman church, and refused his consent to the deposition of Ignatius. To this effect he wrote to the authorities of the Eastern church, calling upon them at the same time to concur in the decrees of the Apostolic see: but subsequently, having obtained full information as to the harsh treatment to which the deposed patriarch had been subjected, he excommunicated Photius, and commanded the restoration of Ignatius ' by the power committed to him by Christ through St. Peter.'

These denunciations produced no effect on the emperor and the new patriarch, and a correspondence between Michael and Nicholas, couched in violent language, continued at intervals for several years. At last, in consequence of a renewed demand on the part of the pope that Ignatius and Photius should be sent to Rome for judgment, the latter prelate, whose ability and eloquence had obtained great influence for him, summoned a council at Constantinople in the year 867 to decree the counter-excommunication of the Western patriarch. Of the eight articles which were drawn up on this occasion for the incrimination of the church of Rome, all but two relate to trivial matters, such as the observance of Saturday as a fast, and the shaving of their beards by the clergy. The two important ones deal with the doctrine of the Procession of the Holy Spirit, and the enforced celibacy of the clergy. The condemnation of the Western Church on these grounds was voted, and a messenger was despatched to bear the defiance to Rome; but ere he reached his destination he was recalled, in consequence of a revolution in the palace at Constantinople. The author of this, Basil the Macedonian, the founder of the most important dynasty that ever occupied the throne of the Eastern empire, had for some time been associated in the government with the emperor Michael; but at length, being fearful for his own safety, he resolved to put his colleague out

Counter-excommunications

of the way, and assassinated him during one of his fits of
drunkenness. It is said that in consequence of this crime
Photius refused to admit him to the Communion; anyhow, one of the first acts of Basil was to depose Photius.
A council hostile to him was now assembled, and was
attended by the legates of the new pope, Hadrian II.
(869). By this Ignatius was restored to his former
dignity, while Photius was degraded, and his ordina-
tions were declared void. So violent was the animosity
displayed against him that he was dragged before the
assembly by the emperor's guard, and his condemnation
was written in the sacramental wine. During the ten
years which elapsed between his restoration and his
death, Ignatius continued to enjoy his high position in
peace, but for Photius other vicissitudes were in store.
On the removal of his rival—so strangely did opinion
sway to and fro at this time in the empire—the current
of feeling set strongly in favour of the learned exile.
He was recalled, and his reinstatement was ratified by
a council (879). But with the death of Basil the Macedonian (886) he again fell from power, for the successor
of that emperor, Leo the Philosopher, ignominiously
removed him, in order to confer the dignity on his
brother Stephen. He passed the remainder of his life
in honourable retirement, and by his death the chief
obstacle in the way of reconcilement with the Roman
church was removed. It is consoling to learn, when
reading of the unhappy rivalry of two men so superior
to the ordinary run of Byzantine prelates, that they
never shared the passions of their respective partisans,
but retained a mutual regard for one another.

We have now to consider the doctrinal questions

which were in dispute between the two churches. Far the most important of these was that relating to the addition of the *Filioque* clause to the Nicene creed. In the first draft of that creed, as promulgated by the council of Nicæa, the article relating to the Holy Spirit ran simply thus : 'I believe in the Holy Ghost.' But in the second general council, that of Constantinople, which condemned the heresy of Macedonius, it was thought advisable to state more explicitly the doctrine of the Church on this subject, and amongst other affirmations the clause was added, 'Who proceedeth from the Father.' Again, at the next general council, at Ephesus, it was ordered that it should not be lawful to make any addition to the creed, as ratified by the council of Constantinople. The fathers of the Western church, however, generally taught that the Spirit proceeds from the Son as well as from the Father, while those of the East preferred to use the expression, 'the Spirit of Christ, proceeding from the Father, and receiving of the Son,' or ' proceeding from the Father through the Son.' It was in the churches of Spain and France that the *Filioque* clause was first introduced into the creed and thus recited in the services, but the addition was not at once approved at Rome. Pope Leo III. early in the ninth century not only expressed his disapproval of this departure from the original form, but, in order to show his sense of the importance of adhering to the traditional practice, caused the creed of Constantinople to be engraved on silver plates, both in Greek and Latin, and thus to be publicly set forth in the church. The first pontiff who authorised the addition was Nicholas I., and against this Photius protested, both during the lifetime of that pope and also in the time of John VIII., when it was condemned by the council held at Constantinople in 879, which is called by the Greeks the eighth general council. It is clear from what we have already seen that Photius was prepared to seize on *any* point of disagreement in order to throw it in the teeth of his opponents, but in this matter the Eastern church had a real grievance to complain of. The Nicene creed was to them, what it was not to the Western church, their only creed, and the authority of the councils, by which its form and wording were determined, stood far higher in their estimation. To add to the one and to disregard the others was, at least in their judgment, the violation of a sacred compact.

The other question, which, if not actually one of doctrine, had come to be regarded as such, was that of the *azyma*, that is, the use of unfermented bread in the celebration of the Eucharist. As far as we can judge from the doubtful evidence on the subject, it seems probable that ordinary, that is, leavened bread, was generally used in the Church for this purpose until the seventh or eighth centuries, when unleavened bread began to be employed in the West, on the ground that it was used in the original institution of the Sacrament, which took place during the feast of the Passover. In the Eastern church this change was never admitted. It seems strange that so insignificant a matter of observance should have been erected into a question of the first importance in the controversy between the two communions, but the reason of this is not far to seek. The fact is that, whereas the weighty

<small>The azyma</small>

matters of dispute—the doctrine of the Procession of the Holy Spirit and the papal claims to supremacy—required some knowledge and reflection in order rightly to understand their bearings, the use of leavened or unleavened bread was a matter within the range of all, and those who were on the look-out for a ground of antagonism found it here ready to hand. In the story of the conversion of the Russian Vladimir we are told that the Greek missionary who expounded to him the religious views of the Eastern church, when combating the claims of the emissaries of the Roman communion, remarked, 'They celebrate the mass with unleavened bread, therefore they have not the true religion.' Still even Photius, when raking together the most minute points of difference between him and his adversaries, did not introduce this one. It was reserved for a hot-headed partisan at a later period to bring it forward as a subject of public discussion.

This was Michael Cerularius, patriarch of Constantinople, with whose name the Great Schism will for ever be associated. The circumstances which led up to that event are as follows. For a century and a half from the death of Photius the controversy slumbered, though no advance was made towards an understanding with respect to the points at issue. In Italy, and even at Rome, churches and monasteries were tolerated, in which the Greek rite was maintained, and similar freedom was allowed to the Latins resident in the Greek empire. But this tacit compact was broken in 1053 by the patriarch Michael, who in his passionate antagonism to everything Western, gave orders that all the churches in Constantinople, in which worship was

<small>Michael Cerularius</small>

celebrated according to the Roman rite, should be closed. At the same time—aroused, perhaps, in some measure by the progress of the Normans in conquering Apulia, which tended to interfere with the jurisdiction still exercised by the Eastern church in that province—he joined with Leo, the archbishop of Achrida and metropolitan of Bulgaria, in addressing a letter to the bishop of Trani in southern Italy, containing a violent attack on the Latin church, in which the question of the *azyma* was put prominently forward. Directions were further given for circulating this missive among the Western clergy. It happened that at the time when the letter arrived at Trani, cardinal Humbert, a vigorous champion of ecclesiastical rights, was residing in that city, and he translated it into Latin, and communicated it to pope Leo IX. In answer, the pope addressed a remonstrance to the patriarch, in which, without entering into the specific charges that he had brought forward, he contrasted the security of the Roman see in matters of doctrine, arising from the guidance which was guaranteed to it through St. Peter, with the liability of the Eastern church to fall into error, and pointedly referred to the more Christian spirit manifested by his own communion in tolerating those from whose opinions they differed. Afterwards, at the commencement of 1054, in compliance with a request from the emperor Constantine Monomachus, who was anxious on political grounds to avoid a rupture, he sent three legates to Constantinople to arrange the terms of an agreement. These were Frederick of Lorraine, chancellor of the Roman church, Peter, archbishop of Amalfi, and cardinal Humbert.

The legates were welcomed by the emperor, but they

unwisely adopted a lofty tone towards the haughty patriarch, who thenceforward avoided all communication with them, declaring that on a matter which so seriously affected the whole Eastern church he could take no steps without consulting the other patriarchs. Humbert now published an argumentative reply to Michael's letter to the pope, in the form of a dialogue between two members of the Greek and Latin churches, in which the charges brought against his own communion were discussed *seriatim*, and especially those relating to fasting on Saturday, and the use of unleavened bread in the Eucharist. A rejoinder to this appeared from the pen of a monk of the monastery of Studium, Nicetas Pectoratus, in which the enforced celibacy of the Western clergy, on which Photius had before animadverted, was severely criticised. The cardinal retorted in intemperate language, and so entirely had the legates secured the support of Constantine, that Nicetas' work was committed to the flames, and he was forced to recant what he had said against the Roman church. But the patriarch was immovable, and for the moment he occupied a stronger position than the emperor, who desired to conciliate him. At last the patience of the legates was exhausted, and on July 16, 1054, they proceeded to the church of St. Sophia, and deposited on the altar, which was prepared for the celebration of the Eucharist, a document containing a fierce anathema, by which Michael Cerularius and his adherents were condemned. After their departure they were for a moment recalled, because the patriarch expressed a desire to confer with them; but this Constantine would not permit, fearing some act of violence on the part of the

The final schism

people. They then finally left Constantinople, and from that time to the present all communion has been broken off between the two great branches of Christendom.

The breach thus made was greatly widened at the period of the Crusades. However serious may have been the alienation between the East and West at the time of their separation, it is clear that the Greeks were not regarded by the Latins as a mere heretical sect, for one of the primary objects with which the first crusade was undertaken was the deliverance of the Eastern empire from the attacks of the Mahometans. But the familiarity which arose from the presence of the crusaders on Greek soil ripened the seeds of mutual dislike and distrust. As long as negotiations between the two parties took place at a distance, the differences, however irreconcilable they might be in principle, did not necessarily bring them into open antagonism, whereas their more intimate acquaintance with one another produced personal and national ill-will. The people of the West now appeared more than ever barbarous and overbearing, and the court of Constantinople more than ever senile and designing. The crafty policy of Alexius Comnenus in transferring his allies with all speed into Asia, and declining to take the lead in the expedition, was almost justified by the necessity of delivering his subjects from these unwelcome visitors and avoiding further embarrassments. But the iniquitous fourth crusade (1204) produced an ineradicable feeling of animosity in the minds of the Byzantine people. The memory of the barbarities of that time, when many Greeks died as martyrs at the stake for their religious convictions,

Effect of the crusades

survives at the present day in various places bordering on the Ægean, in legends which relate that they were formerly destroyed by the pope of Rome. In the case of Mount Athos the story probably arose from the monasteries having been plundered by an agent of Cardinal Benedict, not long after the Frankish occupation of Salonica at the time of that crusade.

Still, the anxiety of the Eastern emperors to maintain their position by means of political support from Western Europe brought it to pass that proposals for reunion were made on several occasions. Even while the Latins were occupying Constantinople, John Ducas Vatatzes, whose court was at Nicæa, entered into communication through the patriarch Germanus with Pope Gregory IX. in the hope of recovering his lost dominions through his mediation. In the year 1233 the pope sent two Dominicans and two Franciscans as his envoys, and they were received with great honour, but in the discussion which ensued neither side would abate anything of their claims, and no agreement was arrived at. A nearer approach to outward reunion was reached some forty years later by the influence of Michael Palæologus, who in the meanwhile had made himself master of Constantinople. Michael was aware that Charles of Anjou, whose daughter was married to the heir of Baldwin, the last of the Latin emperors of the East, was designing to invade his dominions, in order to assert the claims of his son-in-law. With the view of averting this catastrophe, he endeavoured to win the influence of the pope, Gregory X., in his favour, and the price which he undertook to pay for this was the submission of the Greek to the Roman church.

Attempts at reunion

Gregory at this time was exerting himself to organise a crusade, and on this ground, as well as to re-establish the unity of Christendom, he was anxious to secure the good-will of the Greek emperor. He therefore prohibited Charles of Anjou from attacking the empire, and summoned a council to meet at Lyons in 1274, one of the purposes of which was to readmit the Eastern communion within the Catholic church. At this the Greek envoys presented themselves, and after repeating the Creed with the addition of the *Filioque*, they swore to conform to the faith of the Roman church, and to recognise the supremacy of the pope. But when this occurrence was reported in the East, it produced an outburst of indignation, and Michael found himself obliged to remove the patriarch Joseph, and to substitute for him John Beccus, an able and accomplished man who had already convinced himself of the justice of the claims of the Papal See. In order to silence opposition the emperor now proceeded to the most violent measures, and imprisonment, scourging, mutilation, and blinding were resorted to, as in the days of the iconoclastic controversy. Many of the Greeks emigrated to Thessaly, which was in the power of the Wallachians, or to the empire of Trebizond, to avoid signing the hated articles of union. It is due to Beccus to say, that he did all that was in his power to mitigate these atrocities, on one occasion even refusing the Communion to the emperor until he agreed to spare one of his victims. During the rest of Michael's reign the discontent felt by his subjects constantly endangered his throne, and the concordat with Rome was ignored by his successor, Andronicus II.

<small>Council of Lyons</small>

The final attempt at reconciliation was made when the Greek empire was reduced to the direst straits, and its rulers were prepared to purchase the aid of Western Europe against the Ottomans by almost any sacrifice. In the year 1425, when John VI. ascended the throne, he found the Eastern Roman empire reduced to the city of Constantinople, a few neighbouring towns, Thessalonica, and a part of the Peloponnese. In this condition of weakness, the overthrow of the state was only a question of time, unless their deliverance was wrought by a strong combination of the Christian powers; and this could only be brought about through the influence of the Roman pontiff. Accordingly application was made to Pope Eugenius IV., and by him the representatives of the Eastern church were invited to attend the council which was summoned to meet at Ferrara in 1438. The emperor himself and the Greek patriarch Joseph proceeded thither, and in their company, among other officers of church and state, were four men who were destined to make a mark in history—Isidore of Russia and the learned Bessarion, both of whom were afterwards cardinals of the Roman church, Gennadius, who became patriarch of Constantinople under Mahomet II., and the philosopher Gemistus Plethon, whose eloquent advocacy of the views of Plato during this visit to Italy, revived the study of that author in the West. They were provided with galleys by the Pope, and were conveyed to Venice, where a magnificent reception awaited them, and from thence, in the month of March, 1438, they proceeded to Ferrara. There is no need to dwell on the circumstance, which was of primary importance to the

Council of Ferrara

Western Church, that the rival council of Basle was sitting at the same time, nor on the advances which that council had made towards the Byzantine emperor; the Greeks, however, found the assembly to which they had been summoned but thinly attended, and they were themselves exposed to numerous humiliations in their intercourse with the Pope and his subordinates. After a time the plague broke out in Ferrara, and this was made a pretext for transferring the scene of the council to Florence.

The questions in dispute which were to be regarded as of vital importance had been determined on at Ferrara, and were more fully discussed when the council reassembled. These were four—the Procession of the Holy Spirit, with the addition of the *Filioque* clause to the Creed; the use of unfermented bread; purgatory, and the supremacy of the pope. They were debated at great length, and with much obstinacy, but ultimately on all of them, though one or two slight concessions were made to the Greeks, the views of the Latin church were approved. Among the representatives of the Eastern communion great differences of opinion prevailed; and, notwithstanding the arguments of Isidore and Bessarion, who advocated throughout the cause of the union, it required no little urgency, amounting at times to threats on the part of the emperor, to compel the dissidents to conform to the decision of the majority. One of their number, Mark, the stout-hearted bishop of Ephesus, stood firm to the last. In return for these concessions, it was stipulated that the pope should supply vessels and men-at-arms for the defence of Constantinople, and should move the sovereigns of the West

Council of Florence

to espouse the cause of the Greeks. Before the edict of the council was finally ratified, the patriarch Joseph died, and was buried in the baptistery at Florence, but it was subscribed by the pope, the emperor, and the other dignitaries, and was solemnly promulgated in the cathedral of that city (July 6, 1438).

The emperor, however, on his return home, soon discovered that his pilgrimage to the West had been lost labour. Pope Eugenius, indeed, provided him with two galleys and a guard of three hundred men equipped at his own expense, but the hoped-for succours from Western Europe did not arrive. His own subjects were completely alienated by the betrayal of their cherished faith; the clergy who favoured the union were regarded as traitors, and the churches where they ministered were deserted; and the Zealots—as those now called themselves who were strictest in their religious observances and in the maintenance of the orthodox belief —exerted themselves in strenuous opposition. But the deluge was approaching, which was to involve them all in common ruin. John Palæologus himself did not survive to see the final catastrophe; but within fifteen years from the council of Florence Constantinople was captured by the Turks, and the empire of the East had ceased to exist.

Repudiated by the Greeks

CHRONOLOGICAL TABLE

OF

PRINCIPAL EVENTS REFERRED TO.

A.D.
- 325   Council of Nicæa (first general council).
- 330   Foundation of Constantinople.
- 378   Defeat of Valens by the Goths.
- 380   Suppression of paganism by Theodosius.
- 381   Council of Constantinople (second general council).
- 395   Arcadius and Honorius emperors (division of the empire).
- 431   Council of Ephesus (third general council).
- 442   Attila invades the Eastern empire.
- 451   Council of Chalcedon (fourth general council).
- 476   End of Western Roman empire.
- 482   *Henoticon* of Zeno.
- 527   Justinian emperor.
- 547   Rome taken by Belisarius.
- 553   Second council of Constantinople (fifth general council).
- 571   Birth of Mahomet.
- 622   Hejira of Mahomet.
- 622–8   Persian campaigns of Heraclius.
- 638   *Ecthesis* of Heraclius.
- 639   Syria conquered by Omar.
- 640   Egypt conquered by Amrou.
- 648   *Type* of Constans.
- 668   Constantine Pogonatus emperor.
- 672–9   Constantinople besieged by Moawyah.
- 680   Third council of Constantinople (sixth general council).
- 716   Leo the Isaurian emperor.

A.D.
726	First edict against images.
741	Constantine Copronymus emperor.
747	Great plague at Constantinople.
751	End of exarchate of Ravenna.
754	Iconoclast council at Constantinople.
775	Constantine VI. emperor and Irene regent.
787	Second council of Nicæa (seventh general council).
800	Charles the Great crowned emperor of the West.
813	Leo the Armenian emperor.
820	Michael the Stammerer emperor.
829	Theophilus emperor.
842	Michael the Drunkard emperor and Theodora regent.
842	Final restoration of images.
857	Deposition of Ignatius: Photius made patriarch.
863	Cyril and Methodius in Moravia.
864	Conversion of Bogoris.
867	Basil the Macedonian emperor.
879	Council at Constantinople (eighth general council of the Greeks).
913	Constantine Porphyrogenitus emperor.
963	Nicephorus Phocas emperor.
969	John Zimisces emperor.
976	Basil the Slayer of the Bulgarians emperor.
980	Baptism of Vladimir.
1018	Conquest of Bulgarian kingdom of Achrida.
1042	Constantine Monomachus emperor.
1045	Overthrow of the Armenian kingdom.
1054	Separation of the Greek and Latin churches.
1081	Alexius Comnenus emperor.
1095	First Crusade.
1204	Fourth Crusade and capture of Constantinople.
1261	Michael Palæologus recovers Constantinople.
1274	Council of Lyons.
1282	Andronicus II. emperor.
1347	Cantacuzene emperor.
1354	Ottoman Turks cross into Europe.
1402	Bajazet defeated by Timour at Angora.
1425	John VI. emperor.
1438	Councils of Ferrara and Florence.
1453	Capture of Constantinople by the Ottomans.

INDEX.

ABULPHARAGIUS

ABULPHARAGIUS, 75, 80
Abyssinian Church, its Monophysitism, 83; its conversion attempted by Rome, 83; its Jewish customs, 83
Achrida (Ochrida), Bulgarian capital, 19, 144-146
Acominatus (Michael), Archbishop of Athens, 45
Agatho (pope), 90
Alexius Comnenus, 23, 98, 185
Almshouses, 68
Anastatius (patriarch), 106
Anatolius, writer of hymns, 128
Andrew the Kalybite, 109
Andrew of Crete, writer of canons, 129
Andrewes, Bishop, use of the Eastern liturgies in his 'Devotions,' 50
Antioch, becomes a national centre, 72
Apollinaris, of Alexandria, 81
Arianism, its influence, 34
Armenians, their conversion, 84; their Eutychianism, 85; their history, 85; their influence, 86
Army, its iconoclast feeling, 105
Assemani, 91
Athanasius (patriarch), his reforms, 168

C.H.

BULGARIAN

Athos, Mount, 153, 155 foll.
Augustine, Saint, hardly known in the Eastern Church, 33
Azyma, question of, 181, 189

BAGRATIDÆ, overthrow of their kingdom in Armenia, 22, 86
Barlaam, 165
Barsumas, 75
Basil I. (emperor), the Macedonian, 21, 143, 178; captures Tephrice, 96
Basil II. (emperor), the 'Slayer of the Bulgarians,' 19, 145, 150, 176
Basil, Saint, founder of cœnobi e system, 158, 163, 169
Basiliscus, 54
Beccus (patriarch), 187
Bishops, Eastern, their moral and social influence, 57; their judicial power, 58-60; dissociated from the people, 67
Bogomilians, their views, 97, 98; their treatment by Alexius Comnenus, 98, 99
Bogoris, 141-3
Bohemia, conversion of, 139
Bulgarian Church, 174; its patriarchate, 145; its independence, 145, 146

O

BULGARIANS

Bulgarians, their wars with the Empire, 18, 19; conversion of, 140 foll.; overthrow of their kingdom, 145

Byzantine Empire, its greatness, 11, 12, 17; date of its commencement, 17; its history, 17-28

CALLIOPAS, 89
Caloyer, 157
Canons of odes, in hymn-writing, 127
Cantacuzene (emperor), 165, 166, 170
Caroline Books, 124
Chalcedon, council of, its effects, 79
Chaldæan Church, 75 foll.
Charitable institutions, 68
Charles the Great, successor to Constantine VI., 13; his views on images, 124
Cherson, 89, 135, 151
Christians of St. Thomas, 78
Church, description of a Byzantine, 48, 49
Church and State, union of, 38, 52; reasons for it, 55; influence on the State, 56; on the Church, 57
Clement of Alexandria, 102
Clement of Ochrida, 143
Clement of Rome, his remains, 135, 152; statue of, 145
Comneni, their dynasty, 23
Constans, his *Type*, 88
Constantine the Great, his conversion, 1; his administrative system, 2-6
Constantine Pogonatus, summons the sixth œcumenical council, 90; persecutes the Paulicians, 94
Constantine Copronymus, transports Paulicians into Thrace, 96; his iconoclasm, 108-110

EASTERN

Constantine VI., 111, 114, 117
Constantine Monomachus, 183
Constantine Palæologus, 27
Constantine, or Silvanus, founder of the Paulicians, 93
Constantinople, its position, 7; its political importance, 8; its Greek inhabitants, 9
Coptic Church, (see Egyptian)
Cosmas, hymn-writer, 129
Councils, General, their Eastern character, 34-36; importance attached to them by the Eastern Church, 36
Crucifix, disallowed in the Eastern Church, 125
Crucifixion, abolished in Constantine's time, 56
Crusades, how regarded in the Eastern Empire, 24; effect of on the Greeks, 185
Cyprus, Maronites in, 91
Cyril of Alexandria, 72
Cyril, apostle of the Slavonians, 133 foll.; invents the Slavonic alphabet, 133; preaches to the Khazars, 134; converts the Moravians, 136

DECRETALS, the False, 175
Dendrites, 162
Dionysius of Agrapha, his 'Guide to Painting,' 126
Dioscorus, 72, 81
Disarmament of the population, 4

EASTER salutation, 63
Eastern Church, its dignity, 29; the parent of theology, 30; its speculative tendencies, 33; its orthodoxy, 35; its stationary character, 37; its isolation, 39; its austerity, 39, 40; its attitude towards the laity, 42, 62, 67; its love of learning,

EASTERN

44; its types of character, 45-47; its organisation, 47; its liturgies and vestments, 50, 51
Eastern Empire, circumstances of its foundation, 1; causes of its vitality, 6; sketch of its history, 12 foll.
Edessa, seminary at, 75, 76
Egypt, the native region of Monophysitism, 72
Egyptian (Coptic) Church, 81; its decline, 82
Emblems, Christian, 102
Emperor, ecclesiastical supremacy of, 53-55
Ephesus, council of, 72, 74
Etchmiadzin, 86
Ethiopian Church (see Abyssinian)
Eugenius IV. (pope), 188
Eustathius, Archbishop of Thessalonica, 44, 168
Eutychian and Monophysite views, 79
Exarchate, loss of, 20, 124, 173

FASTS, their number and severity, 40, 158
Ferrara, council of (see Florence)
Filioque, the clause, 139, 180, 187, 189
Finlay, on the influence of the parochial clergy, 68; on the iconoclastic period, 123
Florence, council of, 27, 189
Formalism, causes of in the Eastern Church, 38, 39
Frankfort, synod of, 124

GALLERIES for women in churches, 50
Gemistus Plethon, 188
Germanus (patriarch), 105, 128
Greek language, its influence on theology, 31, 32

JOHN

Greek race, degenerated from Alexander's time, 64; revived by Christianity, 64; its relation to the other races, 71
Gregory the Illuminator, converts the Armenians, 84
Gregory II. (pope), 106

HADRIAN I. (pope), 113
Hadrian II. (pope), 138, 179
Heraclius, his struggle with Persia, 15; his Monothelitism, 87; his *Ecthesis*, 88
Hermits, 160-163
Hesychasts, 165
Heterodoxy, how connected with nationality, 36, 71
Hospitals, 68
Humbert, Cardinal, 183, 184
Hymnology of the Eastern Church, 126; history of the art, 127-129

ICONOCLASTIC controversy, 100 foll.; its connection with politics, 101; how regarded in Western Europe, 123, 124
Iconostasis, the use of it not primitive, 41
Ignatius (patriarch), 176-179
Image-worship, growth of, 102, 103; restored by Irene, 111; by Theodora, 121
Irene, her support of image-worship, 111 foll.; her treatment of her son, 115

JACOBITES, 79; their present state, 80
Jacobus Baradæus, 79
Jews of the Dispersion, 29
John VIII. (pope), 139, 181
John VI. (emperor), 188 foll.
John the Grammarian, 120-122

JOHN

John Damascene, defends images, 107; his sacred poetry, 127, 129
Joseph of the Studium, hymn-writer, 129
Julian, his failure to revive paganism, 2
Justinian, character of his reign, 14, 68; his edict *De tribus capitulis*, 54; his persecuting spirit, 74, 76, 79, 81

KHAZARS, 134
Kieff, 136, 148, 152, 153

LAITY, position of the, 42
Latin Empire of the East, 25
Latin language unsuitable for theological distinctions, 32
Learning, fostered by the Eastern Church, 44
Leo the Isaurian, his reforms, 17; his iconoclasm, 103 foll.; his intolerance, 104
Leo the Khazar, 111
Leo the Armenian, 115; his death, 118, 119
Leo IX. (pope), 183
Liturgies of the Eastern Church, 50
Lyons, council of, 187

MACEDONIAN Greeks, origin of, 10; their character, 10
Macedonian dynasty in Byzantine empire, 21, 22
Mahomet II. gives judicial power to Greek bishops, 59
Maronites, 90, 91
Marriage of parochial clergy, 43
Martin I. (pope), his treatment by Constans, 89
Maximus, 88, 89
Megaspelæon, monastery of, 170
Melchite, 74

NESTORIANS

Meteora, monasteries of, 170
Methodius (patriarch), 122
Methodius, apostle of the Slavonians, 133, 138-140
Mezrop, Saint, 85
Michael Cerularius (patriarch). 182-185
Michael the Drunkard, 123, 142, 147, 176
Michael the Stammerer, 118-120, 124
Michael Palæologus, regains Constantinople, 25; conforms to the Roman Church, 186
Milman, Dean, on statues and pictures, 125
Missions, of the Nestorians, 76; of the Eastern Church, 132 foll.
Monasteries, Greek, description of, 157; sites of, 169, 170
Monastic system, 155 foll.; theory of it, 159
Monks, persecution of by Constantine Copronymus, 109; by Leo the Armenian, 116; their mode of life, 157, 158
Monophysites, in Syria, 79; in Egypt, 81
Monothelite controversy, 87-90
Moravia, conversion of, 136 foll.
Music, Byzantine, 40
Mystery, a characteristic of the Eastern Church, 41; perhaps traceable to the influence of the court, 42

NAUM, 145
Neale, Dr., his translations of Greek hymns, 46, 127, 129
Nestor, the historian, 148, 152
Nestorianism, 74; takes refuge in Persia, 75
Nestorians, their missions, 76; attacked by Timour, 77; by the Kurds, 77; their present state, 77, 78

NESTORIUS

Nestorius, 72
Nicæa, first Council of, its Eastern character, 34; represented in frescoes, 37; second Council of, 113
Nicephorus (patriarch), 116
Nicephorus Phocas, 21, 164
Nicholas I. (pope), 138, 143, 175, 176, 180

OCHRIDA (see Achrida)
Olga, conversion of, 148
Organisation of the Eastern Church, 47, 48
Orphanages, 68
Orphanotrophos, 69
Orthodoxy, intensity of it in the Eastern Church, 36, 65; a link between the emperors and the people, 55; took the place of nationality, 65; caused the fusion of the Slavonians with the Greeks, 66; festival of, 122
Oskold and Dir, 146, 147

PACHOMIUS, 162
Painting, Byzantine, 39
Palæologi, dynasty of, 26, 27
Papacy, growth of its power, 172, 175
Paphnutius, opposes clerical celibacy, 43
Parochial clergy, their connection with the people, 67, 68
Patriarch of Constantinople, how appointed, 47; his subordinate position, 61
Patriarchates, the Eastern, 47, 61, 173
Paul (patriarch), 112
Paulicians, their views, 92, 93; their persecutions, 95, 96
Penitentiary founded by Justinian and Theodora, 68
Persecution of heretics, 73, 74, 79, 94, 96

SLAVONIC

Pestilence in the Byzantine Empire, 20
Philippopolis, headquarters of the Paulicians, 96
Photius, 143, 147, 176-179
Pictures, Byzantine, 124, 126, 156
Popular character of the Eastern Church, 62
Preaching, rare in the Eastern Church, 62
Procession of the Holy Spirit, controversy on, 178, 180
Provincial Churches regarded with suspicion, 73; their clergy liable to be accused of heresy, 73

RABULAS, 75
Rastislav, 137, 139
Ravenna, captured by the Lombards, 21
Romanus, hymn-writer, 128
Rome, bishop of, his independent position, 60
Russian Church, Greek character of, 153
Russians, conversion of, 146, 152

SAMUEL of Bulgaria, 145
Sassanidæ, encourage heretical sects, 75
Semantron, 51
Separation of the Eastern and Western Churches, 171 foll.
Sergius (patriarch), supports Monothelite views, 87; composes hymns, 128
Sergius, Paulician teacher, 95
Siganfu, inscription of, 76
Sketes, 161
Slavery, modified by the influence of the Church, 69; how extinguished, 70
Slavs, their conversion, 132 foll.
Slavonic alphabet, 133, 137

SLAVONIC

Slavonic settlers introduced into Greece, 20, 66; assimilated by the Greeks, 66
Statues, proscribed in the Eastern Church, 125
Stephen, the hermit, 110
Studium, monastery of, 117
Stylites, 162
Sumelas, monastery of, 170
Suspicious character of the imperial government, 73
Syria, the native region of Nestorianism, 72; adopts Monophysite views, 79
Syrians, influential in the early Armenian Church, 85

TARASIUS, appointed patriarch, 112
Taxation in the Eastern Empire, 3, 67
Tephrice, 96
Theodora (empress), restores images, 121
Theodore Graptos, 121
Theodore Studita, his views on slavery, 69; on toleration, 117; his defence of images, 117; his hymns, 117, 129
Theodosius the Great, established Christianity as the religion of the state, 12, 53; increased the judicial power of the bishops, 59
Theology, how it arose as a science, 30
Theophilus (emperor), 120

ZIMISCES

Thera, eruption of, 105
Timour, defeats Bajazet, 27; nearly exterminates the Chaldæan Church, 77
Tranquillity, Oriental love of, 165
Transfiguration, festival of, 156; light of, 165
Tribute of Christian children to the Ottomans, 46

VARANGIANS, 147
Vestments of the Eastern Church, 51
Vladimir, his conversion, 149–152
Vulgar tongue, use of in services, 43, 138

WESTERN CHURCH, practical character of its theology, 33, points of contrast with the Eastern, 33, 41, 45, 60, 62, 103, 159, 171 foll.
Western Empire, effect of its extinction, 13
Women, exclusion of from Mount Athos, 157

ZAGORA, 142
Zealots, 190
Zeno, his *henoticon*, 54, 81
Zimisces, 22; transports Paulicians into Thrace, 96; conquers Bulgaria, 145

EPOCHS OF CHURCH HISTORY.

Edited by the Very Rev. M. CREIGHTON, LL.D.
BISHOP OF PETERBOROUGH.

Fcp. 8vo. price 2s. 6d. each.

THE ENGLISH CHURCH IN OTHER LANDS. By the Rev. H. W. TUCKER.

THE HISTORY OF THE REFORMATION IN ENGLAND. By the Rev. GEORGE G. PERRY.

A HISTORY OF THE UNIVERSITY OF OXFORD. By the Hon. G. C. BRODRICK.

A HISTORY OF THE UNIVERSITY OF CAMBRIDGE. By J. BASS MULLINGER, M.A.

THE CHURCH OF THE EARLY FATHERS. By A. PLUMMER, D.D.

THE CHURCH AND THE ROMAN EMPIRE. By the Rev. A. CARR.

THE CHURCH AND THE PURITANS (1570-1660). By H. OFFLEY WAKEMAN, M.A.

THE EVANGELICAL REVIVAL IN THE EIGHTEENTH CENTURY. By the Rev. J. H. OVERTON.

THE CHURCH AND THE EASTERN EMPIRE. By the Rev. H. F. TOZER.

HILDEBRAND AND HIS TIMES. By the Rev. W. R. W. STEPHENS.

THE ENGLISH CHURCH IN THE MIDDLE AGES. By the Rev. W. HUNT, M.A.

THE POPES AND THE HOHENSTAUFEN. By UGO BALZANI.

THE ARIAN CONTROVERSY. By H. M. GWATKIN, M.A.

THE COUNTER-REFORMATION. By A. W. WARD.

WYCLIFFE AND EARLY MOVEMENTS OF REFORM. By REGINALD L. POOLE, M.A.

London: LONGMANS, GREEN, & CO.

EPOCHS OF MODERN HISTORY.

Edited by C. COLBECK, M.A.

19 vols. fcap. 8vo, with Maps, price 2s. 6d. each volume.

AIRY'S ENGLISH RESTORATION AND LOUIS XIV. 1648–1678.
CHURCH'S BEGINNING OF THE MIDDLE AGES.
COX'S CRUSADES.
CREIGHTON'S AGE OF ELIZABETH.
GAIRDNER'S HOUSES OF LANCASTER AND YORK.
GARDINER'S THIRTY YEARS' WAR, 1618–1648.
GARDINER'S FIRST TWO STUARTS AND THE PURITAN REVOLUTION, 1603–1660.
GARDINER'S (Mrs.) THE FRENCH REVOLUTION, 1789–1795.
HALE'S FALL OF THE STUARTS, AND WESTERN EUROPE, from 1678–1697.
JOHNSON'S NORMANS IN EUROPE.
LONGMAN'S FREDERICK THE GREAT AND THE SEVEN YEARS' WAR.
LUDLOW'S WAR OF AMERICAN INDEPENDENCE, 1775–1783.
McCARTHY'S EPOCH OF REFORM, 1830–1850.
MOBERLY'S THE EARLY TUDORS.
MORRIS'S AGE OF ANNE.
MORRIS'S THE EARLY HANOVERIANS.
SEEBOHM'S PROTESTANT REVOLUTION.
STUBBS'S THE EARLY PLANTAGENETS.
WARBURTON'S EDWARD THE THIRD.

EPOCHS OF ANCIENT HISTORY.

Edited by the Rev. Sir G. W. COX, Bart., M.A., and by C. SANKEY, M.A.

10 vols. fcap. 8vo, with Maps, price 2s. 6d. each volume.

BEESLEY'S GRACCHI, MARIUS, AND SULLA.
CAPES'S EARLY ROMAN EMPIRE, from the Assassination of Julius Cæsar to the Assassination of Domitian.
CAPES'S ROMAN EMPIRE of the SECOND CENTURY, or the Age of the Antonines.
COX'S ATHENIAN EMPIRE, from the Flight of Xerxes to the Fall of Athens.
COX'S GREEKS AND PERSIANS.
CURTEIS'S RISE OF THE MACEDONIAN EMPIRE.
IHNE'S ROME TO ITS CAPTURE BY THE GAULS.
MERIVALE'S ROMAN TRIUMVIRATES.
SANKEY'S SPARTAN and THEBAN SUPREMACIES.
SMITH'S ROME AND CARTHAGE.

LONDON : LONGMANS, GREEN, & CO.

MESSRS. LONGMANS, GREEN, & CO.'S
CLASSIFIED CATALOGUE
OF
WORKS IN GENERAL LITERATURE.

History, Politics, Polity, and Political Memoirs.

Abbott.—A HISTORY OF GREECE. By EVELYN ABBOTT, M.A., LL.D. Part I.—From the Earliest Times to the Ionian Revolt. Crown 8vo., 10s. 6d. Part II.—500-445 B.C. Cr. 8vo., 10s. 6d.

Acland and Ransome.—A HANDBOOK IN OUTLINE OF THE POLITICAL HISTORY OF ENGLAND TO 1890. Chronologically Arranged. By the Right Hon. A. H. DYKE ACLAND, M.P., and CYRIL RANSOME, M.A. Crown 8vo., 6s.

ANNUAL REGISTER (THE). A Review of Public Events at Home and Abroad, for the year 1892. 8vo., 18s.

Volumes of the ANNUAL REGISTER for the years 1863-1891 can still be had. 18s. each.

Armstrong.—ELIZABETH FARNESE; The Termagant of Spain. By EDWARD ARMSTRONG, M.A., Fellow of Queen's College, Oxford. 8vo., 16s.

Arnold.—Works by T. ARNOLD, D.D., formerly Head Master of Rugby School.

INTRODUCTORY LECTURES ON MODERN HISTORY. 8vo., 7s. 6d.

MISCELLANEOUS WORKS. 8vo., 7s. 6d.

Bagwell.—IRELAND UNDER THE TUDORS. By RICHARD BAGWELL, LL.D. 3 vols. Vols. I. and II. From the first Invasion of the Northmen to the year 1578. 8vo., 32s. Vol. III. 1578-1603. 8vo., 18s.

Ball.—HISTORICAL REVIEW OF THE LEGISLATIVE SYSTEMS OPERATIVE IN IRELAND, from the Invasion of Henry the Second to the Union (1172-1800). By the Rt. Hon. J. T. BALL. 8vo., 6s.

Besant.—THE HISTORY OF LONDON. By WALTER BESANT. With 74 Illustrations. Crown 8vo. School Reading-book Edition, 1s. 9d.; Prize-book Edition, 2s. 6d.

Buckle.—HISTORY OF CIVILISATION IN ENGLAND AND FRANCE, SPAIN AND SCOTLAND. By HENRY THOMAS BUCKLE. 3 vols. Crown 8vo., 24s.

Creighton.—HISTORY OF THE PAPACY DURING THE REFORMATION. By MANDELL CREIGHTON, D.D., LL.D., Bishop of Peterborough. 8vo. Vols. I. and II. 1378-1464. 32s. Vols. III. and IV. 1464-1518. 24s. Vol. V. 1517-1527. 15s.

Crump.—A SHORT INQUIRY INTO THE FORMATION OF POLITICAL OPINION, from the reign of the Great Families to the advent of Democracy. By ARTHUR CRUMP. 8vo., 7s. 6d.

De Tocqueville.—DEMOCRACY IN AMERICA. By ALEXIS DE TOCQUEVILLE. 2 vols. Crown 8vo., 16s.

Fitzpatrick.—SECRET SERVICE UNDER PITT. By W. J. FITZPATRICK, F.S.A., Author of 'Correspondence of Daniel O'Connell'. 8vo., 7s. 6d.

Freeman.—THE HISTORICAL GEOGRAPHY OF EUROPE. By EDWARD A. FREEMAN, D.C.L., LL.D. With 65 Maps. 2 vols. 8vo., 31s. 6d.

History, Politics, Polity, and Political Memoirs—*continued.*

Froude.—Works by JAMES A. FROUDE, Regius Professor of Modern History in the University of Oxford.

THE HISTORY OF ENGLAND, from the Fall of Wolsey to the Defeat of the Spanish Armada.
Popular Edition. 12 vols. Crown 8vo., 3s. 6d. each.
Silver Library Edition. 12 vols. Crown 8vo., 3s. 6d. each.

THE DIVORCE OF CATHERINE OF ARAGON: the Story as told by the Imperial Ambassadors resident at the Court of Henry VIII. *In usum Laicorum.* Crown 8vo., 6s.

THE SPANISH STORY OF THE ARMADA, and other Essays, Historical and Descriptive. Crown 8vo., 6s.

THE ENGLISH IN IRELAND IN THE EIGHTEENTH CENTURY. 3 vols. Cr. 8vo., 18s.

SHORT STUDIES ON GREAT SUBJECTS. 4 vols. Cr. 8vo., 3s. 6d. each.

CÆSAR: a Sketch. Cr. 8vo., 3s. 6d.

Gardiner.—Works by SAMUEL RAWSON GARDINER, M.A., Hon. LL.D., Edinburgh, Fellow of Merton College, Oxford.

HISTORY OF ENGLAND, from the Accession of James I. to the Outbreak of the Civil War, 1603-1642. 10 vols. Crown 8vo., 6s. each.

A HISTORY OF THE GREAT CIVIL WAR, 1642-1649. 4 vols. Cr. 8vo., 6s. each.

THE STUDENT'S HISTORY OF ENGLAND, With 378 Illustrations. Cr. 8vo., 12s.

Also in Three Volumes.
Vol. I. B.C. 55—A.D. 1509. With 173 Illustrations. Crown 8vo. 4s.
Vol. II. 1509-1689. With 96 Illustrations. Crown 8vo. 4s.
Vol. III. 1689-1885. With 109 Illustrations. Crown 8vo. 4s.

Greville.—A JOURNAL OF THE REIGNS OF KING GEORGE IV., KING WILLIAM IV., AND QUEEN VICTORIA. By CHARLES C. F. GREVILLE, formerly Clerk of the Council. 8 vols. Crown 8vo., 6s. each.

Hart.—PRACTICAL ESSAYS IN AMERICAN GOVERNMENT. By ALBERT BUSHNELL HART, Ph.D., &c. Cr. 8vo., 6s.

Hearn.—THE GOVERNMENT OF ENGLAND: its Structure and its Development. By W. EDWARD HEARN. 8vo., 16s.

Historic Towns.—Edited by E. A. FREEMAN, D.C.L., and Rev. WILLIAM HUNT, M.A. With Maps and Plans. Crown 8vo., 3s. 6d. each.

BRISTOL. By the Rev. W. HUNT.
CARLISLE. By MANDELL CREIGHTON, D.D., Bishop of Peterborough.
CINQUE PORTS. By MONTAGU BURROWS.
COLCHESTER. By Rev. E. L. CUTTS.
EXETER. By E. A. FREEMAN.
LONDON. By Rev. W. J. LOFTIE.
OXFORD. By Rev. C. W. BOASE.
WINCHESTER. By Rev. G. W. KITCHIN, D.D.
YORK. By Rev. JAMES RAINE.
NEW YORK. By THEODORE ROOSEVELT.
BOSTON (U.S.) By HENRY CABOT LODGE.

Horley.—SEFTON: A DESCRIPTIVE AND HISTORICAL ACCOUNT. Comprising the Collected Notes and Researches of the late Rev. ENGELBERT HORLEY, M.A., Rector 1871-1883. By W. D. CARÖE, M.A. (Cantab.), Fellow of the Royal Institute of British Architects, and E. J. A. GORDON. With 17 Plates and 32 Illustrations in the Text. Royal 8vo., 31s. 6d.

Joyce.—A SHORT HISTORY OF IRELAND, from the Earliest Times to 1608. By P. W. JOYCE, LL.D. Crown 8vo., 10s. 6d.

Lang.—ST. ANDREWS. By ANDREW LANG. With 8 Plates and 24 Illustrations in the Text, by T. HODGE. 8vo., 15s. net.

Lecky.—Works by WILLIAM EDWARD HARTPOLE LECKY.

HISTORY OF ENGLAND IN THE EIGHTEENTH CENTURY.
Library Edition. 8 vols. 8vo., £7 4s.
Cabinet Edition. ENGLAND. 7 vols. Cr. 8vo., 6s. each. IRELAND. 5 vols. Crown 8vo., 6s. each.

HISTORY OF EUROPEAN MORALS FROM AUGUSTUS TO CHARLEMAGNE. 2 vols. Crown 8vo., 16s.

HISTORY OF THE RISE AND INFLUENCE OF THE SPIRIT OF RATIONALISM IN EUROPE. 2 vols. Crown 8vo., 16s.

History, Politics, Polity, and Political Memoirs—*continued*.

Macaulay.—Works by LORD MACAULAY.

COMPLETE WORKS.
   Cabinet Ed. 16 vols. Pt. 8vo., £4 16s.
   Library Edition. 8 vols. 8vo., £5 5s.

HISTORY OF ENGLAND FROM THE ACCESSION OF JAMES THE SECOND.
   Popular Edition. 2 vols. Cr. 8vo., 5s.
   Student's Edition. 2 vols. Cr. 8vo., 12s.
   People's Edition. 4 vols. Cr. 8vo., 16s.
   Cabinet Edition. 8 vols. Pt. 8vo., 48s.
   Library Edition. 5 vols. 8vo., £4.

CRITICAL AND HISTORICAL ESSAYS, WITH LAYS OF ANCIENT ROME, in 1 volume.
   Popular Edition. Crown 8vo., 2s. 6d.
   Authorised Edition. Crown 8vo., 2s. 6d., or 3s. 6d., gilt edges.
   Silver Library Edition. Crown 8vo., 3s. 6d.

CRITICAL AND HISTORICAL ESSAYS.
   Student's Edition. 1 vol. Cr. 8vo., 6s.
   People's Edition. 2 vols. Cr. 8vo., 8s.
   Trevelyan Edition. 2 vols. Cr. 8vo., 9s.
   Cabinet Edition. 4 vols. Post 8vo., 24s.
   Library Edition. 3 vols. 8vo., 36s.

ESSAYS which may be had separately price 6d. each sewed, 1s. each cloth.

   Frederick the Great.
   Lord Bacon.
   Addison and Walpole.
   Croker's Boswell's Johnson.
   Hallam's Constitutional History.
   Warren Hastings (3d. swd., 6d. cl.).
   Lord Clive.
   The Earl of Chatham (Two Essays).
   Ranke and Gladstone.
   Milton and Machiavelli.
   Lord Byron, and The Comic Dramatists of the Restoration.

SPEECHES. Crown 8vo., 3s. 6d.

MISCELLANEOUS WRITINGS.
   People's Ed. 1 vol. Cr. 8vo., 4s. 6d.
   Library Edition. 2 vols. 8vo., 21s.

MISCELLANEOUS WRITINGS AND SPEECHES.
   Popular Edition. Cr. 8vo., 2s. 6d.
   Student's Edition. Crown 8vo., 6s.
   Cabinet Edition. Including Indian Penal Code, Lays of Ancient Rome, and Miscellaneous Poems. 4 vols. Post 8vo., 24s.

Macaulay.—Works by LORD MACAULAY—*continued*.

SELECTIONS FROM THE WRITINGS OF LORD MACAULAY. Edited, with Occasional Notes, by the Right Hon. Sir G. O. Trevelyan, Bart. Crown 8vo., 6s.

May.—THE CONSTITUTIONAL HISTORY OF ENGLAND since the Accession of George III. 1760-1870. By Sir THOMAS ERSKINE MAY, K.C.B. (Lord Farnborough). 3 vols. Crown 8vo., 18s.

Merivale.—Works by the Very Rev. CHARLES MERIVALE, late Dean of Ely.

HISTORY OF THE ROMANS UNDER THE EMPIRE.
   Cabinet Edition. 8 vols. Cr. 8vo., 48s.
   Silver Library Edition. 8 vols. Cr. 8vo., 3s. 6d. each.

THE FALL OF THE ROMAN REPUBLIC: a Short History of the Last Century of the Commonwealth. 12mo., 7s. 6d.

Parkes.—FIFTY YEARS IN THE MAKING OF AUSTRALIAN HISTORY. By Sir HENRY PARKES, G.C.M.G. With 2 Portraits (1854 and 1892). 2 vols. 8vo., 32s.

Prendergast.—IRELAND FROM THE RESTORATION TO THE REVOLUTION, 1660-1690. By JOHN P. PRENDERGAST, Author of 'The Cromwellian Settlement in Ireland'. 8vo., 5s.

Round.—GEOFFREY DE MANDEVILLE: a Study of the Anarchy. By J. H. ROUND, M.A. 8vo., 16s.

Seebohm.—THE ENGLISH VILLAGE COMMUNITY Examined in its Relations to the Manorial and Tribal Systems, &c. By FREDERIC SEEBOHM. With 13 Maps and Plates. 8vo., 16s.

Smith.—CARTHAGE AND THE CARTHAGINIANS. By R. BOSWORTH SMITH, M.A., Assistant Master in Harrow School. With Maps, Plans, &c. Cr. 8vo., 3s. 6d.

Stephens.—PAROCHIAL SELF-GOVERNMENT IN RURAL DISTRICTS: Argument and Plan. By HENRY C. STEPHENS, M.P. 4to., 12s. 6d. Popular Edition. Cr. 8vo., 1s.

History, Politics, Polity, and Political Memoirs—*continued.*

Stephens.—A HISTORY OF THE FRENCH REVOLUTION. By H. MORSE STEPHENS, Balliol College, Oxford. 3 vols. 8vo. Vols. I. and II. 18s. each.

Stubbs.—HISTORY OF THE UNIVERSITY OF DUBLIN, from its Foundation to the End of the Eighteenth Century. By J. W. STUBBS. 8vo., 12s. 6d.

Thompson.—POLITICS IN A DEMOCRACY: an Essay. By DANIEL GREENLEAF THOMPSON, Author of 'A System of Psychology,' &c. Cr. 8vo., 5s.

Todd.—PARLIAMENTARY GOVERNMENT IN THE COLONIES. By ALPHEUS TODD, LL.D. [*In the Press.*

Tupper. — OUR INDIAN PROTECTORATE: an Introduction to the Study of the Relations between the British Government and its Indian Feudatories. By CHARLES LEWIS TUPPER, Indian Civil Service. Royal 8vo., 16s.

Wakeman and Hassall.—ESSAYS INTRODUCTORY TO THE STUDY OF ENGLISH CONSTITUTIONAL HISTORY. By Resident Members of the University of Oxford. Edited by HENRY OFFLEY WAKEMAN, M.A., and ARTHUR HASSALL, M.A. Crown 8vo., 6s.

Walpole.—Works by SPENCER WALPOLE.
HISTORY OF ENGLAND FROM THE CONCLUSION OF THE GREAT WAR IN 1815 TO 1858. 6 vols. Crown 8vo., 6s. each.
THE LAND OF HOME RULE: being an Account of the History and Institutions of the Isle of Man. Cr. 8vo., 6s.

Wylie.—HISTORY OF ENGLAND UNDER HENRY IV. By JAMES HAMILTON WYLIE, M.A., one of H. M. Inspectors of Schools. 3 vols. Vol. I., 1399-1404. Crown 8vo., 10s. 6d. Vol. II. [*In the Press.* Vol. III. [*In preparation.*

Biography, Personal Memoirs, &c.

Armstrong.—THE LIFE AND LETTERS OF EDMUND J. ARMSTRONG. Edited by G. F. ARMSTRONG. Fcp. 8vo., 7s. 6d.

Bacon.—LETTERS AND LIFE, INCLUDING ALL HIS OCCASIONAL WORKS. Edited by J. SPEDDING. 7 vols. 8vo., £4 4s.

Bagehot.—BIOGRAPHICAL STUDIES. By WALTER BAGEHOT. 8vo., 12s.

Boyd.—TWENTY-FIVE YEARS OF ST. ANDREWS, 1865-1890. By A. K. H. BOYD, D.D., Author of 'Recreations of a Country Parson,' &c. 2 vols. 8vo. Vol. I., 12s. Vol. II., 15s.

Carlyle.—THOMAS CARLYLE: a History of his Life. By J. A. FROUDE.
1795-1835. 2 vols. Crown 8vo., 7s.
1834-1881. 2 vols. Crown 8vo., 7s.

Fabert.—ABRAHAM FABERT: Governor of Sedan and Marshal of France. His Life and Times, 1599-1662. By GEORGE HOOPER, Author of 'Waterloo,' 'Wellington,' &c. With a Portrait. 8vo., 10s. 6d.

Fox.—THE EARLY HISTORY OF CHARLES JAMES FOX. By the Right Hon. Sir G. O. TREVELYAN, Bart.
Library Edition. 8vo., 18s.
Cabinet Edition. Crown 8vo., 6s.

Hamilton.—LIFE OF SIR WILLIAM HAMILTON. By R. P. GRAVES. 3 vols. 15s. each.
ADDENDUM TO THE LIFE OF SIR WM. ROWAN HAMILTON, LL.D., D.C.L., 8vo., 6d. sewed.

Hassall.—THE NARRATIVE OF A BUSY LIFE: an Autobiography. By ARTHUR HILL HASSALL, M.D. 8vo., 5s.

Havelock.—MEMOIRS OF SIR HENRY HAVELOCK, K.C.B. By JOHN CLARK MARSHMAN. Crown 8vo., 3s. 6d.

Macaulay.—THE LIFE AND LETTERS OF LORD MACAULAY. By the Right Hon. Sir G. O. TREVELYAN, Bart.
Popular Edition. 1 vol. Cr. 8vo., 2s. 6d.
Student's Edition. 1 vol. Cr. 8vo., 6s.
Cabinet Edition. 2 vols. Post 8vo., 12s.
Library Edition. 2 vols. 8vo., 36s.

Marbot.—THE MEMOIRS OF THE BARON DE MARBOT. Translated from the French by ARTHUR JOHN BUTLER, M.A. Crown 8vo., 7s. 6d.

Montrose.—DEEDS OF MONTROSE: THE MEMOIRS OF JAMES, MARQUIS OF MONTROSE, 1639-1650. By the Rev. GEORGE WISHART, D.D. (Bishop of Edinburgh, 1662-1671). Translated, with Introduction, Notes, &c., and the original Latin, by the Rev. ALEXANDER MURDOCH, F.S.A. (Scot.), and H. F. MORELAND SIMPSON, M.A. (Cantab.). 4to., 36s. net.

Biography, Personal Memoirs, &c.—*continued*.

Seebohm.—THE OXFORD REFORMERS—JOHN COLET, ERASMUS AND THOMAS MORE: a History of their Fellow-Work. By FREDERIC SEEBOHM. 8vo., 14s.

Shakespeare.—OUTLINES OF THE LIFE OF SHAKESPEARE. By J. O. HALLIWELL-PHILLIPPS. With numerous Illustrations and Fac-similes. 2 vols. Royal 8vo., £1 1s.

Shakespeare's TRUE LIFE. By JAS. WALTER. With 500 Illustrations by GERALD E. MOIRA. Imp. 8vo., 21s.

Sherbrooke.—LIFE AND LETTERS OF THE RIGHT HON. ROBERT LOWE, VISCOUNT SHERBROOKE, G.C.B., together with a Memoir of his Kinsman, Sir JOHN COAPE SHERBROOKE, G.C.B. By A. PATCHETT MARTIN. With 5 Portraits. 2 vols. 8vo., 36s.

Stephen.—ESSAYS IN ECCLESIASTICAL BIOGRAPHY. By Sir JAMES STEPHEN. Crown 8vo., 7s. 6d.

Verney.—MEMOIRS OF THE VERNEY FAMILY DURING THE CIVIL WAR. Compiled from the Letters and Illustrated by the Portraits at Claydon House, Bucks. By FRANCES PARTHENOPE VERNEY. With a Preface by S. R. GARDINER, M.A., LL.D. With 38 Portraits, Woodcuts and Fac-simile. 2 vols. Royal 8vo., 42s.

Wagner.—WAGNER AS I KNEW HIM. By FERDINAND PRAEGER. Crown 8vo., 7s. 6d.

Walford.—TWELVE ENGLISH AUTHORESSES. By L. B. WALFORD, Author of 'Mischief of Monica,' &c. With Portrait of Hannah More. Crown 8vo., 4s. 6d.

Wellington.—LIFE OF THE DUKE OF WELLINGTON. By the Rev. G. R. GLEIG, M.A. Crown 8vo., 3s. 6d.

Wordsworth.—Works by CHARLES WORDSWORTH, D.C.L., late Bishop of St. Andrews.

ANNALS OF MY EARLY LIFE, 1806-1846. 8vo., 15s.

ANNALS OF MY LIFE, 1847-1856. 8vo., 10s. 6d.

Travel and Adventure.

Arnold.—SEAS AND LANDS. By Sir EDWIN ARNOLD, K.C.I.E. With 71 Illustrations. Cr. 8vo., 7s. 6d.

AUSTRALIA AS IT IS; or, Facts and Features, Sketches and Incidents of Australia and Australian Life, with Notices of New Zealand. By A CLERGYMAN. Crown 8vo., 5s.

Baker.—Works by Sir SAMUEL WHITE BAKER.

EIGHT YEARS IN CEYLON. With 6 Illustrations. Crown 8vo., 3s. 6d.

THE RIFLE AND THE HOUND IN CEYLON. 6 Illustrations. Cr. 8vo., 3s. 6d.

Bent.—Works by J. THEODORE BENT, F.S.A., F.R.G.S.

THE RUINED CITIES OF MASHONALAND: being a Record of Excavation and Exploration in 1891. With Map, 13 Plates, and 104 Illustrations in the Text. Cr. 8vo., 7s. 6d.

THE SACRED CITY OF THE ETHIOPIANS: being a Record of Travel and Research in Abyssinia in 1893. With 8 Plates and 65 Illustrations in the Text. 8vo.

Brassey.—Works by LADY BRASSEY.

A VOYAGE IN THE 'SUNBEAM'; OUR HOME ON THE OCEAN FOR ELEVEN MONTHS.

Library Edition. With 8 Maps and Charts, and 118 Illustrations. 8vo., 21s.

Cabinet Edition. With Map and 66 Illustrations. Crown 8vo., 7s. 6d.

Silver Library Edition. With 66 Illustrations. Crown 8vo., 3s. 6d.

Popular Edition. With 60 Illustrations. 4to., 6d. sewed, 1s. cloth.

School Edition. With 37 Illustrations. Fcp., 2s. cloth, or 3s. white parchment.

SUNSHINE AND STORM IN THE EAST.

Library Edition. With 2 Maps and 141 Illustrations. 8vo., 21s.

Cabinet Edition. With 2 Maps and 114 Illustrations. Crown 8vo., 7s. 6d.

Popular Edition. With 103 Illustrations. 4to., 6d. sewed, 1s. cloth.

Travel and Adventure—*continued.*

Brassey.—Works by LADY BRASSEY—*continued.*
  IN THE TRADES, THE TROPICS, AND THE 'ROARING FORTIES'.
    Cabinet Edition. With Map and 220 Illustrations. Crown 8vo., 7s. 6d.
    Popular Edition. With 183 Illustrations. 4to., 6d. sewed, 1s. cloth.
  THREE VOYAGES IN THE 'SUNBEAM'.
    Popular Edition. With 346 Illustrations. 4to., 2s. 6d.
  THE LAST VOYAGE TO INDIA AND AUSTRALIA IN THE 'SUNBEAM'. With Charts and Maps, and 40 Illustrations in Monotone (20 full-page), and nearly 200 Illustrations in the Text from Drawings by R. T. PRITCHETT. 8vo., 21s.

Curzon.—PERSIA AND THE PERSIAN QUESTION. With 9 Maps, 96 Illustrations, Appendices, and an Index. By the Hon. GEORGE N. CURZON, M.P., late Fellow of All Souls' College, Oxford. 2 vols. 8vo., 42s.

Froude.—Works by JAMES A. FROUDE.
  OCEANA: or England and her Colonies. With 9 Illustrations. Crown 8vo., 2s. boards, 2s. 6d. cloth.
  THE ENGLISH IN THE WEST INDIES: or the Bow of Ulysses. With 9 Illustrations. Cr. 8vo., 2s. bds., 2s. 6d. cl.

Howard.—LIFE WITH TRANS-SIBERIAN SAVAGES. By B. DOUGLAS HOWARD, M.A. Crown 8vo., 6s.

Howitt.—VISITS TO REMARKABLE PLACES, Old Halls, Battle-Fields, Scenes illustrative of Striking Passages in English History and Poetry. By WILLIAM HOWITT. With 80 Illustrations. Crown 8vo., 3s. 6d.

Knight.—Works by E. F. KNIGHT, Author of the Cruise of the 'Falcon'.
  THE CRUISE OF THE 'ALERTE': the Narrative of a Search for Treasure on the Desert Island of Trinidad. With 2 Maps and 23 Illustrations. Crown 8vo., 3s. 6d.
  WHERE THREE EMPIRES MEET: a Narrative of Recent Travel in Kashmir, Western Tibet, Baltistan, Ladak, Gilgit, and the adjoining Countries. With a Map and 54 Illustrations. Cr. 8vo., 7s. 6d.

Lees and Clutterbuck.—B. C. 1887: A RAMBLE IN BRITISH COLUMBIA. By J. A. LEES and W. J. CLUTTERBUCK, Authors of 'Three in Norway'. With Map and 75 Illustrations. Cr. 8vo., 3s. 6d.

Nansen.—Works by Dr. FRIDTJOF NANSEN.
  THE FIRST CROSSING OF GREENLAND. With numerous Illustrations and a Map. Crown 8vo., 7s. 6d.
  ESKIMO LIFE. Translated by WILLIAM ARCHER. With 16 Plates and 15 Illustrations in the Text. 8vo., 16s.

Pratt.—TO THE SNOWS OF TIBET THROUGH CHINA. By A. E. PRATT, F.R.G.S. With 33 Illustrations and a Map. 8vo., 18s.

Riley.—ATHOS: or the Mountain of the Monks. By ATHELSTAN RILEY, M.A. With Map and 29 Illustrations. 8vo., 21s.

Rockhill.—THE LAND OF THE LAMAS: Notes of a Journey through China, Mongolia, and Tibet. By WILLIAM WOODVILLE ROCKHILL. With 2 Maps and 61 Illustrations. 8vo., 15s.

Stephens.—MADOC: An Essay on the Discovery of America, by MADOC AP OWEN GWYNEDD, in the Twelfth Century. By THOMAS STEPHENS. Edited by LLYWARCH REYNOLDS, B.A. Oxon. 8vo., 7s. 6d.

THREE IN NORWAY. By Two of Them. With a Map and 59 Illustrations. Cr. 8vo., 2s. boards, 2s. 6d. cloth.

Von Hohnel.—DISCOVERY OF LAKES RUDOLF AND STEFANIE: Account of Count SAMUEL TELEKI'S Exploring and Hunting Expedition in Eastern Equatorial Africa in 1887 and 1888. By Lieutenant LUDWIG VON HOHNEL. With 179 Illustrations and 6 Maps. 2 vols. 8vo., 42s.

Whishaw.—OUT OF DOORS IN TSARLAND; a Record of the Seeings and Doings of a Wanderer in Russia. By FRED. J. WHISHAW. Cr. 8vo., 7s. 6d.

Wolff.—Works by HENRY W. WOLFF.
  RAMBLES IN THE BLACK FOREST. Crown 8vo., 7s. 6d.
  THE WATERING PLACES OF THE VOSGES. Crown 8vo., 4s. 6d.
  THE COUNTRY OF THE VOSGES. With a Map. 8vo., 12s.

Sport and Pastime.
THE BADMINTON LIBRARY.

Edited by the DUKE OF BEAUFORT, K.G., assisted by ALFRED E. T. WATSON.

ATHLETICS AND FOOTBALL. By MONTAGUE SHEARMAN. With 51 Illlustrations. Crown 8vo., 10s. 6d.

BIG GAME SHOOTING. By C. PHILLIPPS-WOLLEY, F. C. SELONS, W. G. LITTLEDALE, &c. With Illustrations. 2 vols. [*In the Press.*

BOATING. By W. B. WOODGATE. With 49 Illustrations. Cr. 8vo., 10s. 6d.

COURSING AND FALCONRY. By HARDING COX and the Hon. GERALD LASCELLES. With 76 Illustrations. Crown 8vo., 10s. 6d.

CRICKET. By A. G. STEEL and the Hon. R. H. LYTTELTON. With Contributions by ANDREW LANG, R. A. H. MITCHELL, W. G. GRACE, and F. GALE. With 63 Illustrations. Cr. 8vo., 10s. 6d.

CYCLING. By VISCOUNT BURY (Earl of Albemarle), K.C.M.G., and G. LACY HILLIER. With 89 Illustrations. Crown 8vo., 10s. 6d.

DRIVING. By the DUKE OF BEAUFORT. With 65 Illustrations. Cr. 8vo., 10s. 6d.

FENCING, BOXING, AND WRESTLING. By WALTER H. POLLOCK, F. C. GROVE. C. PREVOST, E. B. MITCHELL, and WALTER ARMSTRONG. With 42 Illustrations. Crown 8vo., 10s. 6d.

FISHING. By H. CHOLMONDELEY-PENNELL. With Contributions by the MARQUIS OF EXETER, HENRY R. FRANCIS, R. B. MARSTON, &c.

Vol. I. Salmon, Trout, and Grayling. With 158 Illustrations. Crown 8vo., 10s. 6d.

Vol. II. Pike and other Coarse Fish. With 133 Illustrations. Crown 8vo., 10s. 6d.

GOLF. By HORACE G. HUTCHINSON, the Rt. Hon. A. J. BALFOUR, M.P., Sir W. G. SIMPSON, Bart., ANDREW LANG, and other Writers. With 91 Illustrations. Cr. 8vo., 10s. 6d.

HUNTING. By the DUKE OF BEAUFORT, K.G., and MOWBRAY MORRIS. With Contributions by the EARL OF SUFFOLK AND BERKSHIRE, Rev. E. W. L. DAVIES. With 53 Illustrations. Crown 8vo., 10s. 6d.

MOUNTAINEERING. By C. T. DENT, Sir F. POLLOCK, Bart., W. M. CONWAY, DOUGLAS FRESHFIELD, C. E. MATHEWS, C. PILKINGTON. With 108 Illustrations. Cr. 8vo., 10s. 6d.

RACING AND STEEPLE-CHASING. *Racing:* By the EARL OF SUFFOLK AND BERKSHIRE and W. G. CRAVEN. With a Contribution by the Hon. F. LAWLEY. *Steeple-chasing:* By ARTHUR COVENTRY and ALFRED E. T. WATSON. With 58 Illusts. Cr. 8vo., 10s. 6d.

RIDING AND POLO. By Captain ROBERT WEIR, J. MORAY BROWN, the DUKE OF BEAUFORT, K.G., the EARL of SUFFOLK AND BERKSHIRE, &c. With 59 Illustrations. Cr. 8vo., 10s. 6d.

SHOOTING. By Lord WALSINGHAM and Sir RALPH PAYNE-GALLWEY, Bart. With Contributions by LORD LOVAT, A. J. STUART-WORTLEY, &c.
Vol. I. Field and Covert. With 105 Illustrations. Crown 8vo., 10s. 6d.
Vol. II. Moor and Marsh. With 65 Illustrations. Cr. 8vo., 10s. 6d.

SKATING, CURLING, TOBOGANING, AND OTHER ICE SPORTS. By JN. M. HEATHCOTE, C. G. TEBBUTT, T. MAXWELL WITHAM, &c. With 284 Illustrations. Cr. 8vo., 10s. 6d.

SWIMMING. By ARCHIBALD SINCLAIR and WILLIAM HENRY, Hon. Secs. of the Life Saving Society. With 119 Illustrations. Cr. 8vo., 10s. 6d.

TENNIS, LAWN TENNIS, RACQUETS, AND FIVES. By J. M. and C. G. HEATHCOTE, E. O. PLEYDELL-BOUVERIE and A. C. AINGER. With Contributions by the Hon. A. LYTTELTON, W. C. MARSHALL, Miss L. DOD, H. W. W. WILBERFORCE, H. F. LAWFORD, &c. With 79 Illustrations. Crown 8vo., 10s. 6d.

YACHTING. By the EARL OF PEMBROKE, the MARQUIS OF DUFFERIN AND AVA, the EARL OF ONSLOW, LORD BRASSEY Lieut.-Col. BUCKNILL, LEWIS HERRESHOFF, G. L. WATSON, E. F. KNIGHT, Rev. G. L. BLAKE, R.N., and G. C. DAVIES. With Illustrations by R. T. PRITCHETT, and from Photographs. 2 vols. [*In the Press.*

Sport and Pastime—*continued*.
FUR AND FEATHER SERIES.
Edited by A. E. T. WATSON.

THE PARTRIDGE. Natural History, by the Rev. H. A. MACPHERSON; Shooting, by A. J. STUART-WORTLEY; Cookery, by GEORGE SAINTSBURY. With 11 full-page Illustrations and Vignette by A. THORBURN, A. J. STUART-WORTLEY, and C. WHYMPER, and 15 Diagrams in the Text by A. J. STUART-WORTLEY. Crown 8vo., 5s.

THE GROUSE. By A. J. STUART-WORTLEY, the Rev. H. A. MACPHERSON, and GEORGE SAINTSBURY. [*In preparation.*

THE PHEASANT. By A. J. STUART-WORTLEY, the Rev. H. A. MACPHERSON, and A. J. INNES SHAND. [*In preparation.*

THE HARE AND THE RABBIT. By the Hon. GERALD LASCELLES, &c. [*In preparation.*

WILDFOWL. By the Hon. JOHN SCOTT-MONTAGU, M.P., &c. Illustrated by A. J. STUART WORTLEY, A. THORBURN, and others. [*In preparation.*

Campbell-Walker.—THE CORRECT CARD: or, How to Play at Whist; a Whist Catechism. By Major A. CAMPBELL-WALKER, F.R.G.S. Fcp. 8vo., 2s. 6d.

DEAD SHOT (THE): or, Sportsman's Complete Guide. Being a Treatise on the Use of the Gun, with Rudimentary and Finishing Lessons on the Art of Shooting Game of all kinds, also Game Driving, Wild-Fowl and Pigeon Shooting, Dog Breaking, etc. By MARKSMAN. Crown 8vo., 10s. 6d.

Falkener.—GAMES, ANCIENT AND ORIENTAL, AND HOW TO PLAY THEM. By EDWARD FALKENER. With numerous Photographs, Diagrams, &c. 8vo., 21s.

Ford.—THE THEORY AND PRACTICE OF ARCHERY. By HORACE FORD. New Edition, thoroughly Revised and Rewritten by W. BUTT, M.A. With a Preface by C. J. LONGMAN, M.A. 8vo., 14s.

Francis.—A BOOK ON ANGLING: or, Treatise on the Art of Fishing in every Branch; including full Illustrated List of Salmon Flies. By FRANCIS FRANCIS. With Coloured Plates. Cr. 8vo., 15s.

Hawker.—THE DIARY OF COLONEL PETER HAWKER, author of "Instructions to Young Sportsmen". With an Introduction by Sir RALPH PAYNE-GALLWEY, Bart. With 2 Portraits of the Author and 8 Illustrations. 2 vols. 8vo., 32s.

Hopkins.—FISHING REMINISCENCES. By Major E. P. HOPKINS. With Illustrations. Crown 8vo., 6s. 6d.

Lang.—ANGLING SKETCHES. By ANDREW LANG. With 20 Illustrations. Crown 8vo., 7s. 6d.

Longman.—CHESS OPENINGS. By FRED. W. LONGMAN. Fcp. 8vo., 2s. 6d.

Payne-Gallwey.—Works by Sir RALPH PAYNE-GALLWEY, Bart.

LETTERS TO YOUNG SHOOTERS (First Series). On the Choice and Use of a Gun. With 41 Illustrations. Crown 8vo., 7s. 6d.

LETTERS TO YOUNG SHOOTERS. (Second Series). On the Production, Preservation, and Killing of Game. With Directions in Shooting Wood-Pigeons and Breaking-in Retrievers. With 103 Illustrations. Crown 8vo., 12s. 6d.

Pole.—THE THEORY OF THE MODERN SCIENTIFIC GAME OF WHIST. By W. POLE, F.R.S. Fcp. 8vo., 2s. 6d.

Proctor.—Works by RICHARD A. PROCTOR.

HOW TO PLAY WHIST: WITH THE LAWS AND ETIQUETTE OF WHIST. Crown 8vo., 3s. 6d.

HOME WHIST: an Easy Guide to Correct Play. 16mo., 1s.

Ronalds.—THE FLY-FISHER'S ENTOMOLOGY. By ALFRED RONALDS. With 20 Coloured Plates. 8vo., 14s.

Wilcocks. THE SEA FISHERMAN: Comprising the Chief Methods of Hook and Line Fishing in the British and other Seas, and Remarks on Nets, Boats, and Boating. By J. C. WILCOCKS. Illustrated. Crown 8vo., 6s.

Mental, Moral, and Political Philosophy.

LOGIC, RHETORIC, PSYCHOLOGY, ETC.

Abbott.—THE ELEMENTS OF LOGIC. By T. K. ABBOTT, B.D. 12mo., 3s.

Aristotle.—Works by.

THE POLITICS: G. Bekker's Greek Text of Books I., III., IV. (VII.), with an English Translation by W. E. BOLLAND, M.A.; and short Introductory Essays by A. LANG, M.A. Crown 8vo., 7s. 6d.

THE POLITICS: Introductory Essays. By ANDREW LANG (from Bolland and Lang's 'Politics'). Cr. 8vo., 2s. 6d.

THE ETHICS: Greek Text, Illustrated with Essay and Notes. By Sir ALEXANDER GRANT, Bart. 2 vols. 8vo., 32s.

THE NICOMACHEAN ETHICS: Newly Translated into English. By ROBERT WILLIAMS. Crown 8vo., 7s. 6d.

AN INTRODUCTION TO ARISTOTLE'S ETHICS. Books I.-IV. (Book X. c. vi.-ix. in an Appendix.) With a continuous Analysis and Notes. Intended for the use of Beginners and Junior Students. By the Rev. EDWARD MOORE, D.D., Principal of St. Edmund Hall, and late Fellow and Tutor of Queen's College, Oxford. Crown 8vo., 10s. 6d.

Bacon.—Works by.

COMPLETE WORKS. Edited by R. L. ELLIS, J. SPEDDING, and D. D. HEATH. 7 vols. 8vo., £3 13s. 6d.

THE ESSAYS: with Annotations. By RICHARD WHATELY, D.D. 8vo. 10s. 6d.

Bain.—Works by ALEXANDER BAIN, LL.D.

MENTAL SCIENCE. Crown 8vo., 6s. 6d.

MORAL SCIENCE. Crown 8vo., 4s. 6d.

The two works as above can be had in one volume, price 10s. 6d.

SENSES AND THE INTELLECT. 8vo., 15s.

EMOTIONS AND THE WILL. 8vo., 15s.

LOGIC, DEDUCTIVE AND INDUCTIVE. Part I., 4s. Part II., 6s. 6d.

PRACTICAL ESSAYS. Crown 8vo., 2s.

Bray.—Works by CHARLES BRAY.

THE PHILOSOPHY OF NECESSITY: or Law in Mind as in Matter. Cr. 8vo., 5s.

THE EDUCATION OF THE FEELINGS: a Moral System for Schools. Crown 8vo., 2s. 6d.

Bray.—ELEMENTS OF MORALITY, in Easy Lessons for Home and School Teaching. By Mrs. CHARLES BRAY. Cr. 8vo., 1s. 6d.

Crozier.—CIVILISATION AND PROGRESS. By JOHN BEATTIE CROZIER, M.D. With New Preface, more fully explaining the nature of the New Organon used in the solution of its problems. 8vo., 14s.

Davidson.—THE LOGIC OF DEFINITION, Explained and Applied. By WILLIAM L. DAVIDSON, M.A. Crown 8vo., 6s.

Green.—THE WORKS OF THOMAS HILL GREEN. Edited by R. L. NETTLESHIP.

Vols. I. and II. Philosophical Works. 8vo., 16s. each.

Vol. III. Miscellanies. With Index to the three Volumes, and Memoir. 8vo., 21s.

Hearn.—THE ARYAN HOUSEHOLD: its Structure and its Development. An Introduction to Comparative Jurisprudence. By W. EDWARD HEARN. 8vo., 16s.

Hodgson.—Works by SHADWORTH H. HODGSON.

TIME AND SPACE: a Metaphysical Essay. 8vo., 16s.

THE THEORY OF PRACTICE: an Ethical Inquiry. 2 vols. 8vo., 24s.

THE PHILOSOPHY OF REFLECTION. 2 vols. 8vo., 21s.

Hume.—THE PHILOSOPHICAL WORKS OF DAVID HUME. Edited by T. H. GREEN and T. H. GROSE. 4 vols. 8vo., 56s. Or separately, Essays. 2 vols. 28s. Treatise of Human Nature. 2 vols. 28s.

Mental, Moral and Political Philosophy—*continued*.

Johnstone.—A SHORT INTRODUCTION TO THE STUDY OF LOGIC. By LAURENCE JOHNSTONE. With Questions. Cr. 8vo., 2s. 6d.

Jones.—AN INTRODUCTION TO GENERAL LOGIC. By E. E. CONSTANCE JONES, Author of 'Elements of Logic as a Science of Propositions'. Cr. 8vo., 4s. 6d.

Justinian.—THE INSTITUTES OF JUSTINIAN: Latin Text, chiefly that of Huschke, with English Introduction, Translation, Notes, and Summary. By THOMAS C. SANDARS, M.A. 8vo. 18s.

Kant.—Works by IMMANUEL KANT.

CRITIQUE OF PRACTICAL REASON, AND OTHER WORKS ON THE THEORY OF ETHICS. Translated by T. K. ABBOTT, B.D. With Memoir. 8vo., 12s. 6d.

INTRODUCTION TO LOGIC, AND HIS ESSAY ON THE MISTAKEN SUBTILTY OF THE FOUR FIGURES. Translated by T. K. ABBOTT, and with Notes by S. T. COLERIDGE. 8vo., 6s.

Killick.—HANDBOOK TO MILL'S SYSTEM OF LOGIC. By Rev. A. H. KILLICK, M.A. Crown 8vo., 3s. 6d.

Ladd.—Works by GEORGE TURNBULL LADD.

ELEMENTS OF PHYSIOLOGICAL PSYCHOLOGY. 8vo., 21s.

OUTLINES OF PHYSIOLOGICAL PSYCHOLOGY. A Text-Book of Mental Science for Academies and Colleges. 8vo., 12s.

Lewes.—THE HISTORY OF PHILOSOPHY, from Thales to Comte. By GEORGE HENRY LEWES. 2 vols. 8vo., 32s.

Max Müller.—Works by F. MAX MÜLLER.

THE SCIENCE OF THOUGHT. 8vo., 21s.

THREE INTRODUCTORY LECTURES ON THE SCIENCE OF THOUGHT. 8vo., 2s. 6d.

Mill.—ANALYSIS OF THE PHENOMENA OF THE HUMAN MIND. By JAMES MILL. 2 vols. 8vo., 28s.

Mill.—Works by JOHN STUART MILL.

A SYSTEM OF LOGIC. Cr. 8vo., 3s. 6d.

ON LIBERTY. Cr. 8vo., 1s. 4d.

ON REPRESENTATIVE GOVERNMENT. Crown 8vo., 2s.

UTILITARIANISM. 8vo., 5s.

EXAMINATION OF SIR WILLIAM HAMILTON'S PHILOSOPHY. 8vo., 16s.

NATURE, THE UTILITY OF RELIGION, AND THEISM. Three Essays. 8vo., 5s.

Monck.—INTRODUCTION TO LOGIC. By H. S. MONCK. Crown 8vo., 5s.

Ribot.—THE PSYCHOLOGY OF ATTENTION. By TH. RIBOT. Cr. 8vo., 3s.

Sidgwick.—DISTINCTION: and the Criticism of Belief. By ALFRED SIDGWICK. Crown 8vo., 6s.

Stock.—DEDUCTIVE LOGIC. By ST. GEORGE STOCK. Fcp. 8vo., 3s. 6d.

Sully.—Works by JAMES SULLY, Grote Professor of Mind and Logic at University College, London.

THE HUMAN MIND: a Text-book of Psychology. 2 vols. 8vo., 21s.

OUTLINES OF PSYCHOLOGY. 8vo., 9s.

THE TEACHER'S HANDBOOK OF PSYCHOLOGY. Crown 8vo., 5s.

Swinburne.—PICTURE LOGIC: an Attempt to Popularise the Science of Reasoning. By ALFRED JAMES SWINBURNE, M.A. With 23 Woodcuts. Post 8vo., 5s.

Thompson.—Works by DANIEL GREENLEAF THOMPSON.

A SYSTEM OF PSYCHOLOGY. 2 vols. 8vo., 36s.

THE RELIGIOUS SENTIMENTS OF THE HUMAN MIND. 8vo., 7s. 6d.

THE PROBLEM OF EVIL: an Introduction to the Practical Sciences. 8vo. 10s. 6d.

Mental, Moral and Political Philosophy—*continued.*

Thompson. — Works by DANIEL GREENLEAF THOMPSON—*continued.*

SOCIAL PROGRESS. 8vo., 7s. 6d.

THE PHILOSOPHY OF FICTION IN LITERATURE. Crown 8vo., 6s.

Thomson.—OUTLINES OF THE NECESSARY LAWS OF THOUGHT: a Treatise on Pure and Applied Logic. By WILLIAM THOMSON, D.D., formerly Lord Archbishop of York. Post 8vo., 6s.

Webb.—THE VEIL OF ISIS: a Series of Essays on Idealism. By T. E. WEBB. 8vo., 10s. 6d.

Whately.—Works by R. WHATELY, formerly Archbishop of Dublin.

BACON'S ESSAYS. With Annotation. By R. WHATELY. 8vo., 10s. 6d.

ELEMENTS OF LOGIC. Cr. 8vo., 4s. 6d.

ELEMENTS OF RHETORIC. Cr. 8vo., 4s. 6d.

LESSONS ON REASONING. Fcp. 8vo., 1s. 6d.

Zeller.—Works by Dr. EDWARD ZELLER, Professor in the University of Berlin.

HISTORY OF ECLECTICISM IN GREEK PHILOSOPHY. Translated by SARAH F. ALLEYNE. Cr. 8vo., 10s. 6d.

THE STOICS, EPICUREANS, AND SCEPTICS. Translated by the Rev. O. J. REICHEL, M.A. Crown 8vo., 15s.

OUTLINES OF THE HISTORY OF GREEK PHILOSOPHY. Translated by SARAH F. ALLEYNE and EVELYN ABBOTT. Crown 8vo., 10s. 6d.

PLATO AND THE OLDER ACADEMY. Translated by SARAH F. ALLEYNE and ALFRED GOODWIN, B.A. Crown 8vo., 18s.

SOCRATES AND THE SOCRATIC SCHOOLS. Translated by the Rev. O. J. REICHEL, M.A. Crown 8vo., 10s. 6d.

THE PRE-SOCRATIC SCHOOLS: a History of Greek Philosophy from the Earliest Period to the time of Socrates. Translated by SARAH F. ALLEYNE. 2 vols. Crown 8vo., 30s.

MANUALS OF CATHOLIC PHILOSOPHY.
(Stonyhurst Series.)

A MANUAL OF POLITICAL ECONOMY. By C. S. DEVAS, M.A. Cr. 8vo., 6s. 6d.

FIRST PRINCIPLES OF KNOWLEDGE. By JOHN RICKABY, S.J. Crown 8vo., 5s.

GENERAL METAPHYSICS. By JOHN RICKABY, S.J. Crown 8vo., 5s.

LOGIC. By RICHARD F. CLARKE, S.J. Crown 8vo., 5s.

MORAL PHILOSOPHY (ETHICS AND NATURAL LAW). By JOSEPH RICKABY, S.J. Crown 8vo., 5s.

NATURAL THEOLOGY. By BERNARD BOEDDER, S.J. Crown 8vo., 6s. 6d.

PSYCHOLOGY. By MICHAEL MAHER, S.J. Crown 8vo., 6s. 6d.

History and Science of Language, &c.

Davidson.—LEADING AND IMPORTANT ENGLISH WORDS: Explained and Exemplified. By WILLIAM L. DAVIDSON, M.A. Fcp. 8vo., 3s. 6d.

Farrar.—LANGUAGE AND LANGUAGES: By F. W. FARRAR, D.D., F.R.S., Cr. 8vo., 6s.

Graham.—ENGLISH SYNONYMS, Classified and Explained: with Practical Exercises. By G. F. GRAHAM. Fcp. 8vo., 6s.

History and Science of Language, &c.—*continued*.

Max Müller.—Works by F. MAX MÜLLER.
  SELECTED ESSAYS ON LANGUAGE, MYTHOLOGY, AND RELIGION. 2 vols. Crown 8vo., 16s.
  THE SCIENCE OF LANGUAGE, Founded on Lectures delivered at the Royal Institution in 1861 and 1863. 2 vols. Crown 8vo., 21s.
  BIOGRAPHIES OF WORDS, AND THE HOME OF THE ARYAS. Crown 8vo., 7s. 6d.
  THREE LECTURES ON THE SCIENCE OF LANGUAGE, AND ITS PLACE IN GENERAL EDUCATION, delivered at Oxford, 1889. Crown 8vo., 3s.

Roget.—THESAURUS OF ENGLISH WORDS AND PHRASES. Classified and Arranged so as to Facilitate the Expression of Ideas and assist in Literary Composition. By PETER MARK ROGET, M.D., F.R.S. Recomposed throughout, enlarged and improved, partly from the Author's Notes, and with a full Index, by the Author's Son, JOHN LEWIS ROGET. Crown 8vo., 10s. 6d.

Whately.—ENGLISH SYNONYMS. By E. JANE WHATELY. Fcp. 8vo., 3s.

Political Economy and Economics.

Ashley.—ENGLISH ECONOMIC HISTORY AND THEORY. By W. J. ASHLEY, M.A. Crown 8vo., Part I., 5s. Part II., 10s. 6d.

Bagehot.—ECONOMIC STUDIES. By WALTER BAGEHOT. 8vo., 10s. 6d.

Crump.—AN INVESTIGATION INTO THE CAUSES OF THE GREAT FALL IN PRICES which took place coincidently with the Demonetisation of Silver by Germany. By ARTHUR CRUMP. 8vo., 6s.

Devas.—A MANUAL OF POLITICAL ECONOMY. By C. S. DEVAS, M.A. Crown 8vo., 6s. 6d. (*Manuals of Catholic Philosophy.*)

Dowell.—A HISTORY OF TAXATION AND TAXES IN ENGLAND, from the Earliest Times to the Year 1885. By STEPHEN DOWELL (4 vols. 8vo.) Vols. I. and II. The History of Taxation, 21s. Vols. III. and IV. The History of Taxes, 21s.

Jordan.—THE STANDARD OF VALUE. By WILLIAM LEIGHTON JORDAN. 8vo., 6s.

Leslie.—ESSAYS IN POLITICAL ECONOMY. By T. E. CLIFFE LESLIE. 8vo., 10s. 6d.

Macleod.—Works by HENRY DUNNING MACLEOD, M.A.
  THE ELEMENTS OF BANKING. Crown 8vo., 3s. 6d.
  THE THEORY AND PRACTICE OF BANKING. Vol. I. 8vo., 12s. Vol. II. 14s.
  THE THEORY OF CREDIT. 8vo. Vol. I. 10s. net. Vol. II., Part I., 4s. 6d. Vol. II. Part II., 10s. 6d.

Meath.—PROSPERITY OR PAUPERISM? Physical, Industrial, and Technical Training. By the EARL OF MEATH. 8vo., 5s.

Mill.—POLITICAL ECONOMY. By JOHN STUART MILL.
  Silver Library Edition. Crown 8vo., 3s. 6d.
  Library Edition. 2 vols. 8vo., 30s.

Shirres.—AN ANALYSIS OF THE IDEAS OF ECONOMICS. By L. P. SHIRRES, B.A., sometime Finance Under Secretary of the Government of Bengal. Crown 8vo., 6s.

LONGMANS & CO.'S STANDARD AND GENERAL WORKS.   13

Political Economy and Economics—*continued.*

Symes.—POLITICAL ECONOMY: a Short Text-book of Political Economy. With Problems for Solution, and Hints for Supplementary Reading. By J. E. SYMES, M.A., of University College, Nottingham. Crown 8vo., 2s. 6d.

Toynbee.—LECTURES ON THE INDUSTRIAL REVOLUTION OF THE 18th CENTURY IN ENGLAND. By ARNOLD TOYNBEE. 8vo., 10s. 6d.

Wilson.—Works by A. J. WILSON. Chiefly reprinted from *The Investors' Review.*

PRACTICAL HINTS TO SMALL INVESTORS. Crown 8vo., 1s.

PLAIN ADVICE ABOUT LIFE INSURANCE. Crown 8vo., 1s.

Wolff.—PEOPLE'S BANKS: a Record of Social and Economic Success. By HENRY W. WOLFF. 8vo., 7s. 6d.

Evolution, Anthropology, &c.

Clodd.—THE STORY OF CREATION: a Plain Account of Evolution. By EDWARD CLODD. With 77 Illustrations. Crown 8vo., 3s. 6d.

Huth.—THE MARRIAGE OF NEAR KIN, considered with Respect to the Law of Nations, the Result of Experience, and the Teachings of Biology. By ALFRED HENRY HUTH. Royal 8vo., 7s. 6d.

Lang.—CUSTOM AND MYTH: Studies of Early Usage and Belief. By ANDREW LANG, M.A. With 15 Illustrations. Crown 8vo., 3s. 6d.

Lubbock.—THE ORIGIN OF CIVILISATION and the Primitive Condition of Man. By Sir J. LUBBOCK, Bart., M.P. With 5 Plates and 20 Illustrations in the Text. 8vo. 18s.

Romanes.—Works by GEORGE JOHN ROMANES, M.A., LL.D., F.R.S.

DARWIN, AND AFTER DARWIN: an Exposition of the Darwinian Theory, and a Discussion on Post-Darwinian Questions. Part I. The Darwinian Theory. With Portrait of Darwin and 125 Illustrations. Crown 8vo., 10s. 6d.

AN EXAMINATION OF WEISMANNISM. Crown 8vo., 6s.

Classical Literature.

Abbott.—HELLENICA. A Collection of Essays on Greek Poetry, Philosophy, History, and Religion. Edited by EVELYN ABBOTT, M.A., LL.D. 8vo., 16s.

Æschylus.—EUMENIDES OF ÆSCHYLUS. With Metrical English Translation. By J. F. DAVIES. 8vo., 7s.

Aristophanes.—The ACHARNIANS OF ARISTOPHANES, translated into English Verse. By R. Y. TYRRELL. Crown 8vo., 1s.

Becker.—Works by Professor BECKER.

GALLUS: or, Roman Scenes in the Time of Augustus. Illustrated. Post 8vo., 7s. 6d.

CHARICLES: or, Illustrations of the Private Life of the Ancient Greeks. Illustrated. Post 8vo., 7s. 6d.

Cicero.—CICERO'S CORRESPONDENCE. By R. Y. TYRRELL. Vols. I., II., III. 8vo., each 12s.

Clerke.—FAMILIAR STUDIES IN HOMER. By AGNES M. CLERKE. Cr. 8vo., 7s. 6d.

Farnell.—GREEK LYRIC POETRY: a Complete Collection of the Surviving Passages from the Greek Song-Writing. Arranged with Prefatory Articles, Introductory Matter and Commentary. By GEORGE S. FARNELL, M.A. With 5 Plates. 8vo., 16s.

Harrison.—MYTHS OF THE ODYSSEY, IN ART AND LITERATURE. By JANE E. HARRISON. Illustrated with Outline Drawings. 8vo., 18s.

Lang.—HOMER AND THE EPIC. By ANDREW LANG. Crown 8vo., 9s. net.

Classical Literature—*continued*.

Mackail.—SELECT EPIGRAMS FROM THE GREEK ANTHOLOGY. By J. W. MACKAIL, Fellow of Balliol College, Oxford. Edited with a Revised Text, Introduction, Translation, and Notes. 8vo., 16s.

Plato.—PARMENIDES OF PLATO, Text, with Introduction, Analysis, &c. By T. MAGUIRE. 8vo., 7s. 6d.

Rich.—A DICTIONARY OF ROMAN AND GREEK ANTIQUITIES. By A. RICH, B.A. With 2000 Woodcuts. Crown 8vo., 7s. 6d.

Sophocles.—Translated into English Verse. By ROBERT WHITELAW, M.A., Assistant Master in Rugby School: late Fellow of Trinity College, Cambridge. Crown 8vo., 8s. 6d.

Tyrrell.—TRANSLATIONS INTO GREEK AND LATIN VERSE. Edited by R. Y. TYRRELL. 8vo., 6s.

Virgil.—THE ÆNEID OF VIRGIL. Translated into English Verse by JOHN CONINGTON. Crown 8vo., 6s.

THE POEMS OF VIRGIL. Translated into English Prose by JOHN CONINGTON. Crown 8vo., 6s.

THE ÆNEID OF VIRGIL, freely translated into English Blank Verse. By W. J. THORNHILL. Crown 8vo., 7s. 6d.

THE ÆNEID OF VIRGIL. Books I. to VI. Translated into English Verse by JAMES RHOADES. Crown 8vo., 5s.

Wilkins.—THE GROWTH OF THE HOMERIC POEMS. By G. WILKINS. 8vo. 6s.

Poetry and the Drama.

Allingham.—Works by WILLIAM ALLINGHAM.

IRISH SONGS AND POEMS. With Frontispiece of the Waterfall of Asaroe. Fcp. 8vo., 6s.

LAURENCE BLOOMFIELD. With Portrait of the Author. Fcp. 8vo., 3s. 6d.

FLOWER PIECES; DAY AND NIGHT SONGS; BALLADS. With 2 Designs by D. G. ROSSETTI. Fcp. 8vo., 6s.; large paper edition, 12s.

LIFE AND PHANTASY: with Frontispiece by Sir J. E. MILLAIS, Bart., and Design by ARTHUR HUGHES. Fcp. 8vo., 6s.; large paper edition, 12s.

THOUGHT AND WORD, AND ASHBY MANOR: a Play. With Portrait of the Author (1865), and four Theatrical Scenes drawn by Mr. Allingham. Fcp. 8vo., 6s.; large paper edition, 12s.

BLACKBERRIES. Imperial 16mo., 6s.

Sets of the above 6 vols. may be had in uniform half-parchment binding, price 30s.

Armstrong.—Works by G. F. SAVAGE-ARMSTRONG.

POEMS: Lyrical and Dramatic. Fcp. 8vo., 6s.

KING SAUL. (The Tragedy of Israel, Part I.) Fcp. 8vo. 5s.

KING DAVID. (The Tragedy of Israel, Part II.) Fcp. 8vo., 6s.

KING SOLOMON. (The Tragedy of Israel, Part III.) Fcp. 8vo., 6s.

UGONE: a Tragedy. Fcp. 8vo., 6s.

A GARLAND FROM GREECE: Poems. Fcp. 8vo., 7s. 6d.

STORIES OF WICKLOW: Poems. Fcp. 8vo., 7s. 6d.

MEPHISTOPHELES IN BROADCLOTH: a Satire. Fcp. 8vo., 4s.

ONE IN THE INFINITE: a Poem. Cr. 8vo., 7s. 6d.

Armstrong.—THE POETICAL WORKS OF EDMUND J. ARMSTRONG. Fcp. 8vo., 5s.

Poetry and the Drama—*continued.*

Arnold.—Works by Sir EDWIN ARNOLD, K.C.I.E., Author of 'The Light of Asia,' &c.

THE LIGHT OF THE WORLD: or, the Great Consummation. A Poem. Crown 8vo., 7s. 6d. net.
Presentation Edition. With 14 Illustrations by W. HOLMAN HUNT, &c., 4to., 20s. net.
POTIPHAR'S WIFE, and other Poems. Crown 8vo., 5s. net.
ADZUMA: or, the Japanese Wife. A Play. Crown 8vo., 6s. 6d. net.

Barrow.—THE SEVEN CITIES OF THE DEAD, and other Poems. By Sir JOHN CROKER BARROW, Bart. Fcp. 8vo., 5s.

Bell.—Works by Mrs. HUGH BELL.

CHAMBER COMEDIES: a Collection of Plays and Monologues for the Drawing Room. Crown 8vo., 6s.
NURSERY COMEDIES: Twelve Tiny Plays for Children. Fcp. 8vo., 1s. 6d.

Björnsen.—PASTOR SANG: a Play. By BJÖRNSTJERNE BJÖRNSEN. Translated by WILLIAM WILSON. Cr. 8vo., 5s.

Dante.—LA COMMEDIA DI DANTE. A New Text, carefully revised with the aid of the most recent Editions and Collations. Small 8vo., 6s.

Goethe.

FAUST, Part I., the German Text, with Introduction and Notes. By ALBERT M. SELSS, Ph.D., M.A. Cr. 8vo., 5s.
FAUST. Translated, with Notes. By T. E. WEBB. 8vo., 12s. 6d.
FAUST. The First Part. A New Translation, chiefly in Blank Verse; with Introduction and Notes. By JAMES ADEY BIRDS. Cr. 8vo., 6s.
FAUST. The Second Part. A New Translation in Verse. By JAMES ADEY BIRDS. Crown 8vo., 6s.

Ingelow.—Works by JEAN INGELOW.

POETICAL WORKS. 2 vols. Fcp. 8vo., 12s.
LYRICAL AND OTHER POEMS. Selected from the Writings of JEAN INGELOW. Fcp. 8vo., 2s. 6d. cloth plain, 3s. cloth gilt.

Lang.—Works by ANDREW LANG.

GRASS OF PARNASSUS. Fcp. 8vo., 2s. 6d. net.
BALLADS OF BOOKS. Edited by ANDREW LANG. Fcp. 8vo., 6s.
THE BLUE POETRY BOOK. Edited by ANDREW LANG. With 12 Plates and 88 Illustrations in the Text. Crown 8vo., 6s.
Special Edition, printed on Indian paper. With Notes, but without Illustrations. Crown 8vo., 7s. 6d.

Lecky.—POEMS. By W. E. H. LECKY. Fcp. 8vo., 5s.

Leyton.—Works by FRANK LEYTON.

THE SHADOWS OF THE LAKE, and other Poems. Crown 8vo., 7s. 6d. Cheap Edition. Crown 8vo., 3s. 6d.
SKELETON LEAVES: Poems. Crown 8vo., 6s.

Lytton.—Works by THE EARL OF LYTTON (OWEN MEREDITH).

MARAH. Fcp. 8vo., 6s. 6d.
KING POPPY: a Fantasia. With 1 Plate and Design on Title-Page by Sir ED. BURNE-JONES, A.R.A. Crown 8vo., 10s. 6d.
THE WANDERER. Cr. 8vo., 10s. 6d.
LUCILE. Crown 8vo., 10s. 6d.

Macaulay.—LAYS OF ANCIENT ROME, &c. By Lord MACAULAY.

Illustrated by G. SCHARF. Fcp. 4to., 10s. 6d.
——— Bijou Edition. 18mo., 2s. 6d., gilt top.
——— Popular Edition. Fcp. 4to., 6d. sewed, 1s. cloth.
Illustrated by J. R. WEGUELIN. Crown 8vo., 3s. 6d.
Annotated Edition. Fcp. 8vo., 1s. sewed, 1s. 6d. cloth.

Nesbit.—LAYS AND LEGENDS. by E. NESBIT (Mrs. HUBERT BLAND). First Series. Crown 8vo., 3s. 6d. Second Series, with Portrait. Crown 8vo., 5s.

Piatt.—AN ENCHANTED CASTLE, AND OTHER POEMS: Pictures, Portraits and People in Ireland. By SARAH PIATT. Crown 8vo., 3s. 6d.

Poetry and the Drama—*continued*.

Piatt.—Works by JOHN JAMES PIATT.

   IDYLS AND LYRICS OF THE OHIO VALLEY. Crown 8vo., 5s.

   LITTLE NEW WORLD IDYLS. Cr. 8vo., 5s.

Rhoades.—TERESA AND OTHER POEMS. By JAMES RHOADES. Crown 8vo., 3s. 6d.

Riley.—Works by JAMES WHITCOMB RILEY.

   POEMS HERE AT HOME. Fcap. 8vo., 6s. net.

   OLD FASHIONED ROSES: Poems. 12mo., 5s.

Roberts.—SONGS OF THE COMMON DAY, AND AVE: an Ode for the Shelley Centenary. By CHARLES G. D. ROBERTS. Crown 8vo., 3s. 6d.

Shakespeare.—BOWDLER'S FAMILY SHAKESPEARE. With 36 Woodcuts. 1 vol. 8vo., 14s. Or in 6 vols. Fcp. 8vo., 21s.

   THE SHAKESPEARE BIRTHDAY BOOK. By MARY F. DUNBAR. 32mo., 1s. 6d. Drawing-Room Edition, with Photographs. Fcp. 8vo., 10s. 6d.

Stevenson.—A CHILD'S GARDEN OF VERSES. By ROBERT LOUIS STEVENSON. Small fcp. 8vo., 5s.

Works of Fiction, Humour, &c.

Anstey.—Works by F. ANSTEY, Author of 'Vice Versâ'.

   THE BLACK POODLE, and other Stories. Crown 8vo., 2s. boards, 2s. 6d. cloth.

   VOCES POPULI. Reprinted from 'Punch'. With Illustrations by J. BERNARD PARTRIDGE. First Series. Fcp. 4to., 5s. Second Series. Fcp. 4to., 6s.

   THE TRAVELLING COMPANIONS. Reprinted from 'Punch'. With Illustrations by J. BERNARD PARTRIDGE. Post 4to., 5s.

   THE MAN FROM BLANKLEY'S: a Story in Scenes, and other Sketches. With 24 Illustrations by J. BERNARD PARTRIDGE. Fcp. 4to., 6s.

   ATELIER (THE) DU LYS: or, an Art Student in the Reign of Terror. Crown 8vo., 2s. 6d.

     BY THE SAME AUTHOR.

   MADEMOISELLE MORI: a Tale of Modern Rome. Crown 8vo., 2s. 6d.

BY THE SAME AUTHOR—*continued*.

   THAT CHILD. Illustrated by GORDON BROWNE. Crown 8vo., 2s. 6d.

   UNDER A CLOUD. Cr. 8vo., 2s. 6d.

   THE FIDDLER OF LUGAU. With Illustrations by W. RALSTON. Crown 8vo., 2s. 6d.

   A CHILD OF THE REVOLUTION. With Illustrations by C. J. STANILAND. Crown 8vo., 2s. 6d.

   HESTER'S VENTURE: a Novel. Crown 8vo., 2s. 6d.

   IN THE OLDEN TIME: a Tale of the Peasant War in Germany. Crown 8vo., 2s. 6d.

   THE YOUNGER SISTER: a Tale. Cr. 8vo., 2s. 6d.

Baker.—BY THE WESTERN SEA. By JAMES BAKER, Author of 'John Westacott'. Crown 8vo., 3s. 6d.

Works of Fiction, Humour, &c.—*continued*.

Beaconsfield.—Works by the Earl of BEACONSFIELD.
NOVELS AND TALES. Cheap Edition. Complete in 11 vols. Cr. 8vo., 1s. 6d. each.
Vivian Grey.
The Young Duke. &c.
Alroy, Ixion, &c.
Henrietta Temple.
Contarini Fleming, &c.
Venetia. Tancred.
Coningsby. Sybil.
Lothair. Endymion.
NOVELS AND TALES. The Hughenden Edition. With 2 Portraits and 11 Vignettes. 11 vols. Cr. 8vo., 42s.

Comyn.—ATHERSTONE PRIORY: a Tale. By L. N. COMYN. Crown 8vo., 2s. 6d.

Deland.—Works by MARGARET DELAND, Author of 'John Ward'.
THE STORY OF A CHILD. Cr. 8vo., 5s.
MR. TOMMY DOVE, and other Stories. Crown 8vo., 6s.

Dougall.—Works by L. DOUGALL.
BEGGARS ALL. Crown 8vo., 3s. 6d.
WHAT NECESSITY KNOWS. Crown 8vo., 6s.

Doyle.—Works by A. CONAN DOYLE.
MICAH CLARKE: a Tale of Monmouth's Rebellion. With Frontispiece and Vignette. Cr. 8vo., 3s. 6d.
THE CAPTAIN OF THE POLESTAR, and other Tales. Cr. 8vo., 3s. 6d.
THE REFUGEES: a Tale of Two Continents. Cr. 8vo., 6s.

Farrar.—DARKNESS AND DAWN: or, Scenes in the Days of Nero. An Historic Tale. By Archdeacon FARRAR. Cr. 8vo., 7s. 6d.

Froude.—THE TWO CHIEFS OF DUNBOY: an Irish Romance of the Last Century. By J. A. FROUDE. Cr. 8vo., 3s. 6d.

Haggard.—Works by H. RIDER HAGGARD.
SHE. With 32 Illustrations by M. GREIFFENHAGEN and C. H. M. KERR. Cr. 8vo., 3s. 6d.
ALLAN QUATERMAIN. With 31 Illustrations by C. H. M. KERR. Cr. 8vo., 3s. 6d.
MAIWA'S REVENGE; or, The War of the Little Hand. Cr. 8vo., 1s. boards, 1s. 6d. cloth.
COLONEL QUARITCH, V.C. Cr. 8vo., 3s. 6d.

Haggard.—Works by H. RIDER HAGGARD—*continued*.
CLEOPATRA. With 29 Full-page Illustrations by M. GREIFFENHAGEN and R. CATON WOODVILLE. Cr. 8vo., 3s. 6d.
BEATRICE. Cr. 8vo., 3s. 6d.
ERIC BRIGHTEYES. With 17 Plates and 34 Illustrations in the Text by LANCELOT SPEED. Cr. 8vo., 3s. 6d.
NADA THE LILY. With 23 Illustrations by C. H. M. KERR. Cr. 8vo., 6s.
MONTEZUMA'S DAUGHTER. With 24 Illustrations by M. GREIFFENHAGEN. Cr. 8vo., 6s.

Haggard and Lang.—THE WORLD'S DESIRE. By H. RIDER HAGGARD and ANDREW LANG. Cr. 8vo., 6s.

Harte.—IN THE CARQUINEZ WOODS, and other Stories. By BRET HARTE. Cr. 8vo., 3s. 6d.

KEITH DERAMORE: a Novel. By the Author of 'Miss Molly'. Cr. 8vo., 6s.

Lyall.—THE AUTOBIOGRAPHY OF A SLANDER. By EDNA LYALL, Author of 'Donovan,' &c. Fcp. 8vo., 1s. sewed. Presentation Edition. With 20 Illustrations by LANCELOT SPEED. Cr. 8vo., 5s.

Melville.—Works by G. J. WHYTE MELVILLE.
The Gladiators.
The Interpreter.
Good for Nothing.
The Queen's Maries.
Holmby House.
Kate Coventry.
Digby Grand.
General Bounce.
Cr. 8vo., 1s. 6d. each.

Oliphant.—Works by Mrs. OLIPHANT.
MADAM. Cr. 8vo., 1s. 6d.
IN TRUST. Cr. 8vo., 1s. 6d.

Parr.—CAN THIS BE LOVE? By Mrs. PARR, Author of 'Dorothy Fox'. Cr. 8vo., 6s.

Payn.—Works by JAMES PAYN.
THE LUCK OF THE DARRELLS. Cr. 8vo., 1s. 6d.
THICKER THAN WATER. Cr. 8vo., 1s. 6d.

Phillipps-Wolley.—SNAP: a Legend of the Lone Mountain. By C. PHILLIPPS-WOLLEY. With 13 Illustrations by H. G. WILLINK. Cr. 8vo., 3s. 6d.

Robertson.—THE KIDNAPPED SQUATTER, and other Australian Tales. By A. ROBERTSON. Cr. 8vo., 6s.

Works of Fiction, Humour, &c.—*continued.*

Sewell.—Works by ELIZABETH M. SEWELL.
A Glimpse of the World. | Amy Herbert.
Laneton Parsonage. | Cleve Hall.
Margaret Percival. | Gertrude.
Katharine Ashton. | Home Life.
The Earl's Daughter. | After Life.
The Experience of Life. | Ursula. Ivors.
Cr. 8vo., 1s. 6d. each cloth plain. 2s. 6d. each cloth extra, gilt edges.

Stevenson.—Works by ROBERT LOUIS STEVENSON.
STRANGE CASE OF DR. JEKYLL AND MR. HYDE. Fcp. 8vo., 1s. sewed. 1s. 6d. cloth.
THE DYNAMITER. Fcp. 8vo., 1s. sewed, 1s. 6d. cloth.

Stevenson and Osbourne.—THE WRONG BOX. By ROBERT LOUIS STEVENSON and LLOYD OSBOURNE. Cr. 8vo., 3s. 6d.

Sturgis.—AFTER TWENTY YEARS, and other Stories. By JULIAN STURGIS. Cr. 8vo., 6s.

Suttner.—LAY DOWN YOUR ARMS *Die Waffen Nieder:* The Autobiography of Martha Tilling. By BERTHA VON SUTTNER. Translated by T. HOLMES. Cr. 8vo., 7s. 6d.

Thompson.—A MORAL DILEMMA; a Novel. By ANNIE THOMPSON. Cr. 8vo., 6s.

Tirebuck.—Works by WILLIAM TIREBUCK.
DORRIE. Crown 8vo., 6s.
SWEETHEART GWEN. Cr. 8vo., 6s.

Trollope.—Works by ANTHONY TROLLOPE.
THE WARDEN. Cr. 8vo., 1s. 6d.
BARCHESTER TOWERS. Cr. 8vo., 1s. 6d.

Walford.—Works by L. B. WALFORD, Author of 'Mr. Smith'.
THE MISCHIEF OF MONICA: a Novel. Cr. 8vo., 2s. 6d.
THE ONE GOOD GUEST: a Story. Cr. 8vo, 6s.

West.—HALF-HOURS WITH THE MILLIONAIRES: Showing how much harder it is to spend a million than to make it. Edited by B. B. WEST. Cr. 8vo., 6s.

Weyman.—Works by STANLEY J. WEYMAN.
THE HOUSE OF THE WOLF: a Romance. Cr. 8vo., 3s. 6d.
A GENTLEMAN OF FRANCE. Cr. 8vo, 6s.

Popular Science (Natural History, &c.).

Butler.—OUR HOUSEHOLD INSECTS. By E. A. BUTLER. With 7 Plates and 113 Illustrations in the Text. Crown 8vo., 6s.

Furneaux.—THE OUTDOOR WORLD; or, The Young Collector's Handbook. By W. FURNEAUX, F.R.G.S. With 16 Coloured Plates, 2 Plain Plates, and 549 Illustrations in the Text. Crown 8vo., 7s. 6d.

Hartwig.—Works by Dr. GEORGE HARTWIG.
THE SEA AND ITS LIVING WONDERS. With 12 Plates and 303 Woodcuts. 8vo., 7s. net.
THE TROPICAL WORLD. With 8 Plates and 172 Woodcuts. 8vo., 7s. net.
THE POLAR WORLD. With 3 Maps, 8 Plates and 85 Woodcuts. 8vo., 7s. net.

Hartwig.—Works by Dr. GEORGE HARTWIG—*continued.*
THE SUBTERRANEAN WORLD. With 3 Maps and 80 Woodcuts. 8vo., 7s. net.
THE AERIAL WORLD. With Map, 8 Plates and 60 Woodcuts. 8vo., 7s. net.
HEROES OF THE POLAR WORLD. 19 Illustrations. Crown 8vo., 2s.
WONDERS OF THE TROPICAL FORESTS. 40 Illustrations. Crown 8vo., 2s.
WORKERS UNDER THE GROUND. 29 Illustrations. Crown 8vo., 2s.
MARVELS OVER OUR HEADS. 29 Illustrations. Crown 8vo., 2s.
SEA MONSTERS AND SEA BIRDS. 75 Illustrations. Crown 8vo., 2s. 6d.

Popular Science (Natural History, &c.).

Hartwig.—Works by Dr. GEORGE HARTWIG—*continued*.

DENIZENS OF THE DEEP. 117 Illustrations. Crown 8vo., 2s. 6d.

VOLCANOES AND EARTHQUAKES. 30 Illustrations. Crown 8vo., 2s. 6d.

WILD ANIMALS OF THE TROPICS. 66 Illustrations. Crown 8vo., 3s. 6d.

Helmholtz.—POPULAR LECTURES ON SCIENTIFIC SUBJECTS. By HERMANN VON HELMHOLTZ. With 68 Woodcuts. 2 vols. Crown 8vo., 3s. 6d. each.

Lydekker.—PHASES OF ANIMAL LIFE, PAST AND PRESENT. By R. LYDEKKER, B.A. With 82 Illustrations. Crown 8vo., 6s.

Proctor.—Works by RICHARD A. PROCTOR.

And see Messrs. Longmans & Co.'s Catalogue of Scientific Works.

LIGHT SCIENCE FOR LEISURE HOURS. Familiar Essays on Scientific Subjects. 3 vols. Crown 8vo., 5s. each.

CHANCE AND LUCK: a Discussion of the Laws of Luck, Coincidence, Wagers, Lotteries and the Fallacies of Gambling, &c. Cr. 8vo., 2s. boards, 2s. 6d. cloth.

ROUGH WAYS MADE SMOOTH. Familiar Essays on Scientific Subjects. Silver Library Edition. Crown 8vo., 3s. 6d.

PLEASANT WAYS IN SCIENCE. Cr. 8vo., 5s. Silver Library Edition. Crown 8vo., 3s. 6d.

THE GREAT PYRAMID, OBSERVATORY, TOMB AND TEMPLE. With Illustrations. Crown 8vo., 5s.

NATURE STUDIES. By R. A. PROCTOR, GRANT ALLEN, A. WILSON, T. FOSTER and E. CLODD. Crown 8vo., 5s. Silver Library Edition. Crown 8vo., 3s. 6d.

LEISURE READINGS. By R. A. PROCTOR, E. CLODD, A. WILSON, T. FOSTER, and A. C. RANYARD. Cr. 8vo., 5s.

Stanley.—A FAMILIAR HISTORY OF BIRDS. By E. STANLEY, D.D., formerly Bishop of Norwich. With Illustrations. Cr. 8vo., 3s. 6d.

Wood.—Works by the Rev. J. G. WOOD.

HOMES WITHOUT HANDS: a Description of the Habitation of Animals, classed according to the Principle of Construction. With 140 Illustrations. 8vo., 7s. net.

INSECTS AT HOME: a Popular Account of British Insects, their Structure, Habits and Transformations. With 700 Illustrations. 8vo., 7s. net.

INSECTS ABROAD: a Popular Account of Foreign Insects, their Structure, Habits and Transformations. With 600 Illustrations. 8vo., 7s. net.

BIBLE ANIMALS: a Description of every Living Creature mentioned in the Scriptures. With 112 Illustrations. 8vo., 7s. net.

PETLAND REVISITED. With 33 Illustrations. Cr. 8vo., 3s. 6d.

OUT OF DOORS; a Selection of Original Articles on Practical Natural History. With 11 Illustrations. Cr. 8vo., 3s. 6d.

STRANGE DWELLINGS: a Description of the Habitations of Animals, abridged from 'Homes without Hands'. With 60 Illustrations. Cr. 8vo., 3s. 6d.

BIRD LIFE OF THE BIBLE. 32 Illustrations. Cr. 8vo., 3s. 6d.

WONDERFUL NESTS. 30 Illustrations Cr. 8vo, 3s. 6d.

HOMES UNDER THE GROUND. 28 Illustrations. Cr. 8vo., 3s. 6d.

WILD ANIMALS OF THE BIBLE. 29 Illustrations. Cr. 8vo., 3s. 6d.

DOMESTIC ANIMALS OF THE BIBLE. 23 Illustrations. Cr. 8vo., 3s. 6d.

THE BRANCH BUILDERS. 28 Illustrations. Cr. 8vo., 2s. 6d.

SOCIAL HABITATIONS AND PARASITIC NESTS. 18 Illustrations. Cr. 8vo., 2s.

Works of Reference.

Maunder's (Samuel) Treasuries.

BIOGRAPHICAL TREASURY. With Supplement brought down to 1889. By Rev. JAMES WOOD. Fcp. 8vo., 6s.

TREASURY OF NATURAL HISTORY: or, Popular Dictionary of Zoology. With 900 Woodcuts. Fcp. 8vo., 6s.

TREASURY OF GEOGRAPHY, Physical, Historical, Descriptive, and Political. With 7 Maps and 16 Plates. Fcp. 8vo., 6s.

THE TREASURY OF BIBLE KNOWLEDGE. By the Rev. J. AYRE, M.A. With 5 Maps, 15 plates, and 300 Woodcuts. Fcp. 8vo., 6s.

HISTORICAL TREASURY: Outlines of Universal History, Separate Histories of all Nations. Fcp. 8vo., 6s.

TREASURY OF KNOWLEDGE AND LIBRARY OF REFERENCE. Comprising an English Dictionary and Grammar, Universal Gazeteer, Classical Dictionary, Chronology, Law Dictionary, &c. Fcp. 8vo., 6s.

Maunder's (Samuel) Treasuries—*continued.*

SCIENTIFIC AND LITERARY TREASURY. Fcp. 8vo., 6s.

THE TREASURY OF BOTANY. Edited by J. LINDLEY, F.R.S., and T. MOORE, F.L.S. With 274 Woodcuts and 20 Steel Plates. 2 vols. Fcp. 8vo., 12s.

Roget.—THESAURUS OF ENGLISH WORDS AND PHRASES. Classified and Arranged so as to Facilitate the Expression of Ideas and assist in Literary Composition. By PETER MARK ROGET, M.D., F.R.S. Recomposed throughout, enlarged and improved, partly from the Author's Notes, and with a full Index, by the Author's Son, JOHN LEWIS ROGET. Crown 8vo., 10s. 6d.

Willich.—POPULAR TABLES for giving information for ascertaining the value of Lifehold, Leasehold, and Church Property, the Public Funds, &c. By CHARLES M. WILLICH. Edited by H. BENCE JONES. Crown 8vo., 10s. 6d.

Children's Books.

Crake.—Works by Rev. A. D. CRAKE.

EDWY THE FAIR; or, the First Chronicle of Æscendune. Crown 8vo., 2s. 6d.

ALFGAR THE DANE: or, the Second Chronicle of Æscendune. Cr. 8vo., 2s. 6d.

THE RIVAL HEIRS: being the Third and Last Chronicle of Æscendune. Cr. 8vo., 2s. 6d.

THE HOUSE OF WALDERNE. A Tale of the Cloister and the Forest in the Days of the Barons' Wars. Crown 8vo., 2s. 6d.

BRIAN FITZ-COUNT. A Story of Wallingford Castle and Dorchester Abbey. Cr. 8vo., 2s. 6d.

Ingelow.—VERY YOUNG, AND QUITE ANOTHER STORY. Two Stories. By JEAN INGELOW. Crown 8vo., 2s. 6d.

Lang.—Works edited by ANDREW LANG.

THE BLUE FAIRY BOOK. With 8 Plates and 130 Illustrations in the Text by H. J. FORD and G. P. JACOMB HOOD. Crown 8vo., 6s.

Lang.—Works edited by ANDREW LANG—*continued.*

THE RED FAIRY BOOK. With 4 Plates and 96 Illustrations in the Text by H. J. FORD and LANCELOT SPEED. Crown 8vo., 6s.

THE GREEN FAIRY BOOK. With 11 Plates and 88 Illustrations in the Text by H. J. FORD and L. BOGLE. Cr. 8vo., 6s.

THE BLUE POETRY BOOK. With 12 Plates and 88 Illustrations in the Text by H. J. FORD and LANCELOT SPEED. Crown 8vo., 6s.

THE BLUE POETRY BOOK. School Edition, without Illustrations. Fcp. 8vo., 2s. 6d.

THE TRUE STORY BOOK. With 8 Plates and 58 Illustrations in the Text, by C. H. KERR, H. J. FORD, LANCELOT SPEED, and L. BOGLE. Crown 8vo., 6s.

Children's Books—*continued*.

Meade.—Works by L. T. MEADE.
DEB AND THE DUCHESS. Illustrated. Crown 8vo., 3s. 6d.
THE BERESFORD PRIZE. Illustrated. Cr. 8vo., 5s.
DADDY'S BOY. Illustrated. Crown 8vo., 3s. 6d.

Molesworth.—Works by Mrs. MOLESWORTH.
SILVERTHORNS. Illustrated. Cr. 8vo., 5s.
THE PALACE IN THE GARDEN. Illustrated. Crown 8vo., 5s.
THE THIRD MISS ST. QUENTIN. Cr. 8vo., 2s. 6d.
NEIGHBOURS. Illustrated. Cr. 8vo., 6s.
THE STORY OF A SPRING MORNING, &c. Illustrated. Crown 8vo., 2s. 6d.

Reader.— VOICES FROM FLOWERLAND : a Birthday Book and Language of Flowers. By EMILY E. READER. Illustrated by ADA BROOKE. Royal 16mo., cloth, 2s. 6d. ; vegetable vellum, 3s. 6d.

Stevenson.—Works by ROBERT LOUIS STEVENSON.

A CHILD'S GARDEN OF VERSES. Small fcp. 8vo., 5s.

A CHILD'S GARLAND OF SONGS, Gathered from 'A Child's Garden of Verses'. Set to Music by C. VILLIERS STANFORD, Mus. Doc. 4to., 2s. sewed ; 3s. 6d., cloth gilt.

The Silver Library.

CROWN 8vo. 3s. 6d. EACH VOLUME.

Baker's (Sir S. W.) Eight Years in Ceylon. With 6 Illustrations. 3s. 6d.
Baker's (Sir S. W.) Rifle and Hound in Ceylon. With 6 Illustrations. 3s. 6d.
Baring-Gould's (Rev. S.) Curious Myths of the Middle Ages. 3s. 6d.
Baring-Gould's (Rev. S.) Origin and Development of Religious Belief. 2 vols. 3s. 6d. each.
Brassey's (Lady) A Voyage in the 'Sunbeam'. With 66 Illustrations. 3s. 6d.
Clodd's (E.) Story of Creation : a Plain Account of Evolution. With 77 Illustrations. 3s. 6d.
Conybeare (Rev. W. J.) and Howson's (Very Rev. J. S.) Life and Epistles of St. Paul. 46 Illustrations. 3s. 6d.
Dougall's (L.) Beggars All ; a Novel. 3s. 6d.
Doyle's (A. Conan) Micah Clarke : a Tale of Monmouth's Rebellion. 3s. 6d.
Doyle's (A. Conan) The Captain of the Polestar, and other Tales. 3s. 6d.
Froude's (J. A.) Short Studies on Great Subjects. 4 vols. 3s. 6d. each.
Froude's (J. A.) Cæsar : a Sketch. 3s. 6d.
Froude's (J. A.) Thomas Carlyle : a History of his Life.
1795-1835. 2 vols. 7s.
1834-1881. 2 vols. 7s.
Froude's (J. A.) The Two Chiefs of Dunboy. 3s. 6d.
Froude's (J. A.) The History of England, from the Fall of Wolsey to the Defeat of the Spanish Armada. 12 vols. 3s. 6d. each.
Gleig's (Rev. G. R.) Life of the Duke of Wellington. With Portrait. 3s. 6d.
Haggard's (H. R.) She : A History of Adventure. 32 Illustrations. 3s. 6d.
Haggard's (H. R.) Allan Quatermain. With 20 Illustrations. 3s. 6d.
Haggard's (H. R.) Colonel Quaritch, V.C. : a Tale of Country Life. 3s. 6d.
Haggard's (H. R.) Cleopatra. With 29 Full-page Illustrations. 3s. 6d.
Haggard's (H. R.) Eric Brighteyes. With 51 Illustrations. 3s. 6d.
Haggard's (H. R.) Beatrice. 3s. 6d.
Harte's (Bret) In the Carquinez Woods, and other Stories. 3s. 6d.
Helmholtz's (Hermann von) Popular Lectures on Scientific Subjects. With 68 Woodcuts. 2 vols. 3s. 6d. each.
Howitt's (W.) Visits to Remarkable Places. 80 Illustrations. 3s. 6d.
Jefferies' (R.) The Story of My Heart : My Autobiography. With Portrait. 3s. 6d.
Jefferies' (R.) Field and Hedgerow. With Portrait. 3s. 6d.
Jefferies' (R.) Red Deer. With 17 Illustrations. 3s. 6d.
Jefferies' (R.) Wood Magic : a Fable. 3s. 6d.
Jefferies' (R.) The Toilers of the Field. With Portrait from the Bust in Salisbury Cathedral. 3s. 6d.

The Silver Library—*continued*.

Knight's (E. F.) The Cruise of the 'Alerte': the Narrative of a Search for Treasure on the Desert Island of Trinidad. With 2 Maps and 23 Illustrations. 3s. 6d.

Lang's (A.) Custom and Myth: Studies of Early Usage and Belief. 3s. 6d.

Lees (J. A.) and Clutterbuck's (W. J.) B.C. 1887, A Ramble in British Columbia. With Maps and 75 Illustrations. 3s. 6d.

Macaulay's (Lord) Essays and Lays of Ancient Rome. 3s. 6d.

Macleod (H. D.) The Elements of Banking. 3s. 6d.

Marshman's (J. C.) Memoirs of Sir Henry Havelock. 3s. 6d.

Max Müller's (F.) India, what can it teach us? 3s. 6d.

Max Müller's (F.) Introduction to the Science of Religion. 3s. 6d.

Merivale's (Dean) History of the Romans under the Empire. 8 vols. 3s. 6d. ea.

Mill's (J. S.) Political Economy. 3s. 6d.

Mill's (J. S.) System of Logic. 3s. 6d.

Milner's (Geo.) Country Pleasures. 3s. 6d.

Newman's (Cardinal) Apologia Pro Vitâ Suâ. 3s. 6d.

Newman's (Cardinal) Historical Sketches. 3 vols. 3s. 6d. each.

Newman's (Cardinal) Callista: a Tale of the Third Century. 3s. 6d.

Newman's (Cardinal) Loss and Gain: a Tale. 3s. 6d.

Newman's (Cardinal) Essays, Critical and Historical. 2 vols. 7s.

Newman's (Cardinal) The Development of Christian Doctrine. 3s. 6d.

Newman's (Cardinal) The Arians of the Fourth Century. 3s. 6d.

Newman's (Cardinal) Verses on Various Occasions. 3s. 6d.

Newman's (Cardinal) The Present Position of Catholics in England. 3s. 6d.

Newman's (Cardinal) Parochial and Plain Sermons. 8 vols. 3s. 6d. each.

Newman's (Cardinal) Selection from the 'Parochial and Plain Sermons'. 3s. 6d.

Newman's (Cardinal) Sermons bearing upon Subjects of the Day. 3s. 6d.

Newman's (Cardinal) Difficulties felt by Anglicans in Catholic Teaching Considered. 2 vols. 3s. 6d. each.

Newman's (Cardinal) The Idea of a University. 3s. 6d.

Newman's (Cardinal) Biblical and Ecclesiastical Miracles. 3s. 6d.

Newman's (Cardinal) Discussions and Arguments. 3s. 6d.

Newman's (Cardinal) Grammar of Assent. 3s. 6d.

Newman's (Cardinal) Fifteen Sermons Preached before the University of Oxford. 3s. 6d.

Newman's (Cardinal) Lectures on the Doctrine of Justification. 3s. 6d.

Newman's (Cardinal) Sermons on Various Occasions. 3s. 6d.

Newman's (Cardinal) Via Media of the Anglican Church, in Lectures, &c. 2 vols. 3s. 6d. each.

Newman's (Cardinal) Discourses to Mixed Congregations. 3s. 6d.

Phillipps-Wolley's (C.) Snap: a Legend of the Lone Mountain. With 13 Illustrations. 3s. 6d.

Proctor's (R. A.) Other Worlds than Ours. 3s. 6d.

Proctor's (R. A.) Rough Ways made Smooth. 3s. 6d.

Proctor's (R. A.) Pleasant Ways in Science. 3s. 6d.

Proctor's (R. A.) The Orbs Around Us. 3s. 6d.

Proctor's (R. A.) The Expanse of Heaven. 3s. 6d.

Proctor's (R. A.) Myths and Marvels of Astronomy. 3s. 6d.

Proctor's (R. A.) Nature Studies. 3s. 6d.

Smith's (R. Bosworth) Carthage and the Carthaginians. 3s. 6d.

Stanley's (Bishop) Familiar History of Birds. 160 Illustrations. 3s. 6d.

Stevenson (Robert Louis) and Osbourne's (Lloyd) The Wrong Box. 3s. 6d.

Weyman's (Stanley J.) The House of the Wolf: a Romance. 3s. 6d.

Wood's (Rev. J. G.) Petland Revisited. With 33 Illustrations. 3s. 6d.

Wood's (Rev. J. G.) Strange Dwellings. With 60 Illustrations. 3s. 6d.

Wood's (Rev. J. G.) Out of Doors. 11 Illustrations. 3s. 6d.

Cookery, Domestic Management, &c.

Acton.—MODERN COOKERY. By ELIZA ACTON. With 150 Woodcuts. Fcp. 8vo., 4s. 6d.

Bull.—Works by THOMAS BULL, M.D.

HINTS TO MOTHERS ON THE MANAGEMENT OF THEIR HEALTH DURING THE PERIOD OF PREGNANCY. Fcp. 8vo., 1s. 6d.

THE MATERNAL MANAGEMENT OF CHILDREN IN HEALTH AND DISEASE. Fcp. 8vo., 1s. 6d.

www.ingramcontent.com/pod-product-compliance
Lightning Source LLC
Chambersburg PA
CBHW021820230426
43669CB00008B/813